Mundane and More from Memory

Mundane and More from Memory

V. R. REDDY

Orient BlackSwan

MUNDANE AND MORE FROM MEMORY

ORIENT BLACKSWAN PRIVATE LIMITED

Registered Office
3-6-752 Himayatnagar, Hyderabad 500 029, Telangana, India
e-mail: centraloffice@orientblackswan.com

Other Offices
Bengaluru, Chennai, Guwahati, Hyderabad, Kolkata
Mumbai, New Delhi, Noida, Patna, Visakhapatnam

© Orient Blackswan Private Limited 2021
First published by Orient Blackswan Private Limited 2021

ISBN 978-93-5442-088-7

Typeset in
Minion Pro 10.5/12.8 *by*
Le Studio Graphique, Gurgaon 122 007

Printed in India at
Akash Press, New Delhi

Published by
Orient Blackswan Private Limited
3-6-752 Himayatnagar, Hyderabad 500 029, Telangana, India
e-mail: info@orientblackswan.com

*To my grandchildren, Nitya, Megha, Shloka and Abhinav,
watching whom growing up has been a delight to cherish.*

Contents

List of Abbreviations   *ix*
List of Photographs   *xiii*
List of Appendices   *xxi*
Publishers' Acknowledgements   *xxiii*
Preface   *xxv*

1. Genesis — 1
2. Schooling — 11
3. Colleges — 15
4. University of London — 23
5. Siblings and Spouses — 25
6. 1964, the Eventful Year — 30
7. The Wedding — 33
8. Legal Career Threshold — 37
9. Our Family Grows — 40
10. Nukala, the Father Figure — 44
11. Government Pleader — 51
12. Gen 2 — 60
13. Gen 3 — 67
14. Deepika, the Guru — 74
15. Collateral Activities — 76
16. Warmth of Friendship and Rajampet Gallantry — 84
17. Foray into Bar Bodies—Bar Council of India — 86
18. Bar Council of India—Path for Fulfilment — 95
19. Parallel Progress—Professional Career — 119
20. Global Fraternity — 129
21. Introspection — 139

22. Back to Business—Advocate General of Andhra Pradesh	146
23. Additional Solicitor General of India	154
24. Independent Practice and Retirement	167

Appendices   187

Abbreviations

AGM	annual general meeting
AIG	Asian Institute of Gastroenterology
AOR	Advocate on Record
AP	Andhra Pradesh
APGPCL	Andhra Pradesh Gas Power Corporation Limited
APIDC	Andhra Pradesh Industrial Development Corporation
APSEB	Andhra Pradesh State Electricity Board
APSERC	Andhra Pradesh State Electricity Regulatory Commission
ASG	Additional Solicitor General
BAI	Bar Association of India
BC	backward class
BCI	Bar Council of India
BDA	Bangalore Development Authority
BIL	brother-in-law
BL	Bachelor of Law
BTR	Banyan Tree Retreat
CBI	Central Bureau of Investigation
CCI	Cement Corporation of India
CEGAT	Customs, Excise and Gold (Control) Appellate Tribunal
CEO	chief executive officer
CJ	Chief Justice
CLE	continuing legal education
CM	Chief Minister
CNG	compressed natural gas
CV	curriculum vitae
DDA	Delhi Development Authority
ENT	ear, nose, throat
F&B	food and beverage
FL	first year of law school
GP	government pleader
HC	High Court

HPS	Hyderabad Public School
HRC	Hyderabad Race Club
IAS	Indian Administrative Service
IBA	International Bar Association
ICCR	Indian Council for Cultural Relations
ICRISAT	International Crops Research Institute for the Semi-Arid Tropics
IIT	Indian Institute of Technology
ILI	Indian Law Institute
IPC	Indian Penal Code
IPS	Indian Police Service
IT	information technology
KCP	Krishna Commercial Products Ltd.
LLM	Master of Laws
LSE	London School of Economics
LVPEI	L. V. Prasad Eye Institute
MBA	Master of Business Administration
MLA	member of Legislative Assembly
MP	member of Parliament
MRC	Madras Race Club
NBCC	National Buildings Construction Corporation
NHS	National Health Service
NLS	National Law School
NLSIU	National Law School of India University
NTPC	National Thermal Power Corporation
NUJS	National University of Juridical Sciences
ONGC	Oil and Natural Gas Corporation
PA	personal assistant
PG	postgraduate
PIL	public interest litigation
PM	Prime Minister
PMO	Prime Minister's Office
PP	public prosecutor
PS	personal secretary
PSU	public sector undertaking
PTI	Press Trust of India
RBI	Reserve Bank of India
SAARC	South Asian Association for Regional Cooperation

SC	Supreme Court
SG	Solicitor General
SLP	special leave petition
SSLC	Secondary School Leaving Certificate
TPS	Telangana Praja Samithi
TTD	Tirumala Tirupati Devasthanams
UGC	University Grants Commission
UN	United Nations
UP	Uttar Pradesh
UPSC	Union Public Service Commission
VM	village munsif

Names of People

AC	A. C. Subba Reddy
GNR	G. Nageshwar Reddy
GR	G. Ramaswamy
GVK	G. V. Krishna Reddy
JVR	J. Vengal Rao
KBR	K. Brahmananda Reddy
KKV	K. K. Venugopal
KLN	K. L. N. Prasad
KTS	K. T. S. Tulsi
MM	N. R. Madhava Menon
NJR	Nedurumalli Janardhan Reddy
NK	N. K. Jain
NN	N. Narender Reddy
NRC	N. R. C. Reddi
NTR	N. T. Rama Rao
OCR	O. Chinnappa Reddy
PRC	Pitchi Reddy Chinnayya
PRR	P. Ramachandra Reddy
PSN	P. S. Narasimha
PSR	P. Satyanarayana Rao
PV	P. V. Narasimha Rao
SSC	Sakya Singha Chowdhary
TGK	T. G. Krishnamoorthy
TPS	Telangana Praja Samithi

TR	Tata Rao
VBR	K. Vijayabhaskar Reddy
VC	V. C. Mishra
VRR	V. R. Reddy

Photographs

Personal

1. Earliest photograph of VRR with his mother.
2. VRR's father in Western attire.
3. VRR during early school years with his mother.
4. Family photograph; sitting (L to R) mother, Dr Krishna Swaroop, father, paternal grandmother; standing (L to R) Saraswathi, VRR, Prabhavathi, Suguna.
5. VRR at Loyola College, with C. Venkateshwara Rao and M. M. Ramachandran.
6. VRR after graduation.
7. Radha, VRR's wife, as a student of Osmania Medical College, Hyderabad.
8. VRR at his engagement ceremony, with father-in-law Nukala.
9. VRR weds Radha.
10. VRR at wedding dinner, with Radha's cousins Ramesh, Vijay, Janardhan and Vikram.
11. VRR at wedding dinner, with college friends Ankineedu Prasad, Ram Mohan, Krishnamurthy, Ramachandran, Sounderarajan.
12. At Rajampet with grandmother after the wedding.
13. At Rajampet with sister Saraswati, Shiv mama and their children.
14. With aunt and uncle at Korlakunta.
15. Reception dinner at Rajampet; (L to R) P. Venkataseshaiyya, V. Laxman, P. Venkat Reddy and others.
16. VRR with the children.
17. Radha with the children.
18. Family with Mahipal, Saras, and baby Aarathi.
19. With parents Sri. Velakacherla Narasa Reddy and Smt. Jayalakshmamma at Rajampet.

xiv Photographs

20. VRR's family with Mr and Mrs Neelam Sanjeeva Reddy.
21. VRR at centenary celebrations of Secunderabad Club, with president A. Ranga Rao, Jagdish Reddy and other members of the managing committee.
22. VRR speaking on the occasion at Secunderabad Club.
23. VRR being received as a delegate to the Asian Racing Conference at Seoul, Korea; R. Surender Reddy looks on.
24. At the conference with N. N. Reddy, Secretary HRC and Vikram.
25. VRR and Radha at the wedding of Deepika and Shyam, with NTR gracing the occasion.
26. VRR and Radha greeted by NRC and Prabha on their 25th wedding anniversary.
27. K. T. S. Tulsi at the wedding of VRR's son Siddharth and Aditi in Hyderabad.
28. Dr and Mrs P. S. Rao and Mr and Mrs N. G. Reddy at the wedding.
29. Dignitaries at the wedding: K. Vijayabhaskar Reddy, K. Raghunath Reddy, N. Janardhan Reddy, N. Rajyalaksmi Reddy, T. Subbarami Reddy.
30. Siddharth and Aditi with Bapsi and Fali Nariman at the wedding reception, Delhi.
31. With G. Venkat Swamy, Union Minister, R. Surender Reddy, Justice B. P. Jeevan Reddy and VRR.
32. Receiving blessings from Justice V. K. Krishna Iyer at the wedding reception, Delhi.
33. Family photograph at 40th anniversary celebrations of VRR and Radha in Hyderabad.
34. Chilling with the grandchildren in Coonoor.
35. VRR with close friends Sreedharan, Sreekumar and family in Coonoor.
36. VRR's family performing puja for the *punah pratishthan* (reinstallation) of the temple deity at Hatyarala, Rajampet.
37. VRR with A. Changal Reddy, former TTD chairman, and P. Venkat Reddy.
38. VRR with Dr Madan Mohan Reddy and J. C. Diwakar Reddy.
39. VRR with priests and Nagaraja Gupta, Sudhakar, Raghu, Penchallaiyya, Subba Reddy, Mani, Narayana, Subbayya.

40. VRR's daughter Deepika's *rangapravesham*, with her Guru, Sumathi Kaushal, former CM Vengal Rao, former CJ A. Sambashiva Rao and Akkineni Nageshwara Rao.
41. VRR speaking at the inauguration of Deepanjali; (L to R) Geeta Reddy, Jaipal Reddy, M.M.P. Raju and Deepika.
42. VRR with Pandit Birju Maharaj, after presentation of his production *Ritu Samhar*, in which Deepika was chosen to choreograph and present the Kuchipudi segment.
43. Deepika being felicitated by P. V. Narasimha Rao after her performance at Habitat Centre, Delhi.
44. Dignitaries present for the Gajjapuja performance by Shloka and Abhinav; (L to R) VRR, R. Surender Reddy, Dr Y. V. Reddy, Jagdish Mittal, Deepika, Shyam, Uttam Kumar Reddy.
45. Radha lighting the lamp on commencement of Deepika's ballet *Rukmini Krishna*; (L to R) lyricist Sirivennela Seetharama Sastry, former Union home secretary K. Padmanabhaiah, Kavita Kalvakuntla, president Telangana Jagruthi, Dr Jupally Rameswar Rao, chairman My Home Group.
46. After the ballet, Deepika with the sponsors Vasantha and Varaprasad Reddy, dignitaries Vachaspathi Brahmasri Chaganti Koteswara Rao, Ramanachary, advisor to Govt. of Telangana, singer S. P. Balasubramanyam, music composer and vocalist D. S. V. Sastry.
47. Deepika receiving the Andhra Pradesh State Award 'Kalaratna' from CM Dr Y. S. Rajasekhara Reddy in 2007, in the presence of K. R. Suresh Reddy, speaker AP Legislative Assembly.
48. Deepika receiving the Telangana State Award, 2016, from Governor E. S. L. Narasimhan and CM K. Chandrasekhara Rao.
49. President of India, Ram Nath Kovind, conferring Deepika with the National Sangeet Natak Akademi Award 2017, for her contribution to the Kuchipudi dance form.
50. VRR at Rashtrapati Bhavan, with Deepika and family on the occasion.
51. Radha being felicitated by CM K. Rosaiah, in the presence of Dr Geeta Reddy, Minister of Tourism and Culture on the occasion of golden jubilee celebrations of Ravindra Bharati in 2010, in recognition of her "dedicated contribution for the development of Ravindra Bharati"; Radha was the prime artiste in the ballet presented on the auditorium's inauguration in 1961.

52. VRR with Dr M. Veeraraghava Reddy and K. Jayabharath Reddy.
53. VRR with Vinod Poddar on his 70th birthday.
54. Post-retirement, VRR on a holiday with family to Kenya.
55. High school graduation of Nitya, with both grandparents.
56. In Pune for the launch of a book on the Raste family, with Dinesh and Purnima.
57. Siva with bouquets received after the 40th anniversary celebrations of VRR and Radha in Hyderabad.
58. Family get together at Deepika's house, December 2018.
59. Radha on her 75th birthday, with Srilatha Bhupal, Surender Reddy, Jayamala and Dr Indira.
60. General Sebastin and wife with VRR's family.

Professional

61. VRR's felicitation on assumption of office as Advocate General of AP; (L to R) VRR, Katikaneni Jagannadha Rao, President Bar Association, CM N. Janardhan Reddy, Justice M. Jagannadha Rao.
62. CM at the venue; (L to R) VRR, Niroop Reddy, D. Sudarshan Reddy, CM, E. Ayyapa Reddy.
63. CM greeting attendees; (L to R) K. Raja Reddy, CM, C. V. Nagarjun Reddy and others.
64. At the function; (R to L) P. Babul Reddy, Justice A. Seetaram Reddy and others.
65. VRR with Nori Rajeswhar Rao and Justice K. Ramaswamy.
66. (L to R) K. Raja Reddy, VRR, R. Venugopal Reddy, former AG, Ram Mohan Raj.
67. With the CM and K. Madhava Rao, PS to CM.
68. VRR with 'Senior' P. Ramchandra Reddy and colleagues Venkatram Reddy and Nagaseshiah.
69. VRR, chief guest at conference of Indian Lawyers Association; (L to R) Jwala, C. Padmanabha Reddy (President IAL).
70. VRR with Surya Rao (3rd from left), K. Raja Reddy, N. R. Devaraj and others at the conference.
71. VRR with friends, Justice Parvatha Rao and P. Ramachandra Reddy (ex-speaker Legislative Assembly and minister).

Photographs xvii

72. VRR speaking at the IAL Zonal conference in Vijayawada; on the dais, Karavadi Venkateswarlu (Ongole) and others.
73. CJ Obul Reddi Memorial Lecture delivered by Justice A. M. Ahmadi; (L to R) Prof. Ranbir Singh (Director NALSAR), VRR, Justice Jayachandra Reddy, Justice Devinder Gupta CJ AP, Justice A. M. Ahmadi (ex-CJI), P. Shivshankar (partly seen).
74. Pandit Govind Ballabh Pant Birth Centenary Seminar; on the dais (L to R) advocate K. J. Sethna, CJI R. S. Pathak, ex-President Shankar Dayal Sharma, VRR, former Union law minister V. Shankaranand.
75. VRR and members of BCI with guests of honour.
76. Jawaharlal Nehru birth centenary seminar at Jaipur; (L to R) N. K. Jain, CJI J. S. Verma, Justice E. S. Venkatramaiah, VRR, R. N. Bishnoi.
77. VRR speaking at Commemorative Conference on 40 Years of The Advocates Act, 1961, organised by BAI at Goa in 2001.
78. VRR, with Justice Lahoti lighting a lamp to inaugurate the All India Moot Court Competition held by University College of Law, Karnataka University, Dharwar, in 2001.
79. BCI Trust workshop on constitutional litigation at Shimla; (L to R) VRR, N. R. Madhava Menon, K. D. Sood, P. P. Rao and others.
80. VRR with Madhava Menon, Ramakrishna Hegde, Justice R. S. Pathak, at workshop organised by NLSIU and BCIT in Bangalore.
81. VRR receiving Justice Hidayatullah, Vice President of India, Ashoknath Banerjee, Governor of Karnataka and others at NLSIU's inaugural function.
82. At the inauguration of NLSIU on 25 February 1984, Justice Hidayatullah, CJI Y. V. Chandrachud, CJI Ramakrishna Hegde, Karnataka CM, CJ Malimath, Governor Banerjee, Ranjit Mahanti, BCI Chairman Ram Jethmalani, VRR and others.
83. Justice Chandrachud and wife with Justice Malimath, Shetty, Upendra Baxi, Ranjit Mahanti, Rangaraj, Tippana, VRR and others.
84. Justice Y. V. Chandrachud unveiling the foundation plaque.
85. Ram Jethmalani.
86. Justice Bharucha with CJI A. S. Anand and VRR.
87. VRR and other members of the executive committee at the 2000 convocation.

88. VRR at inaugural of Centre for Education and Training in Human Rights, with Justice Krishna Iyer, Michael Kirby (Australian judge), Puvaiyya, Prof. Madhava Menon and others.
89. VRR with law officer colleagues at the Supreme Court; standing (L to R) Ashok Desai AG, VRR, Andhyarujina SG; sitting (L to R) K. N. Bhatt, Usgaonkar, Altaf Ahmad.
90. Government staff of VRR when he was an ASG during Siddharth's wedding. Pandyan (attender), Vijay Kumar (PA), Khanna (PS), junior advocates Pragasam and Nageswar Reddy.
91. With former president, S. D. Sharma.
92. VRR and other delegates on a visit to China, with the Vice Minister for Justice, China.
93. VRR with Ashok Desai and other Indian delegates at the IBA Conference, Buenos Aires.
94. VRR and Anil Divan in Rio de Janeiro in front of the statue of Christ the Redeemer.
95. VRR and Anil Divan with Anjali Varma and her husband in Peru.
96. VRR with former IBA president Kumar Shankar Das, his wife, and the incumbent IBA president.
97. VRR at IBA's Asian Regional Conference in Delhi.
98. VRR and Radha at the Law Asia Conference in Manila.
99. VRR (as Vice President BAI) at the All India Lawyers Convention organised by BAI; on the dais, Fali Nariman (President BAI), Anil Divan and Gaurishanker.
100. VRR with Lalit Bhasin at the BAI conference on criminal justice.
101. VRR at dinner hosted by P. S. Narasimha, to felicitate him and his family during their visit to Delhi on the occasion of Deepika receiving the National Sangeet Natak Akademi Award from the President of India; (L to R) Justice Madan Lokur, Umapathi, Dayan Krishan, Nikhil Nayyar, Sunil, VRR, R. S. Suri, Sharma.
102. P. H. Parekh with VRR.
103. Parasaran with Deepika, P. S. Narasimha and VRR.
104. VRR receiving Soli Sorabjee.
105. VRR and Deepika with Abhishek Singhvi.
106. VRR with K. K. Venugopal, Attorney General.
107. VRR with M. L. Verma.

108. VRR and P. S. Narasimha with Vikas Singh.
109. VRR with Jaideep Gupta and Justice V. K. Rao.
110. (L to R) Pragasam, Venkat Reddy, Nageshwar Reddy, Venkat Ramani, Sanjay Hegde, Krishnan Venugopal.
111. VRR and Deepika with Justice L. Narasimha Reddy.
112. (Sitting L to R) P. S. Narasimha, Pragasam, Radha, VRR and Deepika; (standing L to R) Siddharth, Vijayabhaskar, Venkat Reddy, Nageshwar Reddy, Shyam, Choudhury, Abhilasha and Kannan.
113. At conference commemorating 60 years of BAI on 3 December 2019, VRR with Parasaran, BAI President Lalit Bhasin; seen Krishnayan Sen.
114. VRR with Vikramjit Banerjee, Justice Ravindra Bhat, Prof. Upendra Baxi, Priya Hingaroni.
115. VRR receiving the plaque of honour and distinction from Justices Indira Banerjee and Ravindra Bhat; seen Ashok Desai, Prashant and Lalit Bhasin.
116. The plaque being presented to VRR.

Appendices

1. 'Justice Delivery System', speech delivered by V. R. Reddy, as Chairman, Bar Council of India, at the National Convention of Lawyers on 22 August 1989, New Delhi. — 187
2. 'Practice of Law in the Multimedia Era—An Indian Perspective', paper presented by V. R. Reddy at the Regional Conference of the International Bar Association on 5 November 1999, New Delhi. — 190
3. 'The Role of Bar and Bench in Administration of Justice', address by V. R. Reddy as guest speaker at the golden jubilee celebrations of the Rajasthan High Court on 4 September 1999, Jodhpur. — 196
4. 'Reminiscences and Random Thoughts', V. R. Reddy's article, penned on '40 Years of The Advocates Act, 1961', published in a commemorative volume on the occasion of the Bar Association of India Conference, 30 September–1 October 2001, Goa. — 202
5. 'Judges and Medals', V. R. Reddy's article published in *The Indian Advocate*, The Journal of Bar Association of India, 21: 27–31, 2003. — 218
6. 'V. R. Reddy's Elevation Welcomed', report in the *Deccan Chronicle*, 4 August 1991, Hyderabad, on V. R. Reddy's appointment as Additional Solicitor General of India. — 223
7. 'Sydney to Sydney—A Lawyer's Lament', V. R. Reddy's article sent to the President of the District Court Bar Association, Kadapa, along with his covering letter of 20 February 2008. — 224
8. 'Kadapotsavam', an invitation to V. R. Reddy from the Kadapotsavam Committee, Cuddapah, to attend the first Kadapotsavam, from 28 January to 1 February 2003. — 230

Publishers' Acknowledgements

For granting permissions to reproduce copyright material in this volume, the publishers and the author thank the following:

Deccan Chronicle, for 'Man Who Took Rajampet Places', by Radha Viswanath, previously published 21 August 1999, New Delhi.

Deccan Chronicle, for 'V. R. Reddy's Elevation Welcomed', previously published 4 August 1991, Hyderabad.

The Bar Association of India, for 'Reminisces and Random Thoughts', previously published in the Commemorative Volume on '40 Years of The Advocates Act, 1961', on the occasion of the Bar Association of India Conference, 30 September–1 October 2001, Goa.

The Bar Association of India, for 'Judges and Medals', previously published in *The Indian Advocate*, The Journal of Bar Association of India, 21: 27–31, 2003.

The National Law School of India University, for the letter on p. 112.

Preface

For one with no literary pretensions and writing skills, writing a memoir was rightly considered to be a stupendous and unessential task. And so when Krishnayan Sen, who worked with me as a Junior Advocate in Delhi, came up with this idea of I narrating the experiences of my life and professional career, I was wary of biting the bait. Smart that he is, Krishnayan made it sound simple, saying, "Sir! Spare an hour dictating to me your experiences". I remember brushing aside the suggestion offhand, saying that I do not consider myself one with accomplishments to make the narrative interesting, let alone inspirational, to readers. But then, Krishnayan proved himself to be a die-hard motivator by relentlessly coaxing me to get down to penning my memoir. His efforts finally bore fruit and I got down to it some years after I quit practice and moved back to Hyderabad, after a twenty-year-long stint in Delhi practicing before the Supreme Court, initially as Additional Solicitor General of India and later as Senior Advocate.

My writings, mostly on scribbling pads, would often get interrupted when recalling dates and, with fading memory, the chronology of events posed a problem and I had to trouble my former juniors and associates, Nagarjun, Nageshwar, Sunil, Sudesh, and Kannan, besides Krishnayan. For information relating to family I would always count on my dear wife, Radha, who would, in fact, surprise me by producing old documents such as invites for important events like our marriage, *gruhapravesam* (housewarming), our daughter Deepika's *rangapravesam* (debut). Shyam, my son-in-law, with his awesome digital skills helped produce neatly-bound typed copies of the manuscript. Above all, it is the frequent enquiries on its progress by my cousin Venu—nay, Thambi (younger brother in Tamil), as he was known to my friends in our school days in Madras—Dr Y. V. Reddy, former governor of the Reserve Bank of India (RBI), and a prolific writer himself, that spurred me on to keep pace and not give up mid-way.

Now that the task hesitantly undertaken is completed, what some great minds had to say helps me overcome self-doubt regarding the purpose and content of the end product.

> Our task is not to leave a record of what happened on this date for those who will inherit the Earth; history will take care of that. Therefore, we will speak about our daily lives, about the difficulties we have had to face. That is all the future will be interested in...
>
> —Paulo Coelho, *Manuscript Found in Accra* (2013)

William Zinsser, in his invaluable book *On Writing Well* (2016), has the following to say under the chapter 'Writing Family History and Memoir':

> Writers are custodians of memory and that is what this chapter is about; how to leave some kind of record of your life and the family you were born into—it can be an informal history, written to tell your children and your grandchildren about the family they were born into. Whatever it is, it is an important kind of writing.

He then adds pithily, "Memories too often die with their owner and time often surprises us by running out" (Zinsser 2016).

That said, I conclude, borrowing the words of Coelho (2013), "I leave for those who come after me everything I learned in life and career. May they make good use of it."

Editor's Note
Honorifics such as Sri. and Smt. used for certain individuals, seniors and noted public figures by the author have been omitted with his consent as per editorial norms to maintain uniformity in style.

References
Coelho, Paulo. 2013. *Manuscript Found in Accra*. HarperCollins.
Zinsser, William. 2016. *On Writing Well: The Classic Guide to Writing Non-Fiction*. Harper Perennial.

1 Genesis

Man who took Rajampet places

Though he has gone places Supreme Court lawyer and former Additional Solicitor-General Velakacherla Rajagopala Reddy says that he always longs to return to his native place

This Rayalaseema luminary refuses to stay away from his roots, notwithstanding his busy schedules and other professional work. Velakacherla Rajagopala Reddy makes not less than three visits an year to Rajampet, where he was born and where he spent his childhood. "I visit it as often as I can," is how the practising Supreme Court lawyer and former Additional-Solicitor General puts it.

As to why he undertakes the tiring journey, given the fact that each visit is very brief, generally not exceeding three days, Rajagopala Reddy has a simple answer. "The visits somehow refresh me because, I think, I interact with people as a person and not as a lawyer, holding some office. Also, they are a great learning experience for me — I try to educate myself on what is really happening at that level and how people look at life and society in general," he says. For the Rajampet residents, who have known the Velakacherla family for decades, it came as a pleasant surprise when Rajagopala Reddy continued with his regular visits even after the death of both his parents. "I have no family members who live in the ancestral home. Only the house, which I have made over for a school," he says. Rajagopala Reddy combined his love for rural India and legal education by instituting a scholarship in the National Law School. The scholarship, instituted in memory of his father, Velakacherla Narasa Reddy, is given to students who have undergone a part of their early education in a village school. Weightage is given to students with rural background, because, Reddy believes, students from villages and small towns are at a comparative disadvantage when it comes to higher education. "Maybe my agricultural background, deep affinity for rural India, gives me this bias in favour of such students," he says.

What impresses the legal luminary is the unmistakable thirst for education in and around the small town of Rajampet. "I feel sad that the government has not been able to meet the demand, despite the State being constitutionally obliged to provide elementary education to all children up to the age of 14. The result is that people with the means send their children to private schools which have mushroomed in the area", he says. Over the years, the area has grown; development is noticeable in more ways than one.

The former Advocate-General of Andhra Pradesh, a post he resigned when he became the first additional solicitor-General of India in August 1991, in which capacity he represented the Central and various State governments in a number of cases, says he is a "one-generation phenomenon" in his family for having taken to law as vocation.

(As told to Radha Viswanath in New Delhi)

That, I think, was a hugely complimentary statement from a popular English daily of the region, *Deccan Chronicle*, particularly in its special issue of 21 August 1999 on the occasion of the launch of its Rayalaseema edition. What made it all the more gratifying was sharing space on the first page with Dr Y. S. Rajasekhara Reddy, the dynamic leader of the (then) State of Andhra Pradesh, and Dr Y. V. Reddy, legendary economist-administrator and (then) RBI governor, both of whom also hailed from the Kadapa district in Rayalaseema. In context of that catchy headline, it may be apt to dwell upon my association with Rajampet from its genesis.

It all started with the event of the birth of a male child to my parents, Velakacherla Narasa Reddy and Jayalakshmamma, on a date not borne out by any authentic record.

My ancestral village, Seetharamapuram, was part of Poli, which was a revenue village and major gram panchayat in the erstwhile taluk of Rajampet (now a *mandal*) of Cuddapah, lately Kadapa district. Seetharamapuram, from which Rajampet town is about three kilometres as the crow flies, had no motorable road. There was only a cart track for double bullock carts which, after traversing a distance on the tank bund, had to skirt around the Poli tank on a track made by cutting the rocky slope of a hillock. Negotiating that stretch used to be quite an experience, what with the cart tilting to one side, the inmates having to either get off and hold it or move to the side to prevent it from tumbling over. When there was no water in the tank, one could comfortably go across the tank bed, cutting the distance by half. We used to have a specially made cart with a curved canopy for protection against sun and rain, and there were two bullocks specially meant to draw the cart and a designated cart driver, Chengaiah, a short-tempered six-footer who used to chew paan all the time. He used to be the man to go to, to put in place anyone who misbehaved with me and also to teach me swimming in the well. Father used to commute to Rajampet in the cart to attend to fruit commission agency business, and for official dealings of the gram panchayat, of which he was continuously the president and sarpanch for over fifty years from its inception. His initial foray into politics and public life was when he got elected in his early twenties to the District Board, defeating a much senior person and successful businessman from Rajampet town, Ambati Ramaswamy. Those were the days when the franchise was limited to those who satisfied the requirement of ownership of property, etc. Father used to very fondly remember his association with senior leaders of the district during that time, who were men of indisputable integrity. As time passed, he gradually lost interest in politics, except when he worked in support of the Swatantra Party, founded by C. Rajagopalachari, of which Naru Ranga Reddy, my sister Prabha's father-in-law, was a staunch supporter and leader in the district. For one who believed in traditional values of integrity and the spirit of service in public life, later years caused him disillusionment.

Father was the village munsif (VM), a hereditary office, traditionally referred to by villagers as the 'Reddy' of the village. In his treatise, *Castes and Tribes of Southern India* (1909), Edgar Thurston observes: "Reddi is the usual title of the Kapus and is the title by which the Village Munsif is called in the Telugu country, regardless of the caste to which he may belong". Though Father had this hereditary office, he never worked as such and used to frequently secure long leave and nominate someone else to act on his behalf. When I was born, since I had the hereditary right to succeed him to the post, he obtained leave till I could take charge after attaining the age of majority. It was an interesting experience for me to prepare for the test for the post of VM, held in the office of the Sub Collector, Rajampet, while I was still in college, and complete the same successfully to be able to take charge. I formally took charge, and an educated villager was nominated to carry on as VM in my place. This hereditary system of village munsifs was abolished when N. T. Rama Rao took over as Chief Minister, leading to protracted litigation in the High Court and Supreme Court.

Going back to Father's younger days, there were no schools easily accessible in rural areas, let alone colleges for higher education. In his time, the only high school was in Nandaluru presumably, since it was then a taluk town, Rajampet becoming headquarters in the later years. There were apparently no hostel facilities then, with the result that only children of town-dwellers had access to schooling. This must have been a serious deterrent even for progressive parents of agriculturist families in villages to provide education for their children. Father seems to have lived with a family as a paying guest in Nandaluru for his schooling. He had to discontinue and get back to the village after the passing away of his father to take over management of family affairs. It's a pity, really, that Father didn't have an opportunity to complete his schooling, since his aptitude for education was noticeable even to us in our younger days. He had apparently engaged a tutor to come and stay in the village and teach him English, which facilitated his reading of *The Hindu*, *Bhavan's Journal* and the like during his later years. He would closely go through the drafts prepared by his lawyers and other well-educated persons and, on occasion, make significant changes.

My mother Yellamma (originally given name), renamed Jayalakshmamma from the time of marriage, is the third daughter of Kasireddy Gangi Reddy and Subbamma of Patur village, which is about three kilometres from Nandaluru railway station on the Madras-Bombay railway line of the then Southern Railway. Nandaluru is one station beyond Rajampet while proceeding from Madras towards Bombay, and together with Nagireddipalli, was a town with a high school, etc.

Patur, as I can recall, was a more prosperous village compared to Seetharamapuram, primarily on account of it being a riverside village with large swathes of wetland on which paddy could be grown year after year, water being available for irrigation in abundance both from the river channel and the nearby tank. Landowners like my grandfather and the families of his cousins used to lease out small parcels of land to *ryot*s on crop-sharing basis, and exercised sufficient clout over them to use their services when needed. In the street extending from the Sri Rama temple T-junction were the houses of Mother's cousins and relatives, all prosperous families, and in Pedduru, on the right side of the junction, there were many Raju and Balija families, while residing in a prominent building there was Dharmayya, the *karnam* of the village and incidentally the arch rival of my uncles. On the other side, where the primary school was located, was the 'Turakapalli' hamlet and V. M. Krishna Reddy's house.

Mother had three brothers and two sisters. She was the second after Korlakunta *peddamma* (elder aunt). Then came the three brothers, followed by the youngest, Ammanemma (Ammanakka—she being relatively very young, Saraswathi, my elder sister, started addressing her as *akka* or sister, and we all followed the same). The eldest of the brothers was Ram *mama* (Rami Reddy); the second, Shiv mama (Shivarami Reddy); and the third, Ramachandra mama (Ramachandra Reddy). Of the three, Ram mama was big-built and had machismo. He quit studies before graduation, married Indirakka, daughter of Barrister Pamidi Bayappa Reddy of Anantapur. Indirakka was a fair, slim and graceful lady. For some time before she passed away, about more than a year ago, she was afflicted by dementia and used to live with her older son Dr Madan Mohan Reddy; a doctor by qualification and politician by inclination, he represented the Rajampet Assembly constituency for a term in the Legislative Assembly.

Indirakka's younger son, Jyothishkar, a successful entrepreneur, lives in Madras while her daughter Subhashini, married to a doctor, lives in Hyderabad.

I had visited Indirakka during her brief cognisant period and mentioned to her, with love and gratitude, that I could vividly recall her combing my hair before sending me to school in Patur. She sweetly responded, gesturing with a hand, "You were a small child then". Yes, I was small, since my schooling there in Patur was up to third class or so. I used to walk to the school past the temple, and one day on the way back, I told Ramachandra mama, who was sitting on the temple platform, of a teacher being harsh to me, which led to the teacher concerned getting a drubbing from him. No wonder Ramachandra mama didn't much value education and dropped out of school. He used to be mostly in Patur, supervising agriculture, except for his brief visits to Pondicherry to spend time at the Aurobindo Ashram. I can't say how much spiritual *gyan* (knowledge) he acquired there, though I do remember the imported goodies he used to bring from there—including French deodorants—Pondicherry being a French colony, with a more liberal import policy.

Shiv mama, the only graduate amongst them, had a happy-go-lucky attitude and enjoyed life in his youth. My hunch is that his father had a special liking for him since with all the time spent with his doctor friends in Madras, Shiv mama could help his father, who suffered from severe diabetes and related ailments, with palliative care. Notable among Shiv mama's doctor friends were Dr H. T. Veera Reddy, Dr Veerabhadra Reddy, Dr Ram Mohan Rao and others. His very close non-medical friend was K. Venkatrami Reddy, son of K. Koti Reddy and Ramasubbamma, who was then an engineer high up in the Madras Corporation, living in Chenoy Nagar, and there was also P. Rama Rao, Town Planning Engineer of the Corporation, living close by. Venkatrami Reddy was the man to go to for me when I needed to buy a pre-owned car for Father or have his car repaired. He used to take me to the TVS Company workshop, and from there we would go to Irani Café next to Buharis for his favourite cream cakes and small samosas.

Ram mama owned a Jeep, army disposal, with a four-wheel drive suited to traverse the sandy track in the river near Gundlur, which he had to cross on his way to Rajampet from Patur. When we moved to

Rajampet from the village, Ram mama used to come there practically every other day to spend time in the *mandi*, the fruit commission agency Kodur Orange Producers' office, or on his way to Anasamudram near Pullampet where he had developed a sizeable estate on family lands lying fallow. Mother used to make special food for her brother on his visits, and if chicken or mutton was not available, it used to be boiled eggs, with two earmarked for him. While in Rajampet, spending time during my school or college vacations, I used to accompany him to Anasamudram for the opportunity of driving the Jeep. Must say, driving a Jeep—which required one to pump the brake pedal more than once to make it work—in the difficult terrain of the *kaccha* road created by bulldozers on the edge of a hillock was a hair-raising experience. I used to enjoy it, and that experience stood me in good stead in later years when I had opportunities to drive on uneven Indian roads as well as motorways and autobahns in Europe, besides the winding mountain roads in the Swiss Alps. I felt quite distressed when disputes arose between Mother's brothers in the matter of partitioning family properties between them.

If I am to ever boast of an exposure to life in a typical rural agricultural family, it was when I spent time intermittently with my aunt at Korlakunta village. Peddamma, who was older than Mother, was married to V. P. Gangi Reddy (*Peddaiah*) of Korlakunta village, about twenty miles from Rajampet. Since they had no children, Mother used to send me on and off to spend time with them. Peddaiah typified a rural middle-class landowner. Their house was unique as successive partitions in their family led to the family house being divided into a row of small dwelling units. If there was something being said by Aunt to her husband at meal time, the lady from the third house might pipe in to add or elaborate. Though they had individual dwelling units, life there was like one huge family living together. Peddaiah used to smoke *beedies* and would proudly drive a bullock cart laden with paddy bags from the fields during harvest time. Peddamma used to make tasty food, with more of non-vegetarian items including pork. She could make homemade cottage cheese (*paneer*) and make delicious masala fry with it. Tumblers full of coffee used to be consumed in the morning and evening. Amidst such an ambience, Peddaiah's father preserved space for his pious lifestyle. After his bath, clad in saffron attire, he would read religious texts and chant his prayers. When that was done, he used to wrap the books reverentially in a saffron cloth and put the bundle on the rafters of the verandah. As a child, I found his pious ways awe-inspiring, while I was fascinated by the lifestyle of his son Peddaiah, a middle-aged, macho, rural landowner whose life revolved around his lands and crops. The only concession for sophistication he made was to switch to Charminar cigarettes in later years while visiting us or others in towns. Peddamma and Peddaiah used to spend time in Tirupati with Saraswathi and Shiv mama, who used to provide them all the medical care and comforts needed in old age. The presence and company of Saraswathi's three children—Nani (Dr Krishna Swarup), Geetha and Sai—was, I am sure, the best palliative for the elderly couple who were practically bedridden.

The families on both sides, paternal and maternal, were essentially landowning agriculturists, though my maternal grandfather had a sizeable money-lending business as well. On my paternal side, till after Father's marriage, when he started a fruit commission agency business along with his brother-in-law Ram mama and another, the family was solely dependent on agriculture. The family owned a considerable extent of wetlands in Poli village and dry lands in Seetharamapuram, Chinillugaripalli, Kichamambapuram and Mandaram villages. The lands in Mandaram village to a large extent went to the share of Tirumal Reddy, Father's younger brother, who took his share in the family properties and settled in Mandaram after his marriage. His sons, except the last one, ended as school dropouts, presumably on account of a pampered early childhood. His three daughters married well; the eldest, Sujatha, married the late Ella Reddy, who was a successful lawyer and Chairman of the State Bar Council. Their sons Sudhir and Sunil, two active entrepreneurs, were for long executing highways and other infrastructural projects as contractors. Their firm, a highly-rated infrastructure major, has lately suffered, apparently on account of vastly diversified and expanded operations.

From what I heard in my younger days, agriculture was not lucrative back then. As a family elder in an old Telugu movie pithily puts it to his progeny: "Agriculture was never a profit-oriented occupation; it was a way of life", and perhaps it continues to be so for a vast majority of the rural population. In our area, the farmers were not growing cash crops, like in the later years, and the mainstay was paddy and a few short-term rabi crops. Farmers had to depend solely on timely rains and when they did not receive sufficient rainfall, they were in dire straits. Though in such times a few families like ours could manage with stored grains, small-scale farmers, tenants and agricultural labourers found it hard to have even a frugal meal. In those days, the worth of a family would be gauged by the number of pairs of bullocks they owned, since agricultural operations depended solely on bullocks for ploughing, transportation and baling water out of wells. It was said that my family had to often sell gold to pay the land revenue when the crops failed, which was not infrequent. For anyone with some business sense, it would have seemed utterly imprudent to retain lands fetching little or no income, with liability to pay revenue besides maintaining farm servants and cattle. But then, for the farming families, prestige lay in the extent of land owned and, as stated above, agriculture was never viewed from the angle of profitability.

This became abundantly clear to me when I took over the reins of management after Father passed away in 1990. I had to send money all the time to maintain the lands and gardens, leave alone earning profit. Advocate Nagaraja Gupta, my friend and neighbour in Rajampet, used to take care of my affairs, particularly passing on money to Raghuramaiah (Raghu) for managing agricultural operations, and he would often tell me how dismal the cost–benefit ratio was. But then, the legacy that I represent being what it is, I never ever thought of winding up the show. I can recall writing to the then Chief Minister Chandrababu Naidu on management of water reserves in a rain-starved area like Rajampet. Statistics would reveal that this small pocket of area around Rajampet has over the years been a rain shadow area; often during monsoon, heavy rainfall stops at Kodur on the south and Cuddapah on the other side. With the result, Poli Tank, with land over 1,400 acres as its *ayacut*, doesn't get filled, and the wetlands which depend on water from the tank remain fallow. Ironically, those wetlands are classified as being of the highest *taram*, the scale used for levy of land revenue in the settlement records for classification of lands during British rule, with reference to fertility, irrigation and other factors contributing for yield. During one of my visits, it struck me that the poor record of water availability in Poli Tank meant that all those lands were lying fallow and unproductive.

Genesis

Having surrendered all the wetlands we owned there as excess land under the Land Ceiling Act of 1969, my family had no interest in the irrigation water for those wetlands. However, seeing the vast expanse of those lands lying fallow year after year used to be deeply saddening. So, my proposal was to classify such tanks, with reference to rainfall data and the number of consecutive years during which it remained dry as percolation tanks disallowing water for cultivation of the wetlands under its ayacut; and pay an amount determined as expense for converting the soil of such wetlands to be made usable for dry crop cultivation, and possibly some subsidy for sinking wells. With the tank retaining what little water was received for longer periods in the summer months, wells in many neighbouring villages would have plenty of water available at a lesser depth. This would provide a boost to well-irrigated cultivation in all those villages, besides reducing the cost of bore wells and electricity consumed for the farmers. When there was no response from the CM on my proposal, I mentioned it to S. V. Prasad, Secretary to the CM, whom I had known for long, and sent him a copy of my representation, which of course was of no avail. What I found most disappointing is the lack of awareness of the travails of the farmers of those villages owing to this unfortunate natural phenomenon of scanty rains. These thoughts engaged my mind then and are, I imagine, alive in my mind today on account of the legacy of a farming background. The turnaround came in the later years when progressive farmers like Father started growing cash crops like banana, sugarcane and turmeric, and raised citrus orchards. While in the village, I vividly recall walking with Father in the evenings to the orchards and fields, where he would go to check on the work done earlier in the day by the farm servants and daily wagers.

The source of water for irrigation was open wells, with water levels dipping if the tank went dry for long. There being no electricity, water had to be baled by the traditional method using bullocks. I remember Father getting a 'Russell Newberry' 10 HP oil engine to operate water pumps besides a sugarcane crusher to make jaggery. The mechanic who operated such an engine in the cinema theatre had to come to formally open the crate and make a trial operation. It's a different matter that, over the years, one of our farm servants became an expert at the operation and maintenance of oil engines, electric motors, etc.

A few years later, Father bought a tractor made in Russia, which was good value for its price and could be conveniently used with paddle wheels for preparing wetlands for paddy cultivation.

Father used to be quite passionate about farming and was known to be an aficionado of diverse crops and orchards, besides being a progressive farmer. He is known to have procured bulbs of a green variety of bananas from the southern districts of Tamil Nadu and was a pioneer in planting them in our area. Growing this variety of bananas is even now very popular amongst farmers in the area since it is highly fetching. Of course, now there is a sea change, with tissue culture making planting of bulbs obsolete and better road transport facilities making access to markets in far-off cities like Delhi easy. The villages where we had lands being located amidst hillocks, dry lands suitable for farming were available only in small pockets. This necessitated the conversion of grazing lands into cultivable land to create large enough and commercially viable plots for raising orchards or for agriculture. While such a plot closer to the village was used for raising a citrus orchard besides bananas and turmeric cultivation, for a mango orchard a larger plot was considered desirable. This led to planting a mango orchard on an island in the middle of the river in Kichamambapuram village. The family had a major share in that 'Inam Shotriam' village, where there is a cluster of temples on the riverside and the place is known as Hatyarala. There in the river Cheyyeru, and about two kilometres from the temples on its bank, an island got formed with sandy soil, and Father availed of it to plant a mango orchard of more than fifty acres. Our family retained this and other dry lands, surrendering all wetlands owned when the agricultural Land Ceiling Act came into force in the year 1969.

Looking back, it must be said that farming DNA seems to prevail over the rest in me as well. This is perhaps attributable more to the environment as there was hardly any focus on education in rural areas.

2   Schooling

While in the village, schooling for my two elder sisters Saraswathi and Prabhavathi (Prabha) and myself must have been a ticklish problem for our parents. There being no school in the village, one could only attend school in Rajampet, which had classes from primary to sixth form (Secondary School Leaving Certificate or SSLC level). Our parents therefore maintained a house near the school in Rajampet for us with a cook-cum-caretaker, and after a couple of years decided to shift my sisters to Madras for proper education. Pausing here, I need to advert to my mother's progressive mind and strong-willed nature. As is to be expected of one born and brought up in and married into families of rural landowners, she had a feudal mindset which manifested while dealing with domestic staff and other villagers. She had, at the same time, a highly compassionate nature in extending help to whoever sought it. More significantly, Mother was remarkably progressive in matters like education for girls, etc. It is her strong will that led to my two elder siblings Saraswathi and Prabha being sent to a convent school, Santhome Convent (St. Raphael's Girls School) in Madras. It is worth recalling what, in Mother's words, led to her determination in this regard despite the cost and logistical issues involved. Father had admitted her into hospital in Madras for the delivery of her first two children. While in the hospital, Mother apparently used to hear the doctors, nurses and others conversing in English, without being able to follow what was said since she had no English education, though she was proficient in Telugu. That disability, according to her, made her resolve to ensure that her daughters shall not suffer such a handicap, and so choose convent education for them.

The anglicised education and exposure to lifestyle in the convent was complemented by the classical Carnatic music that my sisters were made to learn while spending summer vacation and other holidays in the village. A violinist from one of the neighbouring villages used to come and teach them violin and Carnatic vocals, and how I wish

Mother had not left me out of this exercise since I often used to repeat the lyrics of *Thyagarayakeerthanas* to test my sisters' memory. After schooling, Saraswathi and Prabha joined Queen Mary's College in Madras, from where they graduated, becoming the first graduates in the family. There may not have been any women graduates at that time in Rajampet area, though at about the same time, two other ladies—coincidentally of the same name, Prabhavathi—hailing from Rajampet area, graduated from Madras University. The senior amongst them is P. Prabhavathi of Rajampet, a close friend of my sisters, who later married Yugandhar, a highly regarded Indian Administrative Service (IAS) officer; and if one considers Ivanka Trump during her recent visit to Hyderabad referring to that city, in laudatory terms, as the place where Satya Nadella, an icon of information technology (IT), had his education, one can claim that Rajampet is the mother of IT since Nadella is the distinguished son of P. Prabhavathi. The other highly regarded lady graduate of the time from the area was K. Prabhavathamma, who was elected as member of the Legislative Assembly from Rajampet constituency after the passing away of her husband Konduru Mara Reddy, a former member of Legislative Assembly (MLA) who commanded great respect and was regarded as a gentleman-politician even at a very young age.

With my sisters shifting to Madras for their education, I was left alone, and so a house with domestic staff in Rajampet was not found worthwhile to maintain. Forced by circumstances, I was made a paying guest in the house of a teacher, the rent and cost of boarding being met by the family. Besides basic provisions like rice and dal, which were regularly delivered to ensure wholesome food for me, Mother would also send eggs and fruits, which I, of course, used to share with the host family. Must say, it was quite uneventful, with me living away from the family, without any significant progress in studies and no pleasant memories to recall as such; nay, I would rather wipe out the memories of my time as a house guest.

At about that time, i.e., in about 1950, when I was in third form or eighth standard, my uncle, Yaga Pitchi Reddy, my mother's younger sister Ammanemma's husband and father of my cousins Dr Y. V. Reddy (Venu) and Dr Y. R. K. Reddy (Babu), came to be posted as a senior administrative officer in the Madras State Secretariat. He was, I think, director of the Rayalaseema Development Board in the Secretariat. This led to my moving to Madras to live with them, and I joined school there. Initially, for a short while, I was in Kesari High School, and later I completed my schooling from Ramakrishna Mission High School, T Nagar in Madras. Venu and I used to catch a bus from near Lakshmipuram, where my aunt and uncle used to live, to go to Panagal Park in T Nagar. It was bus number 13 on that route then. Every morning some thinking used to go into deciding at which bus stop we were going to board the bus. Of the two bus stops, which were more or less equidistant for us, Gowdiya Matt was the first one the bus would reach. If we boarded the bus there, the fare used to be half anna more and the crowd was less. If we boarded from the later bus stop on the perpendicular road known as Besant Road, the fare used to be half anna less, but more people to push your way through. When Venu, with a brilliant academic career and accomplishments as an economist-administrator—as secretary in the Ministry of Finance and later as deputy governor and then governor of RBI—handled India's economic affairs remarkably deftly, particularly when our fiscal management was in dire straits, I missed no opportunity in taunting him by telling friends that Venu cut his teeth in economics when we used to board bus number 13 to go to school in Madras.

Though Ammanakka, my aunt, used to organise packed lunch for us to carry, if we missed out on that, we used to go to the vegetarian hotel across the road to have Mysore bonda and masala dosa for lunch. In the evenings, we played gully cricket with our friends in the narrow strip of our backyard. I remember using an Australian cork ball, which was more lasting and with less bounce than the ordinary cork ball. There was no need for an umpire as the ball used to bear a touch of the colour of the stumps drawn on the wall. C. Sadasiva Reddy (Sada), who later joined the bar and practiced along with me in the Andhra Pradesh High Court, was a Dattu Phadkar of sorts, though now he claims that he was more into spin of the Subhash Gupte mould. The other regulars were Satya Raju (Satti), who retired as a senior officer in the Revenue Department and member of the Land Grab Tribunal, and Dr R. Ramchandra Reddy (soda glasses, son of R. Ramalinga Reddy, advocate, who later became public prosecutor of Andhra Pradesh in Hyderabad), all from our neighbourhood. That was about the time when international freestyle wrestling bouts came to be organised for the first time in Madras with Dara Singh, King

Kong, Harbans Singh and many others—it was great fun. The princely sum of five rupees for entrance fee was nothing if we consider all the excitement. We used to even try emulating the bouts, having a ring in the upper floor hall with cotton mattresses spread out. I used to give rides to Babu, the youngest in the family, on the bicycle. In between Venu and Babu there was another brother Madhu who, after graduating in law, passed away in a tragic accident while driving a Jeep on the Nandyal–Kurnool road. He was expected to take to the legal profession, and the tragedy denied me a companion in the profession from the family. Sarala (Prameela), their only sister, is married to Dr Prabhakar Reddy, a very amiable person, and they proceeded to the UK and made London their home. In Lakshmipuram there was also M. Jagannadha Rao, who, after a successful career as advocate, rose to adorn the Bench of the Supreme Court, and there was his brother Krishnamohan. On the whole, it was a good and enjoyable life, with an affectionate family and the company of good friends all around.

3 Colleges

My uncle, Pitchi Reddy Chinnayya (PRC), though a senior officer in the government, had no airs about him and was incredibly down-to-earth in his dealings with one and all. He personified poise and equanimity. Ammanakka, my aunt, would of course ensure all creature comforts for the family, besides organising delectable and sumptuous food. I was quite close to PRC and a recipient of his unremitting affection. Here, one incident comes to my mind. Being particularly poor in maths, I was keen to have a private tutor. I mentioned this to PRC, who agreed to arrange one for me. He apparently entrusted the task to a deputy secretary working under him, and when it did not materialise for long, I conjured a plan to make him realise the urgency. Back then, senior officers like him used to wear a cotton jacket and solar *topi* to office. I made a dozen slips of paper, writing on each of them 'Raja's tuition', put one in each pocket of his jacket, one in his spectacles case, and so on, and at the office, a slip of reminder emerging from whichever pocket he put his hand in did the trick. I can recall the distress I felt while I was with him at the Vellore Hospital, where he initially underwent treatment for his urological problem. I was deeply saddened by the news of his passing away while I was in London.

Well, I completed my SSLC with the distinction of making use of every concession in the rule book for scraping through, moved on to intermediate course with biology, chemistry, etc. Deft dissection of frog for brain got me ten upon ten, leading to a momentary fancy for joining a medical course. Needless to say that the marks scored could get me nowhere near there, and so I joined BA Economics and Politics in Loyola College, Madras. Life at the hostel in Loyola was filled with fun and friendship, despite the taunts and invectives hurled at us by the boys of Madras Christian College, Tambaram, while traveling past our hostel in the electric local trains. They wouldn't miss an opportunity to deride us as the 'slaves of Loyola'.

Yes, there were rules to be followed. Inmates had to be in their rooms by 8.00 p.m., unless they were using the library for study and signing in the register there. Father Repinat, a lovable elderly Italian priest who was the warden, used to go around with a long torchlight in hand to see if the inmates were back in their rooms. If we ran out of our pocket money, he would lend us Rs 20, adding it later to the monthly bill. There also used to be an Indian priest as a deputy warden to check on the inmates.

Such rigorous enforcement of discipline would necessarily make young minds innovate methods to circumvent the same. One friend with remarkable activism in this respect was T. G. Krishnamoorthy (TGK), who is presently doing a great deal of social work, apart from associating himself with activities at Puttaparthi. Strangely, I find him disinclined to be reminded of college life, leading me to wonder if all his spiritual and social service activities are meant to be some kind of penance, though I cannot imagine anything sinful in our college life. Besides TGK, I had few others in the hostel like C. Venkateswara Rao, M. M. Ramachandran from Dharmapuri, Gopal (G. K. P. Reddy), K. L. N. Shastry, and the irrepressible Homi Dinshaw Dhanjiboi, with whom I spend quality time now whenever Radha and I are in Coonoor, where Homi has settled after his retirement as a planter with his loving wife Khorshid. Amongst the day scholars were close friends like tennis captain V. Ram Mohan, Joe Abraham, the Challapally brothers (Ammu and Bujji). We, the hostel group, partook in many adventures and activities together, which mostly involved sneaking out for a late show in a downtown theatre. Must say, the hostel management tried to pander to this craving of movie buffs by screening English movies once a week, every Friday, in the Bertram Hall. Since very often it used to be a movie we had already seen or considered not worth seeing, we, particularly TGK and I, used to take off to the city for a more recent English or a Hindi movie in a solitary theatre, 'Star', that used to screen the latest movies. Six different dining facilities catering different cuisines was a somewhat unique feature of Loyola hostel. We all had the luxury of single occupancy rooms. Looking back, must say the contrast in lifestyle and facilities provided by hostels of schools and colleges run by the Ramakrishna Mission and those in Loyola College make the two seem polar opposites.

After completing BA, a professional course was the obvious choice and so I joined the renowned Madras Law College in Chennai. In fact, it being the only law college in the composite Madras State, many of the lawyers and judges in South India were the proud products of Madras Law College. It was a two-year course then, with a student having to successfully complete the first year of law (FL) and passing the first-year exam before moving to the second year. It is perhaps no exaggeration to state that academic activity in the college was marked by a lack of seriousness both amongst the teachers and more so amongst the taught. Daily attendance or roll call was, for long, a shallow formality, with proxies answering in many cases and the more enterprising managing favourable numbers at the end of the year to satisfy the requirement of the university. Frankly, no one is to be blamed for any lack of motivation and commitment. We, in fact, had some excellent teachers like Balasubramaniam and Rajaram among others, and part-timers, notable amongst them being Justice Mohan, who later adorned the Bench of the Supreme Court. The root cause, I believe, was the widely held notion that law for a legal practitioner was something to be learnt on the job, not in class.

To quote from 'Reminiscences and Random Thoughts', my presentation during the conference organised by the Bar Association of India (BAI) on '40 Years of The Advocates Act, 1961', in Goa in 2001 (henceforth referred to as the 'Goa article'; see Appendix 4), published in the commemorative volume brought out on the occasion by BAI:

> Legal education had never enjoyed any particular importance or primacy in the academic world. The 14th Report of the Law Commission headed by Sri. M. C. Setalvad, Attorney General for India, referring to standards in law colleges bemoaned that in the chaotic state of affairs prevailing in a number of these institutions there is hardly a pretence at teaching. The Commission went on further to comment "It is true that our country has produced eminent practitioners in law and learned Judges. Their achievements probably arise from their own intellectual brilliance and capacity rather than from the education received by them at the Universities". Dealing with the steady deterioration in standards, the Commission highlighted lack of motivation amongst the students and lack

of earnestness in teaching as factors leading to the dismal state of legal education. How true it is. Students of early days of Madras Law College remember the opening lecture of one of the popular professors in which he was known to remind his students that "they were there since they could not be elsewhere". There was also this Vice-Chancellor of a University, who had earlier occupied a high position in the Judiciary, who recalled to memory his days as a student of Law, addressing the law faculty of the University, reportedly stated matter of factly that law courses were never serious educational exercises. Thus, there was always this belief that professional knowledge and skills are to be gained by a lawyer more during his initial association with a senior or in courts than through study of law.

The attendance part of it got tightened during my second year, that is, when Sankarnarayanan took over as director, and some students like me had to pay the price by applying for condonation, besides attending college even during the pre-exam preparatory holidays. There was, of course, a library in the college with books neatly stacked on shelves, but hardly any users from among the students. Capsule guides in question-and-answer format were popular and not textbooks, much less the reference volumes in the library. There may have been some exceptions with a few students aiming for medals and distinctions.

Since the newly opened hostel of the Madras Law College was far, involving a long commute, I tried for accommodation at the Catholic Center and was put on the waiting list. Meanwhile I joined a university students' hostel in Broadway which, besides being an old building, was a dump really, facilities wise. It took a while to get used to staying there, what with all the comforts enjoyed at Loyola earlier. The only advantage was that this hostel was within walking distance from college. Must say, attending college was more fun than any serious academic activity. During the second year, i.e., while doing the BL (Bachelor of Law) part, I decided to contest for the post of general secretary of the college union. Campaigning involved addressing classes between lecture periods and pumping hands with supporters giving out flyers at the main entrance. I had no dearth of supporters for campaigning, though the strategy was totally flawed in not paying sufficient attention to meet and humour the students of the two first year of law (FL) sections attending the afternoon session. Considering that large number of students hailed from districts in Tamil Nadu, the fact that I hailed from Andhra state, and was seemingly an urbanite, willy-nilly became an adverse factor amongst a substantial section, while, curiously, I couldn't secure the wholehearted support of the Telugus, who felt peeved that I was mostly amongst the urbanite Tamil supporters. There were, of course, a few exceptions. Notable amongst them being Ch. Sidda Reddy, a highly regarded senior lawyer in Kadapa, the late Rama Raju who was into politics in Rajampet, and Justice P. Venkatram Reddy who retired after a distinguished career as Chief Justice (CJ), Karnataka High Court and Judge, Supreme Court of India. Significantly and mercifully there was no involvement of political parties in the student body elections then, as became commonplace in later years in Hyderabad and elsewhere. Well, the outcome was a narrow loss by three votes to Santhyogarajan. The solace, if any, was that I could poll more than what all the three opposing candidates, including the winner, together had from my BL section, of which they were also members. The downside of the misadventure in practical terms was that friends couldn't help me with attendance as proxies since I came to be known to all the lecturers.

All through the years while I was doing BA in Loyola and law in the Madras Law College, I used to regularly visit Rajampet and spend my holidays there. While there, practically every morning I used to accompany Father in his Jeep or car to Seetharamapuram or on occasions to our Hatyarala mango garden, to be back for lunch. During that time, I started noticing the gradual transformation of rural society. Farm servants and daily wagers had seemingly improved their lifestyle and standards. Use of shirts, sandals, watches became commonplace. Many from the Harijan hamlets of Seetharamapuram and neighbouring villages started working as gang coolies in railways and a significant number in Tirumala Tirupati Devasthanams (TTD). It was immensely heartening to see Harijans from Seetharamapuram in the sanctum sanatorium of the temple as helpers; one of them was in charge of vending gold lockets, etc. They would recognise Father and greet him with respect when we visited the temple, and the warm feeling of oneness always transcended the much-talked about sectorial divide.

While mornings were devoted to visiting the farms and orchards, in the evenings I used to go to what was known as the Officers Club in the compound of the Taluk office and police station. The Officers Club comprised a thatched hut with a table, some chairs for playing cards and a clay court for tennis which was dusty most of the time except when watered with cattle dung and rolled. A few tennis players were lawyers: V. Laxman, A. Chengal Reddy, P. Venkat Reddy, Rama Raju, besides P. Venkat Seshaiah, headmaster, and few others like M. S. Naidu, and some excise officials. Most of them started playing tennis later in life, using their experience in playing ball badminton, which was the most popular sport back then in the region, and so were not adept at ground strokes. Laxman, having played in his college days, stood out as the best player. It used to be fascinating to see this elderly gentleman, Venkatratnam, who used to play bare-feet, clad in a dhoti. He had retired from government service after a long stint in the sub-collector's office. He must have played on the tennis court in the sub-collector's bungalow to keep the officer in good humour. Anticipation was the key to his game, which enabled him to be in place to receive the ball and hit it back into the opposite court, making us marvel at his skill. After tennis, there used to be a game of cards with small stakes of a paisa or so. There used to be a riot of laughter with the wit and humour of Venkat Seshaiah, who would often pull the leg of his friend Venkat Reddy or taunt someone else. About that time, Daljit Arora, IAS, was sub-collector at Rajampet. When his wife joined him, she apparently used to accompany him to the club and join the cards table. It used to be hilarious to hear Venkat Seshaiah describe the tricky situations experienced by the other players in dealing with a lady at the table, starting with the mode of address and other courtesies. Though I had known Daljit Arora—having been invited for tea when I visited Rajampet the first time after his posting—I was not there when Mrs Arora joined him, and so missed out on all the fun and confusion amongst the patriarchal players of Rajampet.

After I secured the BL degree, since practicing law was the goal, I had to think of commencing apprenticeship, a pre-enrolment requirement back then, in Hyderabad—it being the seat of the High Court of Andhra Pradesh. I chose Koka Ramachandra Rao's office for my apprenticeship since he handled a variety of civil litigation. Though

Rao couldn't take me in as he already had two apprentices, which was the maximum permitted by the Bar Council rules, I felt gratified when he tried to seek a relaxation of the rule to accommodate me. Since that didn't seem feasible, I joined the office of Justice O. Chinnappa Reddy (OCR), who was then a noted criminal lawyer, handling a large volume of work including heavy civil matters. There were seven to eight juniors in his office, the senior-most amongst them being C. Padmanabha Reddy, who in later years stood tallest among criminal lawyers, with an unparalleled reputation for integrity, and came to be truly acknowledged as a people's lawyer. To my knowledge, no litigant who sought to engage him was ever turned away for incapacity to pay even a modest fee. Must say, C. Padmanabha Reddy truly imbibed the spirit of service as the ethos of the profession, for which his mentor Justice O. Chinnappa Reddy, an eminent lawyer and legendary judge himself, came to be recognised in the country. Very association with the office was a matter of immense pride, and I had developed close relationships with all the juniors. One of the juniors was D. Raja Reddy, who had married my younger sister, Suguna. For some months when Suguna was not in Hyderabad, being away in Rajampet, I used to stay in their home in Agapura and commute to the senior's office from there in Raja's Ford Prefect car.

    About that time, I developed a fascination for going to the United Kingdom for pursuing further studies in law. That was also the time when there were severe restrictions for release of foreign exchange, and a course of study in law certainly did not qualify for such release. B. Gopala Reddy was then minister of state in the Central Ministry of Finance. I approached him during one of his visits to Hyderabad through his close associate Parthasarathy, who was then an MP representing the Rajampet constituency. The rules being stringent, no help was forthcoming. This was overcome with my sister Prabha and brother-in-law Dr N. R. C. Reddi, who was then working in London, insisting on my going to London and offering to take care of my financial requirements. One hurdle crossed, the next was the serious problem of persuading my parents, Father particularly, to allow me to go abroad, since Father knew as well as I did that any further qualification may not benefit me greatly in my career as a lawyer in India. Though there were a few barristers practicing in Madras, generally there wasn't as much prestige attached to foreign educational qualifications in the south back then as there was in Calcutta and elsewhere. Looking back, I think it was the opportunity to travel and get an exposure to university life, particularly since I had the advantage of my sister and brother-in-law living in London, which ultimately led to my going to the UK.

Plate 1 Earliest photograph of VRR with his mother.

Plate 2 VRR's father in Western attire.

PLATE 3 VRR during early school years with his mother.

PLATE 4 Family photograph; sitting (L to R) mother, Dr Krishna Swaroop, father, paternal grandmother; standing (L to R) Saraswathi, VRR, Prabhavathi, Suguna.

Plate 5 VRR at Loyola College, with C. Venkateshwara Rao and M. M. Ramachandran.

Plate 6 VRR after graduation.

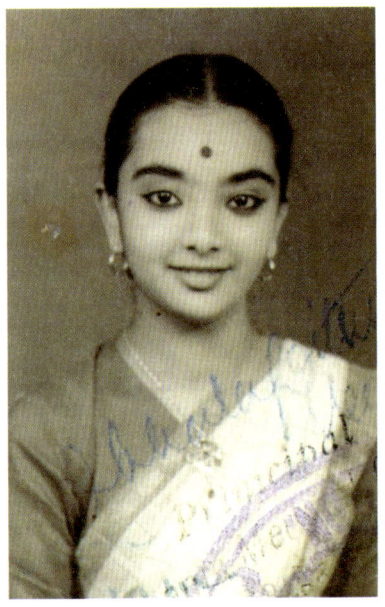

PLATE 7 Radha, VRR's wife, as a student of Osmania Medical College, Hyderabad.

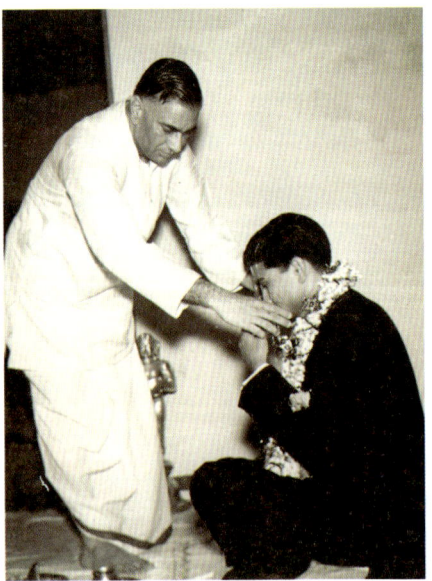

PLATE 8 VRR at his engagement ceremony, with father-in-law Nukala.

Plate 9 VRR weds Radha.

Plate 10 VRR at wedding dinner, with Radha's cousins Ramesh, Vijay, Janardhan and Vikram.

PLATE 11 VRR at wedding dinner, with college friends Ankineedu Prasad, Ram Mohan, Krishnamurthy, Ramachandran, Sounderarajan.

PLATE 12 At Rajampet with grandmother after the wedding.

PLATE 13 At Rajampet with sister Saraswati, Shiv mama and their children.

PLATE 14 With aunt and uncle at Korlakunta.

PLATE 15 Reception dinner at Rajampet; (L to R) P. Venkataseshaiyya, V. Laxman, P. Venkat Reddy and others.

PLATE 16 VRR with the children.

Plate 17 Radha with the children.

Plate 18 Family with Mahipal, Saras, and baby Aarathi.

PLATE 19 With parents Sri. Velakacherla Narasa Reddy and Smt. Jayalakshmamma at Rajampet.

PLATE 20 VRR's family with Mr and Mrs Neelam Sanjeeva Reddy.

Plate 21 VRR at centenary celebrations of Secunderabad Club, with president A. Ranga Rao, Jagdish Reddy and other members of the managing committee.

Plate 22 VRR speaking on the occasion at Secunderabad Club.

PLATE 23 VRR being received as a delegate to the Asian Racing Conference at Seoul, Korea; R. Surender Reddy looks on.

PLATE 24 At the conference with N. N. Reddy, Secretary HRC and Vikram.

Plate 25 VRR and Radha at the wedding of Deepika and Shyam, with NTR gracing the occasion.

Plate 26 VRR and Radha greeted by NRC and Prabha on their 25th wedding anniversary.

PLATE 27 K. T. S. Tulsi at the wedding of VRR's son Siddharth and Aditi in Hyderabad.

PLATE 28 Dr and Mrs P. S. Rao and Mr and Mrs N. G. Reddy at the wedding.

PLATE 29 Dignitaries at the wedding: K. Vijayabhaskar Reddy, K. Raghunath Reddy, N. Janardhan Reddy, N. Rajyalaksmi Reddy, T. Subbarami Reddy.

PLATE 30 Siddharth and Aditi with Bapsi and Fali Nariman at the wedding reception, Delhi.

PLATE 31 With G. Venkat Swamy, Union Minister, R. Surender Reddy, Justice B. P. Jeevan Reddy and VRR.

PLATE 32 Receiving blessings from Justice V. K. Krishna Iyer at the wedding reception, Delhi.

4   University of London

Regarding the course options, I got hold of a London University publication which gave details of various courses on offer in law. I was excited to find a diploma course listed as 'Academic Postgraduate Diploma in Law'. This made it easier to persuade my parents to agree, it being only a one-year course.

The diploma course was essentially a shorter version of the Master of Laws (LLM) postgraduate degree. While LLM had four subjects, the diploma had three, and the marks to be secured in the exam were ten per cent less for the diploma course, being of a shorter duration. For candidates who graduated from non-common law countries, English legal history was compulsory. Others, like me, could choose any other subject instead. My subjects were Law of International Institutions, Comparative Study of Constitutions of Australia, Canada and India, besides Tort and Contracts, which I opted for instead of English Legal History.

The international law lectures were by Dr Shwartzenberger in the University College and seminars by Dr Chang. Lectures on the Indian Constitution were by Prof. Alan Gledhill, Administrative Law by Prof. DeSmith in London School of Economics (LSE), and Tort and Contracts lectures used to be in Kings College. One year passed in no time, attending lectures and seminars at different venues and studying in the cosy rooms of the library of the School of Oriental Studies in Russell Square. Most of the time during that period I was staying with NRC (Dr N. R. C. Reddi) and Prabha, initially in Tooting Bec and later in Leytonstone, commuting by tube. After some time, I moved to lodgings in Earls Court where a couple of my college friends from Madras were also staying. The University schedule was a rewarding experience, which gave me some idea of what a proper university education and curriculum ought to be.

I had an occasion to attend a law lecture at Harvard while visiting the US during the years of my practice in the Supreme Court. My wife and I were in the US, visiting my sister-in-law, Saras, and her husband Mahipal, living in Millbury near Boston. We somehow came into contact with our dear ebullient friend P. H. Parekh, a busy lawyer in the Supreme Court, heading the law firm founded by him, who was attending some summer courses at the Harvard Law School. Praveen, as is his wont, insisted that we meet up for lunch at his friend's place. There we met Harish Salve, who was also attending summer lectures at Harvard University. When I evinced interest to attend one of them, Harish took me along to the one he was attending that afternoon. It turned out to be a lecture on a topic of jurisprudence. Must say, the professor, by his informal style, made even that dry topic incredibly interesting. Having had exposure, though briefly, on either side of the Atlantic, I could notice the difference in the styles of teaching and, more importantly, what was significantly lacking in legal education in India.

After my diploma course, I was advised by Ramachandra Reddy, the only person from this area who was doing an LLM in London University at that time, to try and see if I could pursue a PhD, though admission to PhD was only for those who completed their PG degree (LLM). Ramachandra was obviously unaware of my future plans of legal practice, and may have assumed that I had inclinations to be an academic. At his insistence, I met Prof. Gledhill, who was not very helpful.

After securing my diploma, with a view to spend some free time in London, I approached the student counsellor's office and secured temporary employment in the Social Welfare Department of the government, which needed manpower to collate data in their office. I used to receive weekly payment in cash, neatly put into an envelope. During this period, I made a trip to the Scandinavian countries to see the much-touted concept of 'welfare-state' pursued there, particularly by Sweden. After some procrastination, enjoying my free time, mostly at the University of London Union and with friends, I made my booking with Lloyd Triestino to sail back home.

5 Siblings and Spouses

Looking back, I have fond memories of close and affectionate association with my three sisters and, more particularly, their spouses (my brothers-in-law).

My eldest sibling, Saraswathi, was from her younger days an embodiment of equanimity and compassion. She had a spirituality-oriented mindset and a highly forgiving nature marked by boundless affection to all within the family and beyond. She chose to be a vegetarian from a young age, barring the consumption of eggs, which I should imagine must have been necessitated by the limited choice of food on offer for a vegetarian during her stay in the Catholic boarding school. I can recall being induced to convert to vegetarianism, which, of course, didn't last for long with me. After her graduation, Saraswathi got married to our maternal uncle, Shivaram Reddy (Shiv mama), as was the customary practice amongst many families in those days. I suppose such practices—unmindful of the advice of medical science, which may not have been so vocal back then as in later years, to avoid marriage between close blood relations—may have stemmed from the desire to maintain close relations with daughters even after they were married.

Shiv mama, a science graduate, was immensely popular with contemporaries of his college days and used to spend much time with them in Madras, trying to pitch upon a profitable enterprise. After his marriage, he became a civil contractor on the advice of Ramanujula Naidu, the first registrar of the newly-established Sri Venkateswara University at Tirupati. Naidu was a lecturer in the college where Shiv mama was a student in Madras, and was very fond of him. Since, at its inception, many civil works were to be executed for the university, he induced Shiv mama—in whose integrity he had full faith—to take up such works as a civil contractor. Shiv mama and Saraswathi thus came to live in Tirupati for many years. Tirupati, besides being a highly popular pilgrim centre, had become a hub of sorts for education and medical care, and there used to be a stream of visitors to their house, and Saraswathi would unfailingly extend hospitality to them with a smile, regardless of their economic or social status. Many used to count on Shiv mama for help in securing admission to colleges, and *darshan* at the temple, and whatever be the nature of help sought and whoever the seeker, high or low, Shiv mama used to attend to it even at the cost of his own contract business. He was a non-smoker and teetotaller who used to spend time at the club playing cards, the pastime he enjoyed most. It was not the money changing hands at the table that enamoured him, since he would gladly play with family members including children and could be seen enjoying the same. Youngsters in the family used to love his company as much as the seniors did. In my younger days in Madras, I used to count on Shiv mama for helping me with my shopping and admission to college. He was so very familiar with Madras that he knew where to find the best deals, be it woollen wear or footwear, you name it, and he was acquainted with the shopkeepers, particularly in China Bazar, Broadway and those areas.

Their two sons, Krishna Swaroop (Nani) and Sai Sreenath, completed medicine and law courses respectively, and their only daughter Geetha was married to Janardhan, a bank executive, while in Tirupati. Shiv mama passed away after battling oral cancer for about three years. Sadly, his second son, Sai, a very affectionate young man, passed away prematurely at a young age, leaving behind his devoted wife Manasa and children Sravya and Suhrud. Swaroop worked in hospitals abroad after doing his MD, and is now a highly regarded paediatric consultant in Hyderabad. It is indeed a tragedy that Saraswathi should pass away while I was penning this memoir, on 7 December 2017, a year after being afflicted by cancer.

I have had closer association with Prabha, my second sister, who spent many years in the UK, along with her husband Dr N. R. C. Reddi (NRC). NRC was the son of Naru Ranga Reddi, a noted lawyer at Cuddapah who was a minister in the Madras Cabinet, headed by C. Rajagopalachari. NRC passed out of Stanley Medical College in Madras and served briefly as a doctor in government hospitals before proceeding to UK for his postgraduate qualification. He secured his Fellowship of the Royal Colleges of Surgeons and specialised in orthopaedics, securing a Master of Surgery. Prabha, who joined him little later in UK, completed a postgraduate diploma course in social studies at London University, and then worked for sometime in a children's hospital of the National Health Service (NHS) as a hospital almoner. My initial period in London I spent with them, and the affection they showered on me is something I cherish. Prabha used to fix breakfast for me before dashing off for her work and would manage to organise supper after returning from work, with some items of Indian cuisine thrown in. Those were not the days with Indian restaurants, takeaways and Indian stores in abundance, as one finds in London now. For spices, condiments and Indian vegetables, one had to go to Pathak Stores, and Veeraswamy was the restaurant known for fine dining with authentic Indian food. With NRC's affable and warm-hearted persona and Prabha's immensely hospitable nature coupled with the ability to produce delectable food to suit the Indian palate, must say, they were a hugely popular Indian couple. NRC was a sought-after visitor for all my friends. He was BIL (brother-in-law) to all of them and they used to troupe into my room whenever he came to visit me in my digs.

The eldest of their children, Sarath, who had spent some years in Rajampet during childhood and had schooling mostly in Hyderabad Public School, is an IIT-ian from Madras. He later did his MBA from University of Chicago, and is now founder-CEO of a venture capital firm, living in Chennai with his ebullient spouse, Meena. Their daughter Padma, who graduated from Birmingham University, is married to the lovably friendly K. K. Ashok, who, with his irrepressible wit, is delightful company. Ashok's father, the late K. Krishna Murthy, was a barrister who chose to become a corporate entrepreneur. He would nevertheless reel off legal maxims while spending time with me during my visits to Chennai. Ashok's mother, Akkamma, was a noted social entrepreneur who took many initiatives for the upliftment of women by creating institutions for their education and vocational training, and was the president of the Andhra Mahila Sabha. Before Padma's marriage to Ashok, at the instance of NRC and Prabha, I had to gather some information on the family, and so I asked my friend Ram Mohan if he knew them. Ram's response was, "Oh, them, of course I know them. They play tennis at the Gymkhana and are known for having their rackets strung in London". Being the tennis captain of my college, tennis was always foremost on Ram's mind. Padma and Ashok live in Chennai, and Ashok successfully lives down his zamindari background of Kattuputtur near Trichy in Tamil Nadu. Padma had developed a flair for stained glass artwork and used to make beautiful pieces in a small workplace that she created for herself at home. Sirish, after schooling in Rugby public school, graduated from Cambridge and secured his MBA from Insead in Paris. He is a busy entrepreneur, presently working on a start-up with good potential, along with Kavitha, his wife, who was with the BBC while she was with her parents, Shevak and Gul Tahilyani, in London. Shevak is such good company that we both love to spend time together during his visits to Hyderabad.

Suguna, my younger sister, married Dorigallu Raja Reddy (Raja) after her graduation. Raja, who had done his law, continued his stint as a lawyer after his marriage for a short period in Hyderabad. In fact, we used to attend the chambers of O. Chinnappa Reddy, he as a junior and I as an apprentice. Raja gave up practice and was with the Hindustan Shipyard in Vizag for a while before moving to Hyderabad to try his hand as an entrepreneur. He was a soft-spoken genial person of great equanimity and humility. The heart ailment which led to his passing away prematurely was shocking. Suguna, who chose to be a homemaker, puts to good use her intellect and innate organisational ability. Their son Vandith is an entrepreneur in the hospitality sector. Their daughter Nita is married to V. Srikar Reddy, a reputed real estate developer in Chennai; Srikar is also a great help to me in managing my interests in Chennai.

Raja's father, Venkataranga Reddy, who personified the typical patriarch of a joint family, was a fine person and had a lot of affection for me. I used to enjoy sitting with him on the platform in the front veranda, whenever I visited Dorigallu, to partake in the mid-morning coffee ritual with *palaharalu* (snacks). More interesting used to be to follow his aides reporting to him on various matters. Raja's father apparently did not consider the environment in Dorigallu conducive for peaceful living, and so packed off Raja to Hyderabad. It is a different matter that Raja, much later, tried his hand at politics, unsuccessfully contesting polls for Legislative Assembly. And just as well, for Raja, with his pleasant and decent nature, would have been unsuited for the rough and tumble of politics at that level.

Before signing off here it must be said that I was fortunate in enjoying the bonhomie and affection of the spouses of my three sisters, which oftentimes surpassed what may have been forthcoming from my own siblings—a blessing indeed.

6 1964, the Eventful Year

On my return from England, the first step to move forward in life was to enrol myself as advocate to commence practice. Not much deliberation was called for on this as I was clear in my mind that I would pursue my chosen career as a lawyer. Venue-wise, too, decision-making did not pose any problem as it had to be in the High Court of Andhra Pradesh in Hyderabad. Since by then the requirement of apprenticeship before enrolment was dispensed with, there was no need for me to complete the remainder of a few months left on account of my departure to London before completing one year of apprenticeship. I had also appeared for and passed the Bar Council exam, a pre-enrolment requirement, before leaving for abroad. I therefore immediately applied for enrolment, which by then had become a simple procedure of appearing before the enrolment committee of the State Bar Council, dispensing with the practice of appearance before the Chief Justice's court, with a senior lawyer proposing the candidate for enrolment. On 16 March 1964, I appeared before a committee of which J. Seethamahalakshmamma, mother of Justice Eshwari Prasad, was a member. Parallel to all this was my parents' move to get me married. Mother had started scouting for a suitable bride, visiting Hyderabad and spending time with Ammanakka, her younger sister. It wasn't long before her efforts bore fruit.

Pitchi Reddy Chinnayya's (PRC) younger brother, Shivashankar Reddy (Shankarayyachinnayya), who joined government service as an officer in the labour department and moved on to become commissioner Provident Fund, in which post he later retired, had married Snehalathamma, eldest daughter of a senior political leader—a stalwart, really, in Andhra State and later in Andhra Pradesh—A. C. Subba Reddy (AC) of the Anam family in Nellore district. He was closely associated, and on friendly terms, with Nukala Ramachandra Reddy (Nukala), senior Congress leader of Telangana hailing from Warangal district and a minister in the cabinet headed by K. Brahmananda Reddy as Chief Minister. This association between the two leaders and their families seems to have led to the proposal of my marriage with Radhika (Radha), elder daughter of Nukala.

When the proposal was broached to me, I had no reason not to seriously consider it. Firstly, my parents, more importantly, Father, who was not one to be enamoured by wealth or fame, seemed more than inclined to the match. Father had this perception of Nukala's reputation as a man of integrity and that of his family as unostentatious and one abiding by traditional family values. Looking back, I can say that, as one brimming with self-worth and the confidence of making good in the career I was about to embark on, more weightage was given to the education and the widely known simple and unassuming nature of the prospective bride from the standpoint of compatibility. Though dowry as a factor was not uncommon, it had mercifully not crossed the mind of anyone in the family since no such thing was involved when my sisters got married, and allowing the same to be factored in even remotely would have been a matter of compromising one's self-respect. In fact, when I heard a hint from Mother that it would be nice for the bride to have some select piece of jewellery, I vetoed it when it came to my notice.

From our side, decision-making was relatively easy since Nukala was a noted political leader, and the family's background and standing were well known in close circles of relatives and friends. On the other hand, I should imagine that it would have been rather complex for them to decide, with no personal knowledge of our family hailing from far-off Rajampet in an altogether different region. After they formed a favourable opinion, Radha's parents left the task of sizing me up to R. Surender Reddy (Surender), Nukala's brother-in-law, who was close to their family and in whose judgement they had implicit faith in most matters concerning the family. In later years, my close association with Surender made him guide, friend and philosopher to me.

Another of Nukala's relatives, G. Upender Reddy (Upender), who had married Nukala's eldest brother's daughter, also became a much-admired associate of mine. Upender was particularly known for his large-hearted, hospitable nature. Deep affection and an extremely helpful nature were traits noticeable not only in him, but seem to have run in the family. I have observed this trait in the late G. Surender Reddy, Upender's younger brother, and also in their sister Sucharita, wife of Dr P. C. Reddy (PC), the Founder Chairman of Apollo Hospitals. A legend and pioneer in the field of medical care in India, he has, by his pioneering initiatives in the private sector, made not only his family and friends but the country proud. A wise man once bemoaned that on account of advances in science, medical men sometimes fail to realise the importance of the psychological effect that their personality has on their patients, and said that, "If a doctor is to fulfil his role, he must learn the art of spreading sunshine and hope by his very presence and speech in every sick room that he enters" (Kulapati K. M. Munshi). Such advice is meant for lesser mortals. Blessed are doctors like PC who are born with it.

Speaking about the wonderful couple, Sucharita and PC, it is apt to quote Pranay Gupte—author of PC's remarkable biography *The Healer*—who, speaking from the heart, said, "I can think of few other couples that have enriched each other's existence as Sucharita and Pratap Chandra Reddy have".

While practicing in Delhi, I had the privilege of being an independent director on the Board of Directors of Indraprastha Apollo, a joint venture of their group with the Government of NCR Delhi. This gave me some insight into the professionalism and commitment that marked the successful administration of the Apollo Hospitals. One of PC's daughters, Suneeta Reddy, was the managing director, and I could see that the many entities of the group were managed responsibly and professionally by the four daughters of PC—Preeta Reddy, Suneeta Reddy, Sangita Reddy and Shobhana Kamineni—who are recognised as notable women entrepreneurs of India.

7 The Wedding

So, there was this boy-meets-girl scene enacted at the tea meet on the back lawns of 'Eruvaka', A. C. Subba Reddy's (AC) ministerial home, organised by Snehalathamma. It might be apt to add a word about human relationships here. Relationships, including those amongst blood relations and other family members, are what we make of them. Shankarayyachinnayya was not a blood relation. His relationship to us was through Pitchi Reddy Chinnayya (PRC), his elder brother. We used to stay under one roof in PRC's house for a few years in Madras. That led to my close association with Shankarayyachinnayya. When he got his first daughter, Nirupama, married in Hyderabad, the venue was the Exhibition Grounds near Gandhi Bhavan. This was a few years after my marriage and, having gained experience in the ways of life in Hyderabad social circles, I was trying to help out at the wedding dinner, which led to an elderly family friend seriously asking me how I was related to Shankarayyachinnayya. Obviously, he found my active role in trying to help rather odd. It was really an awkward question, but then that's how some people react when they notice others bonding in a manner that they are unfamiliar with.

After the meeting over tea on the lawns of AC's official residence, things moved swiftly, with the key players expressing their assent. For whatever reason, Radha's parents preferred the wedding to be conducted towards the end of the year in November and seemed keen to have a formal engagement function meanwhile, which was fixed in May that year. We had no issues with that. The engagement ceremony, which seemed rather elaborate, was performed at the then 'Gadwal House' near Punjagutta junction. Raja Krishnaram Bhoopal, Raja of Gadwal Samasthan, had married Radha's aunt, her mother's youngest sister, Srilatha Bhoopal. Prabha, coincidentally, was visiting at the time from UK, and I recall her active participation on behalf of the family. On the evening of the function, there came the news of P. V. G. Raju, a minister in the AP cabinet, meeting with a road accident in Punjab.

Since he was close to Nukala as a cabinet colleague and, more so, as a personal friend, Nukala—who was known to be a reticent person—was found all the more reticent that evening.

After the engagement, when the courts reopened, I started living in the New MLAs' Quarters, from where I used to go to my senior, P. Ramchandra Reddy's office in Hardikar Bagh, and then to the high court, to be back at lunch break. Lunch used to come from Radha's place, and I am sure my mother-in-law Bharathi Devi (Bharathi aunty)—who in many ways personified the traditional values of Indian womanhood—would personally oversee every meal sent for me. In the evening, I mostly used to visit their place and have dinner with them, that is, after a movie or Tank Bund outing with Radha. Though Radha's parents were generally known to be conservative traditionalists, thankfully, they had no issues with Radha going out with me. As I didn't then have a car myself, these outings used to be in her Fiat 1100, bearing the number 555. She had a driver, an elderly man clad in a dhoti who would often greet you with 'Jai Sitaram', and so came to be known as Jai Sitaram. After driving us to the movie house, or on some other outing and back, he would leave, and a tip of one or two rupees used to please him immensely. There was, to his utter disappointment, a break in this routine when I got into the driver's seat one day and asked him to go home. His jaw dropped in shock. He had apparently assumed that I couldn't drive, and hence his routine of driving the car for us in the evenings followed by the daily tip.

After this carefree life of post-engagement courtship, the wedding ceremony was fixed for 25 November 1964, the only date I can now readily recall, reflecting the significance attached to the same. Once the date was fixed, Radha's family got busy with all the preparatory work. The marriage ceremony was to be on the lawns of 'Green Lands' Begumpet, which was earlier the official residence of N. Sanjeeva Reddy while he was the CM and thereafter—with Brahmananda Reddy, his successor, opting for 'Ananda Nilayam'—it was made a State Guest House; it had swathes of lawns which could accommodate the *mandap* and the large number of guests expected. KCP Guest House, next to the Electricity Board's office in Khairatabad, was the accommodation for me, my family members and guests from Rajampet. G. Upender Reddy (Upender) was in charge of arrangements at that guest house. The manner in which guests from the village and Rajampet accommodated in the outer rooms of the guest house were looked after under Upender's personal care made their stay for those couple of days in Hyderabad memorable for them, to the extent that many of them used to narrate it as folklore for months and years. Though initially I couldn't take their narrative—which seemed an exaggeration—seriously, over time, when I got to know Upender well, I could quite well understand their exuberance while recalling their experiences. I could then quite well figure that their narration, if anything, could only have been an understatement.

It was a late evening wedding, and back then, late November in Hyderabad used to be cold. Many who came from Rajampet and those areas, clad in just dhoti and shirt without any warm clothing, felt the weather to be far too chilly for comfort. The next day there was a reception in the evening at the same venue, which Nukala apparently left to M. R. Appa Rao, a minister and his close friend, to organise. There was a dance performance by film artist Rajasulochana. After all the guests left, I moved into Radha's house in Hyderguda, and blissful married life commenced in a simple, serene manner.

Our honeymoon, so called, was a driving trip in Radha's car meant to be without any fixed schedule. Since I had a great fascination for road trips without any pre-arranged itinerary, I decided upon Bangalore and beyond in Karnataka. It was, however, not to be so. When we got to Bangalore, I decided to drop by and see Mari Gowda, director of horticulture, who used to live in a large bungalow in Cubbon Park. I had earlier met him when I visited Bangalore along with Shiv mama, his friend, and found him to be very friendly person, and so the visit was more a courtesy call. He was seemingly pleased, and when he got to know of our plans to visit a few places in Karnataka, he insisted on giving us an itinerary and a typed programme was promptly delivered at our hotel. The journey was to start with a visit to Nandi Hills, to spend a night in the guest house—spruced up for the Queen's visit sometime earlier—booked for us (the Queen's Suite), and from there we were to drive towards Mangalore, up to Thirthahalli, en route visiting Jog Falls, Brindavan Gardens and all the other tourist spots. Since the guest houses at various places were under control of the department headed by Mr Gowda, messages were sent out in advance to expect us. All the guest houses and traveller's bungalows were incredibly clean, with a cook who could organise at short notice a meal for the night. We used to leave early every morning and pick up a vegetarian breakfast from one of the roadside vegetarian hotels to eat in the car and drive on. As I can recall, the drive ended at Agumbe, on the Western Ghats, to have that beautiful view of the sun setting beyond the Arabian Sea.

Then we drove back all the way to Chennai to show Radha my favourite jaunts of college days like the Chinese restaurants, Buharis, etc., and to reminisce the days of my carefree student life there. There used to be one Chinese restaurant right next to Buharis on Mount Road, which students would normally patronise. T. G. Krishnamoorthy (TGK) and I, particularly after our Loyola days when I was doing law and he was into his family business, used to have dinner at the Chunking Chinese, on the first floor of the Musee Musicals building, before a late movie in one of the three or four theatres showing English movies. It was a simple but exclusive diner run by a Chinese family, with a few other Chinese people who worked elsewhere doubling up as waiters at dinner time. A few Westerners living in Madras could be seen having shark fin soup and other exotic stuff. For TGK and I, it was always some soup followed by 'Flied lice and flied plawns' (fried rice and fried prawns); we were never tired of eating those same dishes with their homemade chilli sauce. And so I took Radha to my favourite Chinese diner, particularly since we often used to have dinner at the famous Nanking in Secunderabad. There, to my utter disappointment, the first thing she did was to sniff at the plate kept in front of her, and the frown on her face was a tell-all. Well, favourites, I suppose, are often irrational choices.

8   Legal Career Threshold

Must say, the eventful year of 1964—with milestones in both professional career and personal life—set the tone for the future that unfolded. Joining the office of P. Ramachandra Reddy (PRR) was by no means a random decision. Considering my past association with Justice O. Chinnappa Reddy's (OCR) office and the close relations I had developed with most of the juniors there, it perhaps should have been the first choice; but then, considering the predominant nature of work there, I would have to gravitate to criminal work and be branded as a criminal lawyer. Not that I was averse to practicing criminal law, but two considerations primarily seemed to have weighed with me.

Firstly, if I could claim exposure to any particular branch of law useful for practice in the High Court during my academic career, it was constitutional litigation, since I had the comparative study of constitutions of India, Canada and Australia in my brief PG course in London University. Secondly, the major chunk of criminal cases, as I could see, were from the Rayalaseema districts, known for its hard-core factionalism, and there were many lawyers hailing from there already practicing criminal law. As such, the office of PRR practically became the automatic choice. As the principal government pleader, PRR was dealing with most of the government litigation on the civil side, including writ petitions. Since I had no previous acquaintance with PRR, I was taken to him by lawyer-politician C. Kulasekhar Reddy on my request. PRR, on knowing my background, readily agreed to have me as a junior, and thus started my devilling in his office. There were already more than half-a-dozen juniors working in his office. E. Kalyanram, the senior-most, who also hailed from Tirupati like PRR, was the chosen one to assist PRR (whom we all called Senior) in TTD-related and personal cases. O. Adinarayana Reddy was the mainstay, who together with S. Ramachandra Reddy, used to handle most of the writ petitions. Mr Shastri handled commercial taxes and related litigation. I fit into the group of other new entrants, whose task was mainly to draft counters on the basis of the paragraph-wise remarks received from the concerned departments. While some of us tried to understand the issue involved before finalising the draft counter with due emphasis on the core defence, those without patience would make do by adding appropriate lingo, like opening the paragraph with "It is submitted", etc. and concluding with a prayer for dismissal of the petition with costs as devoid of any merit. I had friendly relations with the seniors amongst the juniors, starting with Kalyanram, and we would dine out together on some Fridays, calling ourselves the "We 5 Group".

Their warm companionship aside, I also had the opportunity of learning much from my senior colleagues: the skill of infusing confidence in a client from Kalyanram; maintaining a calm demeanour and equanimity from Adinarayan Reddy; a sense of humour from S. Ramachandra Reddy. Sadly, the three seniors in our group have passed away. P. Venkatram Reddy, my contemporary from Madras Law College days, used to be serious and intense in his work even while he was with us in PRR's office. In recognition of the same, Senior had assigned him the task of handling commercial taxes and related cases after Shastri—who used to deal with them—moved on to practice on his own. The exposure and resultant experience in the area led to Venkatram being recognised particularly for his knowledge and expertise in the tax-related branch of law. He had deservedly adorned the Bench as a judge in the High Court of Andhra Pradesh, as chief Justice in the High Court of Karnataka and as judge in the Supreme Court of India. On his retirement after serving the judiciary with distinction, he was made chairman, Law Commission of India and later chairman, Tax Advance Ruling Tribunal. Venkatram keeps himself busy even now, doing arbitration work and visiting the Law Academy in Bhopal, besides assisting judicial administration in diverse ways, leaving very little time for me to meet with him, despite living in the same residential complex.

As far as Senior is concerned, he was totally self-reliant in his preparation of cases, and juniors like me had no opportunity to interact with him or discuss the preparatory process for matters to be argued. PRR's phenomenal memory always stood him in good stead when referring to case laws even while on his feet, and this, in a way, denied us the opportunities to pore over legal digests and find relevant precedents. He, in fact, would off-hand give citations to Nair, the smart attender we had, who would fetch the requisite law reports to his desk. Whatever we could pick up from him was only by following his methodical presentation in court, paying meticulous attention to every nuance and detail.

9   Our Family Grows

Though for some time after marriage we continued living in the Hyderguda house, Nukala, on a whim, decided to move into a government bungalow meant for senior ministers, to which he was entitled. It was perhaps to ensure greater comfort to his newly-married daughter and son-in-law. A bungalow in Begumpet—where there were a couple of such big properties in a huge area—which was occupied by Chief Justice Chandra Reddy, fell vacant on his transfer to Madras High Court, and the family moved into it. It was a huge bungalow with a tennis court and vast open spaces with dense foliage. Next door was P. V. G. Raju, a close friend and ministerial colleague of Nukala.

While there, Radha spent her months of pregnancy and on 15 September 1965, the stork delivered to us a bundle of sublime joy, our daughter, who was named Deepika to rhyme with her mother's name, Radhika. The delivery was in Nilofer Hospital, the government's prominent medical facility for maternity and paediatrics. The noble lady, Dr Seetha, who was close to the family, handled her delivery and she often would recall her first impression on seeing the new-born, that she would be a dancer. This thought may have stemmed from the fact that Radha had herself trained in Bharatanatyam and performed on stage on some occasions, including the opening ceremony of Ravindra Bharathi in 1961 for which Dr S. Radhakrishnan, then vice president of India, was the chief guest. What is traditionally known as the cradle ceremony for the child was performed at the Begumpet house, and thereafter the family moved back to the Hyderguda house. It was the time of political uncertainty in the state. There was considerable dissent building up against K. Brahmananda Reddy (KBR) within the Congress, and AC and Nukala were leading that dissident faction. Simultaneously, there was this movement for a separate Telangana with the Telangana Praja Samithi (TPS), headed by Dr Channa Reddy, gaining ground.

With the shift to Hyderguda, the limited space made it possible for the parents and grandparents to be close to the baby most of the time. Words fail me in describing the sublime joy experienced while rocking the child on my legs, listening to music—mostly from the radio, since those were not the days of TV, and thank God for that! Deepa—as Deepika came to be known in the family, and Deepayya for the tradition-bound domestic staff from Manukota—grew up in the laps of her parents and grandparents, who had more than their share of time with her. In the otherwise sedate life, enlivened by the diversion and joy provided by little Deepa, came this exciting moment of the birth of our second child, a boy, Siddharth, on 20 January 1969. His delivery was also aided by Dr Seetha in Nilofer Hospital, and my going to Rajampet to spend a few days of Sankranti vacation with Father and Mother had apparently caused severe displeasure to my spouse. I was, however, back by the day Siddharth, with his hair like a rock star, arrived. Needless to speak of the mood of delight and elation in the family with the arrival of a daughter followed by a son.

Deepa, with her attractive eyes and looks, was a charmer as a toddler, and her mother and grandparents decided that she should learn classical dance. As a lover of music, I also liked the idea. Sumathy Kaushal, a well-known Kuchipudi dancer, was running a dance school along with her husband Kaushal, who was himself an instrumentalist. Thus Deepa took her baby steps towards what, in the course of time, proved to be a long, fulfilling journey on the glorious path of classical dance, our cultural heritage. She used to go there in the evenings for an hour or more, and her schooling was in Vidyaranya School, started by its founder principal, Shanta Rameshwar Rao. I liked the method of teaching followed there, particularly its ethos of education sans competition. Children were free birds, learning their lessons out of free will as they went along. Siddharth also spent his early years of schooling at Vidyaranya, before he shifted to Hyderabad Public School (HPS).

While Siddharth was in HPS, I may have been signing his periodical reports, but never seriously applied my mind to his grades. However, I took keen interest in his sports activities and had him learn the *mridangam* (a percussion instrument for Carnatic music). The day we went to watch him play a cricket match, as his luck would have it, he was out for a duck. He more than made up for it with his badminton, and was part of the medallist team of three, representing AP at the National Games held in Aizawl in Mizoram. He often had to travel to the districts and other states to play badminton while in school, leading to some attendance issues. So I went to meet the school vice principal, and I can vividly recall his comment on that occasion. After agreeing to condone Siddharth's absence for playing in recognised tournaments, he said it was for me as a parent to think about the adverse impact on his academics at school, and added that while one or two might make it to high levels in sport, parents should give greater importance to education. I was not one to take his advice seriously. Radha and I were more interested in his co-curriculars like elocution, etc. One day, when Siddharth had one such elocution competition while in the primary section, Radha and I had picked him up from school, and I can never forget his comment by way of self-evaluation. He said, "Daddy! Something was happening in my throat when I had to speak out". There you are. It is always pleasurable to relive such intimacy through memories, of the little guy standing on the bench seat of my Fiat 1100 with his arm around my neck while I drove, and every time my foot pressed the brake pedal, my left hand would automatically stretch out to prevent him from falling to the front.

Though I cannot similarly comment on Deepa's grades, I should imagine they were good since her mother seemed happy looking into the reports. I would, of course, closely follow Deepa's progress in her dance.

While life was replete with all elements for a happy family, what with a devoted spouse, the two kids and loving elders bestowing all care and concern, I couldn't resist the nagging urge to move out of the Hyderguda house into an independent house. This essentially stemmed from my keenness to have my office away from the bustle of the minister's house. I started looking for a place nearby and Surender, who got wind of it, offered a small house in Himayat Nagar, on the road in front of the then Gayathri Bhavan, which he owned. Though accommodation was limited, I found it good enough for my immediate purpose. Surender, whose middle name is undoubtedly generosity, took pains to have the interiors remodelled, and Radha and I moved into that house. The veranda and the front room constituted my office and we had two bedrooms, with a large area for a table-tennis table on the first floor. The most significant feature was the location—it was walking distance to the Hyderguda house and my senior's office.

10   Nukala, the Father Figure

It was the time when the agitation for a separate Telangana had peaked, with many leaders, including Dr Channa Reddy, arrested and detained. I had filed many writ petitions on behalf of the late P. Ramchandra Reddy (MLA Sangareddy) and his associates, and it used to be an ordeal driving to the High Court with the agitators, including lawyers from the city civil court and other courts, blocking roads near the High Court. My juniors and I used to have the briefs representing TPS leaders on the car seat to convince the agitators of the need to reach the High Court on time. In other areas of Telangana, like Warangal district, the Naxalite movement with its related violence, together with the separate Telangana movement, led to near failure of law and order, and the personal security of landed gentry in rural areas was in great danger. As a result, many of them left their villages and moved to the city. They wouldn't venture even an occasional visit to their villages. Against this backdrop, Nukala decided to visit Jamallapally, causing concern in the family. Since there was no way to stop him, I accompanied him. While there, at night we used to sleep on the first floor of the *gadi* (bungalow), with firearms and a fellow known to be a good marksman. Villagers used to report about the Naxals visiting the village the previous night and, significantly, enquiring whether Nukala, the 'Dora' was in the gadi. The perception in the village was that the Naxals did not seem keen to harm Nukala, presumably since he was not, in their view, an exploiter.

About that time, there were also the elections to Panchayats. Nukala had to visit the area. While there, he visited Seerole village, following a distress call from his close follower and leader in the village, Venkat Reddy, who said that his opponents were resorting to threats of violence to stop his followers from reaching the polling booths. He pleaded that unless Nukala visits the village, his supporters will be doomed. Nukala, in hindsight, mindlessly went there, and there was an incident of the opposite faction creating a commotion, leading to

Nukala having to fire his revolver into the air. Since he was a dissident leader, the overzealous local police registered a case of attempt to murder under Section 307 of the Indian Penal Code (IPC), and he was arrested to please the ruling dispensation. The trauma caused by the event resulted in his developing some heart-related breathing problem, and the police took him to Warangal and admitted him in the hospital. When I came to know, I rushed to Warangal post-haste and found him to be in a stable condition. There were many local leaders who had gathered out of concern, and one such was P. Purushottam Rao, a highly energetic young leader close to Nukala. I remember seeing him convey to Nukala that the collector, K. R. Venugopal, wanted to visit him. Nukala, not wanting the collector to antagonise the CM and others, wanted Rao to convey to Venugopal his personal request not to visit him under any circumstances. Venugopal's bold and fair mindset as an administrator did not go unnoticed, and it was heartening to see him rise to great heights in the esteem of one and all when he, over time, moved to the Prime Minister's Office (PMO) in Delhi. My bonhomie with and regard for Purushottam Rao, whom I run into occasionally, continues.

Later the next evening, Dr Channa Reddy, the dynamic leader heading the separate Telangana movement, and V. B. Raju, a leader known for his high intellect, came to the Warangal hospital to enquire after Nukala's health. When the doctors assured us that Nukala was in a stable condition with no room for any anxiety, I planned to get back to Hyderabad and I was invited to travel with Dr Channa Reddy and V. B. Raju, who were returning in their car to Hyderabad. There I was, with these two senior leaders of the state, and particularly of Telangana. At some point on the way, Dr Channa Reddy expressed his dismay at the manner in which Nukala, a recognised leader at the state level, got embroiled in a gram panchayat poll, and V. B. Raju's response was that Nukala would not remain in politics but for his commitment to Mahbubabad. That response I always felt was remarkably true. Nukala, despite rising to higher echelons of state politics, was at heart a simple, down-to-earth politician who never deviated from his commitment to serve the people of Mahbubabad, who had drawn him into politics and sustained his leadership. He was always happy in the company of his grassroot-level workers and comfortable amongst the poor and downtrodden. He had no airs about him, even when he was at the pinnacle of his political career. Yet another salutary feature of his mindset was the total lack of urge for riches, which I believe made him stand tall as a politician of high integrity.

Well, such a reputation enjoyed by a political leader is bound to induce journalists like Sitaram, close to many politicians of the time, to fish for something negative to sensationalise. So, there was this report in the tabloid *Anti-Corruption* published by Sitaram, that Nukala was building two houses in Begumpet. It is a different matter that nobody took it seriously. However, I could figure out that this imaginary report must have sprung from the fact that Surender Reddy and his father-in-law, the late Pingle Indrasena Reddy, were building houses for themselves one next to the other on Begumpet Road. Nukala, one known for giving away most of his ancestral lands to Lambadas and other tenants, had only that small house in Hyderguda, which he apparently bought when he became an MLA while he was living in the old MLAs' quarters close by. When the Jubilee Hills Cooperative Housing Society was formed, and plots were allotted to members, Suryanarayana Swamy, the founder president of the society, had earmarked a well-located plot for allotment to Nukala, which he declined. Though I can understand his disinclination to accept a plot as a member, being the revenue minister, what astonished me was the information I had after he passed away—of his surrendering his membership of the Housing Society. I was quite baffled by what was revealed by way of answer when I asked one of his PAs, Seshaiah, who mercifully is with us. Such a clean political life led by him even at the cost of family security, I am sure, would make his progeny and all who were close to him immensely proud. This was evident from the condolence messages and tributes paid by leaders and public personalities representing diverse sections of society, the common thread running through them being the recognition of his impeccable integrity and administrative ability. Be that as it may, the intensity of the Telangana agitation started waning with the exit of KBR as CM becoming near certainty. In late 1971, KBR resigned and TPS merged with the Congress, formally bringing to a close the separatist movement heralded by the TPS. P. V. Narasimha Rao (PV) became Chief Minister, and Nukala was not a member of his cabinet.

We continued to live in the Himayat Nagar house, and Nukala used to visit us practically every evening to spend time with his grandchildren. By then he had developed some health issues. He was, for long, a diabetic, which seemed to have run in his family. The stressful political life made him a hypertensive, requiring constant medical care. There were also signs of developing cardiac problems such as angina. The two doctors in whom he had implicit faith, and who would regularly visit him to keep track of his health, were the noted neurologist Dr M. Veeraraghava Reddy and cardiologist Dr P. Satyanarayana Rao (PSR). These two young specialists took constant care of his health with deep affection and commitment, making them practically part of the family, and the bond has only deepened over the years, even after Nukala's demise. Nukala, who ceased to be a minister, would drive his jeep to come and spend time with us. Troubling him in that manner didn't seem right, and so Radha and I decided to wind up our establishment and move back to the Hyderguda house. Both Nukala and Mother-in-law were immensely happy to have us back.

Going by the press reports of the time, PV seemed like an unsure CM who spent more time in Delhi seeking guidance from the party leadership, than in Hyderabad. To add to his woes there was this Supreme Court judgement upholding Mulki Rules, making only '*Mulkis*'—those who had lived in Telangana region for at least fifteen years—eligible for admission to government colleges and government jobs. This raised hackles among the people of the other regions, and the CM's approach in welcoming the decision as one giving finality to the issue did not help assuage their anger and humiliation. There was a serious division in his cabinet, followed by a separate Andhra agitation, which took an ugly turn with mismanagement of law and order during a meeting called by an NGOs' association in Cuddapah. With the situation going out of hand, Andhra Pradesh was brought under President's Rule, with H. C. Sarin and V. K. Rao as advisors to the governor.

After a few months, when peace prevailed, the Congress high command started working on reinstating a popular government and, commenced the process of choosing the leader to take over as chief minister of the state. Dr Shankar Dayal Sharma, who later became the President of India, together with J. N. Dixit started the consultation process. Important leaders from the state were invited to Delhi for consultations. Nukala, being one of the foremost, had to go to Delhi for a few days. I had to accompany him to ensure that he did not overexert himself. We were staying in the AP guest house, and so were many other leaders. The two names figuring prominently in the political circles and press were Nukala and J. Vengal Rao (JVR). K. C. Pant, son of the erstwhile stalwart and freedom fighter Govind Ballabh Pant, was helping Mrs Indira Gandhi in the selection process. Nukala received a call to see Pant, and we had gone to his house one morning. As Nukala was waiting to be called in, he noticed some kids playing football on the lawns in the front yard. He instinctively went and joined them, and this made news the next day in the Delhi press, which highlighted the fact that Nukala, one of the frontrunners for the CM's post, who is stated to have health problems, was found dribbling a football with children. The report reflected what was touted as a negative factor against choosing Nukala as CM. I have vivid recollections of discussions with young energetic leaders like Purushottam Reddy on the day Nukala decided it was time to return to Hyderabad. Thereafter, the party, following its age-old practice, decided upon JVR as the consensus candidate for the leadership of the legislative party and for the post of CM.

Whatever may have been the doubts expressed in some quarters, Nukala, who embodied decency in politics, never expressed a word of displeasure or dissent. JVR, who held Nukala in high regard, invited him to be the finance minister in his cabinet. When Nukala did not seem enthusiastic about it, I was one of those who thought that there was no valid ground for his hesitation when the CM himself had invited him to join the cabinet. Nukala was sworn in as Minister for Finance and Commercial Taxes. Earlier, as the revenue minister, he had Satyanarayana Swamy as his personal secretary and Narasimha Rao and Seshaiah as his personal assistants. They all served him well, with utmost loyalty and commitment. Satyanarayana Swamy's elder brother, who was chief engineer in the waterworks department, was our immediate neighbour, while the younger Swamy lived a couple of houses away. They were all like family. Nevertheless, I thought the change in portfolio from revenue to finance also called for a change in personal secretaries since there was going to be a great deal more of work in the legislative assembly besides budgetary preparation. I consulted cousin Venu, who, after some thought, suggested the name of Mr J. M. Girglani, an academic teaching at Osmania University before joining the State Civil Service. He was a refugee from Pakistan who came up the hard way and earned a well-deserved reputation for his efficiency and integrity. I passed on the suggestion to Nukala, who agreed and conveyed his decision to E. V. Ram Reddy, senior secretary and an upright officer close to the family. Mr Girglani proved to be the best suited for the job. Nukala used to take his work and responsibility as minister seriously. There was this *India Today* desk diary in which he used to note down, neatly, every point raised by the legislators during the post-budget debate, and try to address each one of them. We had that diary for long after he passed away, though I can't lay my hands on it now. Nukala was chairman of the administrative reforms committee and, as leader of the TPS legislature party, he was leader of the opposition. Whatever be the office he held, he carried himself with great dignity and tried to fulfil his duties with commitment. His courteous and amiable nature endeared him to most of the senior leaders from coastal districts as well.

All this turned out to be short-lived with his passing away in July 1974. In May 1974, he decided to take a break for a few days at Horsely Hills near Madanapally with the family. This was presumably because being in Horsely Hills, within the state, made it easy for him to attend to any urgent work. After a few days there, Radha and I went to Rajampet to spend a couple of days before returning to Hyderabad, while Nukala was to visit Anantapur to call on N. Sanjeeva Reddy, for whom he had great regard, and then return to Hyderabad by road. On the way to Hyderabad from Anantapur, he suffered a heart attack and was taken to the government general hospital in Kurnool. Dr Bhaskar Reddy, superintendent of the hospital, ensured proper care, before Dr P. S. Rao and others reached there from Hyderabad. Nukala was later shifted to Osmania General Hospital, where he was in the ICCU under the care of Dr P. S. Rao and his colleagues. Radha and Mother-in-law used to stay with him, while I also spent most of my time there. Medical care in cardiology had not quite advanced then and interventional therapy skills were unavailable. Doctors depended mainly on medicines and enforced total rest on the patient. After a few days, in the evening of 26 July, his condition worsened, and Dr P. S. Rao thought it best to call in Dr Padmavathi, reputed cardiologist at AIIMS Delhi, to see him, and get a second opinion on the course of treatment to be followed. So, he and I went to JVR, the CM, that night to seek his help for organising Dr Padmavathi's visit to Hyderabad. The CM immediately arranged to have her flown in to Hyderabad the next morning. She came to Osmania and, after examining the patient and discussions with the doctors attending on him, endorsed the course of treatment followed. PSR and I accompanied her back to the guest house in Raj Bhavan. We had barely reached there, when PSR got a call saying that the patient was critical, and we rushed back to find resuscitation efforts being carried out, in vain. Nukala passed away most prematurely at the age of 56.

He was a non-smoker, a teetotaller and a keen sportsman in his younger days, and his passing away while in office as a highly respected senior minister in the cabinet came as a shock to all who had known him. The funeral was conducted with the usual state honours and the obsequies were to be performed by Siddharth, his grandson, and since he was very young at the time, I deputised him in lighting the pyre. What a tragic loss of someone who, with his benevolent, loving nature and stoic persona, was a true father figure in the family.

11 Government Pleader

The sad and untimely demise of Nukala caused deep anguish to the family and the wide circle of friends and admirers; he was only 56, and in the prime of his political career. For many days there used to be a stream of visitors to condole Mother-in-law, and Radha and I had to stay at home with them, particularly Mother-in-law, a frail lady in poor health who was in a state of shock. After that phase was over, Radha and I had to visit senior relatives and dignitaries who had come to offer their condolences. One such visit was to Justice S. Obul Reddy, then the chief justice of AP High Court. When we met him and his wife one afternoon at their house in Malakpet, the CJ, after enquiring about my practice as a lawyer, said that the CM J. Vengal Rao was expected to meet him that evening, presumably to discuss the team of government lawyers under the existing arrangement and to seek advice on improving the effectiveness of representation on behalf of the government. He also said that he might suggest my name for appointment as government pleader (GP) if the CM sought his views in that regard. This came as a surprise to me since I was not there to discuss my career and, considering my relatively young age, I thought he might have an assistant GP's post in mind, and so I told him that I had enough work to keep me occupied. CJ Reddy then clarified that he had a GP's post in mind and said, let us see what the CM wants to discuss. After spending some time with them, Radha and I returned home. Around 7.00 p.m. the CJ called me to say that the CM had come and that when he suggested my name for GP, the CM said, "Oh yes. I know him. That will be a good choice". A few days later, when a new team of government pleaders was appointed for the high court, with V. Rajagopal Reddy as one of them, the intimation went to the wrong person—the senior-most amongst my namesakes. Mr Ratnam, the home secretary, who realised the mistake when the wrong person went to meet him, made sure that the appointment order was delivered to me through a special messenger.

The order itself revealed the subjects allocated and the designation. Against my name it said, "GP for Home". Not familiar with government work, I wasn't sure if there would be sizeable work relating to the Home Department, making it worthwhile for me. I then called Mr Girglani to express my doubts and dilemma. He, I think, spoke to Rao Saheb, the chief secretary, and on his advice wanted me to call on the home secretary, which I did. Mr Ratnam, who was anything but a typical bureaucrat, understood my dilemma and was good enough to explain, showing me the statistics of the number of cases pending per each of the appointees, particularly drawing my attention to a couple of them who had a much smaller number and the punch line he employed, that he chose me particularly for his department, clinched the issue. On the whole, I felt immensely gratified to be chosen as one of the team, with most being senior to me and well-established lawyers. The other members included Sardar Ali Khan, Bar-at-law who later became a judge and after retirement was chairman, Minorities Commission; Sitaram Reddy, a barrister, and Amareshwari, who were elevated to the Bench in course of time. Special mention should be made of my close friend K. Ramaswami, who, after his stint on the Bench of the High Court, was made a judge of the Supreme Court, which office he held with great distinction. Most of us GPs had cubicles for chambers in the main building, while the GP's office and some chambers were in the new block.

While assuming charge as GP I figured I may need some experienced junior to assist me and, particularly, to handle matters independently in some courts. I had with me as juniors A. B. Krishna Reddy, P. M. Reddykrishna and others not quite experienced enough to independently argue cases. I consulted my colleague from PRR's office, S. Ramchandra Reddy, who suggested the name of Ms S. V. Maruthi, who had earlier worked in the office of Venkatram Sastry while he was a GP, and also helped me in convincing her to join as a junior in my office. The work in terms of issues arising in writ petitions was found to be far more varied than imagined. The responsibility of office provided the requisite impetus to work with commitment.

It was about that time that I had the good fortune of getting acquainted with my former associate and committed well-wisher, advocate Narahari Rao Devaraj. He hailed from the Karnam/Patwari family of Wanaparthy, and had worked with the Law Ministry in Delhi for some time before proceeding to the USA for pursuing his legal education further. While in Delhi, he had married the daughter of Baddam Ella Reddy, a senior CPM leader and member of Parliament. When Devaraj decided to start practicing in the High Court, he, for whatever reason, pitched upon my office to join as junior and was not one to take a no. One day he walked into my chambers during lunch recess, introduced himself and expressed his desire to join my office. I was taken aback, since he had obviously gone past the age of a college fresher joining the profession and I had doubts about how he might gel with other juniors, who were much younger but had put in more years in the profession. When he persisted, despite my reservations, I agreed and over the years, he turned out to be more a companion than a junior counsel. Devaraj was quite knowledgeable in politics and current affairs, and was proficient in Telugu besides being fluent in English. Most importantly, what made him an indispensable companion were two traits: he was an interesting conversationalist and had a profound sense of humour. He used to help Deepa in clearing her doubts relating to lyrics of songs in her dance repertoire. My father, otherwise known for his serious disposition, also enjoyed Devaraj's company immensely. Our association was based so much on mutual respect that even after some years I would still address him as Mr Devaraj. After I ceased to be a GP, Devaraj continued as a junior in my office. We would share lunch in my chambers and he would keep me posted on public affairs in the state and the country. Even after I moved to Delhi in 1991, communication between us remained incessant over phone, and the last call he made, before he passed away one morning, was to me the night before.

Well, it is no exaggeration to say that Devaraj is missed so much that even now he is remembered at least once in a couple of days. It may not be inapt to say that he was, in a way, my alter ego, whose commitment to bolster my image as a well-wisher was tremendous. He was overjoyed when I was elected to the Bar Council of India (BCI) and was also present in Delhi when I first got elected as chairman of BCI. I often reminisce on his boundless joy on those occasions. When Deepika was to be honoured by the Government of Andhra Pradesh with the Ugadi Puraskar in May 2007, he was keen that I should come to Hyderabad, regardless of my commitments in Delhi. I owe entirely to Devaraj the deep urge to delve into Telugu language and literature that I developed. In fact, this led to my attempting to pen short verses in Telugu using my limited vocabulary, which might seem amateurish to the knowledgeable. For instance, on that occasion of Ugadi Puraskar, when it didn't seem possible for me, in view of professional commitments, to take the next morning's flight to Hyderabad despite his persistence, I sent him a message using some lyrics from a Telugu film song, urging him to witness the function, treating his eyes as mine. For him, this more than made up for my absence.

Devaraj had this unique ability to vibe well with persons of different sections and age groups. He was close to three Chief Ministers of AP: P. V. Narasimha Rao, J. Vengal Rao and K. Vijayabhaskar Reddy. Not mere acquaintance, oh no, he would engage them in long conversations and convey his opinions on political issues. He was also close to academics in Osmania University and elsewhere. Prof. Jayshankar was one such for whom Devaraj used to work relentlessly to ensure due recognition for the professor's accomplishments. Significantly, he was also close to leaders who were political adversaries, and was respected by both sides. I have personally seen this in the context of his connection with district leaders. Once we were traveling by road from Kurnool and as we reached Jadcherla, Devaraj insisted on taking a detour to visit Sudhakar Reddy, who was contesting the election and was close to me, though Devaraj was also known to be close to the rival candidate. He had great regard and admiration for Jaipal Reddy and would visit him during his election campaign. When Jaipal was to decide upon moving to Delhi and entering Central politics contesting as MP, Devaraj brought him over to my place to provide him some relief from his stressful schedule of meeting his innumerable concerned supporters, and we had a long chat sitting on the lawns of my house. There was this instance of a high functionary making his displeasure against me known to Devaraj. Unable to understand the cause, Devaraj came and put it to me, expecting me to throw some light on it. I realised it must have been on account of what was wrongly perceived by the concerned gentleman to be an adverse comment expressed by me, and which in fact was most positive under the circumstances. Such instances might be mistaken against Devaraj, but since his deep loyalty to me was known to all, what was told to him was presumably intended to be conveyed to me. After his long stint as a junior in my office, Devaraj was appointed as standing counsel for the Central government in the Central Administrative Tribunal and, must say, he enjoyed his work there immensely. The tribunal, which included Surya Rao, former registrar of the High Court, besides the advocates practicing there, held him in high esteem. I find it difficult to curb my urge to go on about this good friend and genuine well-wisher of mine, who departed, leaving a deep vacuum and sense of loss.

It is perhaps apt to advert to my resignation as GP at this stage. I was appointed along with others as GP in 1974–75, when Vengal Rao was Chief Minister, with the united Congress Party in power in the state. Then came the split in the party, with Indira Gandhi heading Congress (I), and the other headed by Brahmananda Reddy, the incumbent president. Vengal Rao and his cabinet remained in the Congress headed by Reddy and contested elections to the state assembly, in which Congress (I), led by Dr Chenna Reddy, succeeded and formed the new government in the state. Yedlapati Venkat Rao held the portfolio of law and courts initially. A few months later, Nadendla Bhaskar Rao, a colleague practicing in the High Court, having been elected MLA, became a cabinet member, and was obliged by the CM, who allocated him the law and courts portfolio, which Bhaskar Rao was apparently keen to have. Immediately after taking over the new portfolio, Bhaskar Rao made a caustic statement in a press conference on 11 April 1978, castigating the government pleaders appointed by the previous government for not resigning to make way for fresh appointments. His statement was widely reported in the press the next day. After I saw it in the morning's newspaper, I had no mind to represent the government in the court and decided to quit. The other GPs, who got wind of it, persuaded me not to act in haste till a collective decision was taken by all the GPs. In deference to their wish I delayed the formal resignation, though I would not attend the court as GP after such ignominy. My colleagues apparently contacted the home secretary, and were informed that though he had also seen the statement of the new law minister, to his knowledge there was no such decision by the government. Being satisfied with that, my colleagues decided to continue in office, and I decided to take an independent decision and on 14 April 1978, I addressed my letter of resignation to the CM, forwarding a copy of the same to the Chief Justice. Having done that, while driving back home from court, I called on M. V. Narayan Rao, IPS, the home secretary, whom I had known personally, to inform him of my resignation through my letter to the CM, since I did not want his department's cases to suffer in the court on account of my non-appearance. After reading through a copy of the letter, Narayan Rao said that while he could understand my reaction, he didn't approve of the last sentence, which stated categorically that I did not wish to be considered for reappointment. I had to tell him that without that statement, the letter may be misread as merely a pressure tactic of sorts to continue as GP, seeking reappointment, which was indeed the farthest from my intention. My resignation was widely reported in the newspapers, leading lawyers all over the state to feel jubilant at what was perceived as an act upholding the dignity and self-respect of the profession. This became evident from the manner in which I polled votes from all districts of AP when I contested elections to the State Bar Council sometime later. Some of the senior members of the bar who were my well-wishers, like K. Jayachandra Reddy, felt that I had overreacted, particularly since the post of GP was considered to be a stepping stone of sorts for elevation to the Bench. The law minister, Bhaskar Rao, tried to wriggle out with some convoluted logic highlighting the tradition of the advocate general having to demit office when there is a change of government, adding that he did not mean to denigrate the government pleaders.

Now to go back to my work as GP, mention must be made of Ms S. V. Maruthi, who joined my office as junior. Must say, her presence made my task much easier as I could count on her to handle matters in some courts while I was busy in the others. She was known for putting up a tough fight without conceding even an inch to the opposite side. She continued in my office even after I ceased to be GP. About that time, she was successful in securing a job in the Union Law Ministry through UPSC selection. After a couple of years there, she presumably started missing the excitement of court work and conveyed to me that she wanted to resign and come back to her desk in my office. I dissuaded her since she was doing well in her job and was expected to be promoted. She heeded my advice, and thankfully she was not only promoted but was also appointed as member of the Customs, Excise and Gold (Control) Appellate Tribunal (CEGAT) in Delhi. This proved to be a tipping point in her career, leading to her appointment as judge, AP High Court. It might be of interest to recount how fate played its part. About that time Justice Pratap was the CJ of High Court of AP, having been transferred from Mumbai. On one of my visits to Hyderabad from Delhi, I sought to call on him as a matter of courtesy and he was happy to receive me. Since he was alone, his family not having shifted, he insisted on my joining him for dinner. During the course of conversation, he expressed some difficulty in finding a suitable lady candidate for inclusion in the list to be sent for appointment of judges. Since he sounded earnest in seeking my views, I told him that if he was willing to go beyond those practicing in court then he could consider Ms Maruthi who was on the CEGAT, having earlier practiced in the high court. The CJ then insisted on my sending him her resume. Ms Maruthi, who didn't think anything would come of it, reluctantly sent me her CV, which I forwarded to the CJ. And bingo! Her name was recommended and cleared by Chief Minister N. Janardhan Reddy's government. The CM enquired about her suitability from me, having seen from her resume that she had earlier worked with me while I was a GP, and she was appointed judge of the AP High Court, perhaps much to the chagrin of the aspiring lady candidates from Hyderabad.

With this feeling of having settled down reasonably well in the profession while enjoying my work as GP, I decided to build a house with enough room to accommodate my office as well. The areas in demand for residential housing were in Punjagutta, Begumpet besides Banjara Hills. With a view to ensure easy access and transport facility for persons visiting my office at home, I pitched upon a plot in Somajiguda, opposite the Irram Manzil colony. Though now it has become a crowded area, back then it was very peaceful, just off the Khairatabad–Punjagutta Road, with adequate public transport facility.

Apart from easy access to the two main roads, the Khairatabad–Punjagutta Road on one side and Raj Bhavan Road on the other, we had come to like the neighbourhood immensely. One house which was already there on the north was that of P. T. Malla Reddy, who had retired as chief engineer irrigation. He and his wife, Bhanu aunty, parents of Dr Surekha, Radha's friend from her college days, were of great help, since theirs was the neighbouring house when we built ours. Two doors away on the west was the house of Dr Narayana, a noted dental surgeon and Padma Shri awardee. His son Dr Mohan, a highly qualified dentist, runs his clinic there now. These past few years, my visits to the area are mostly to have him attend to my dental problems. Dr Mohan is such an excellent dentist that what patients like me undergo at his hands is like admirable artistry. The special care bestowed is, I believe, more on account of his close friendship with my son, Siddharth. Bang in front of us there were the noted surgeon Dr Chalapathi Rao and his wife Dr Ushalakshmi. Their son Dr Raghuram (Raghu) is a renowned oncoplastic surgeon. Without dilating upon his exemplary accomplishments and global recognition, I remain content to say that Raghu's achievements make elders like me, who have seen him rise to great heights, immensely proud. Another regular visitor for Siddharth was Seshu, who wasn't a resident in the area but would probably visit his sister, who lived there, I think, and he could be seen coming with his nephew—a toddler, then—sitting in front on his motorcycle. It was fascinating to learn that the toddler has now grown up to be a popular film actor, Ram, who dances in the role of a romantic hero in Telugu movies. I suppose Seshu and Siddharth have more than made up for not having been neighbours in their younger days by living in the same complex in Hong Kong for some years now.

Speaking about regular young visitors, Deepa used to have many friends visiting her; most regular of them was Purnima, daughter of Dr Nene, who was then chief of the International Crops Research Institute for the Semi-Arid Tropics (ICRISAT), an entity of the United Nations (UN). Imported cars like the Honda and Datsun were available for use of Dr Nene and his family, and during Purnima's visits, one such car used to be parked at our gate, attracting the attention of young people, who would throng to have a closer look at it. The bond Deepa and Purnima developed in those days has become a lasting family friendship, even after they both attained marital status. A few months back there was this function in Pune, where Purnima lives with her husband Dinesh Raste, for the release of an excellent book produced by Dinesh, narrating the history of his family. There was this dance presentation by Deepa with her students on the occasion, and we were all there, enjoying the hospitality of the Raste family. Another close friend of Deepa who used to visit was Parneeta, daughter of a close friend of mine, G. Pitcheshwar Rao, thanks to whom I could watch the Asian Games on a colour TV. We used to have a black-and-white TV, since we hardly spent time watching the insipid programmes of Doordarshan—the only available channel then—and when the Asian

Games were going to be telecast, G. P. Rao, whose family manufactured Bush TVs in their factory in Bangalore, had one delivered to my place. Parneeta, who married Prasad, now lives in Goa, making life one long holiday on the seashore.

Finalising plans for the new house was quite a task for Radha and I, necessitating visits to the architectural firm's office in Secunderabad every Saturday. The two partners of the firm, Anand Sagar and Subhash Narayan, were very helpful in finalising plans suiting our requirement and also overseeing every aspect of construction. Speaking about finalisation of plans for the house, something etched in my memory is the visit of Gunapati Srinivasulu Reddy (Srinivas). When the construction had started, he dropped by while visiting someone in the neighbourhood. Seeing the location of the house at the highest point, and the view from the first floor of the train passing in front of Raj Bhavan, between Khairatabad and Begumpet stations, he strongly advised me to have a balcony next to the master bedroom to sit and enjoy the view, including the passing of the train. Following his advice, I did make provision for a balcony, but which I never could get to use in the manner envisioned by him. Well, Srinivas, a very warm-hearted friend and a highly successful entrepreneur and civil contractor, may not have realised that a lawyer in the early period of his career can rarely find time to indulge in such relaxation. Can't blame him though, since all in his family and close relatives were highly successful entrepreneurs, and his younger brother Ranga Reddy (Ranga), though a qualified lawyer, chose, perhaps wisely, not to make it a career. Radha and I have enjoyed the hospitality of Srinivas, Ranga and other members of their family in get-togethers at their homes, and the company of socialites from different walks of life, besides great food and beverages. Contractor Sudarshan, whom we engaged, pleased us so much with his work that he was engaged for Shyam and Deepika's house as well. We had a formal gruhapravesam puja on 21 March 1976, though we moved into the new house much later.

12 Gen 2

Meanwhile, with the passage of time, life was back to the old routine. Siddharth used to go to HPS in the school bus and Deepa used to pursue her dance training, besides attending school. Her natural talent for dance, particularly for *abhinaya*, was noticeable even in her early years, and her prowess pleased her teacher to the extent that she considered Deepa ready for her *rangapravesam* debut when she was just eleven and in sixth class perhaps. It was to be in December 1976, at Ravindra Bharati, and, being a major event in the life of the young dancer and her family, we were all quite excited. There had to be a photo shoot, to print pictures in the brochure and the invitation. As we enter 'Deepanjali', her institute, we see a black and white picture of Deepa, which was shot at the State Photo Studio in Secunderabad for her brochure. We then had to think of some dignitaries to invite as chief guests to the programme. Since her grandfather Nukala was sadly no more, we decided to invite Chief Minister Vengal Rao, who had close relations with Nukala during his sunset years. I then wanted a litterateur and an artiste. For the first we wanted Dr C. Narayan Reddy, who said he would be away in Chennai, and so I pitched upon Justice Avula Sambasiva Rao, acting Chief Justice, who was known for his Telugu literary prowess. For the second, Akkineni Nageswara Rao was the automatic choice, being a highly regarded leading artiste of Telugu cinema in Hyderabad. All three were kind enough to accede to our request. Deepa impressed the audience in the packed house at Ravindra Bharati with her debut. She had the blessings of the dignitaries and, going by the reviews, dance critics who attended the programme were deeply impressed by her talent and her potential to shape up as a prime artiste. It is indeed gratifying that their words proved prophetic, bringing immense joy to our hearts.

Ravindra Bharati was the only well-equipped auditorium of sizeable capacity at that time in Hyderabad. Radha had performed at the inauguration of Ravindra Bharti by the then vice president of India, Dr Sarvepalli Radhakrishnan in the year 1961. She had portrayed the main role of Chitrangada in a dance ballet based on *Chitrangada* penned by Rabindranath Tagore. Though I was not in the picture at that time, I had heard many, including the renowned dance guru Raja Reddy, recount her performance in laudatory terms. In fact, referring to the plaque in the auditorium premises, I had tried to ascertain whether there were any photographs or documents of the inaugural function, but sadly, the auditorium management had preserved none such—reflecting our woeful lack of sense of history. The solace nonetheless is that there was this call from the Department of Culture, Andhra Pradesh, while we were having a summer break in Coonoor, informing Radha that she was to be felicitated on the occasion of the fifty-year celebrations of Ravindra Bharati. She had to, naturally, rush to Hyderabad to be felicitated with a memento presented by K. Rosaiah, the then Chief Minister of Andhra Pradesh.

One of Deepa's early performances outside Hyderabad was in Delhi. An organisation arranged for her solo performance at the Andhra Pradesh Bhavan auditorium. She was a bit under the weather before the trip and we were a little anxious about her stamina for the performance. I can recall the sense of relief when she finished her first item, and my signalling 'thumbs up' to her after it. When the show ended, there was this gentleman who walked up to me, having figured that I was the artiste's father. He handed over one of his visiting cards and wanted us to call him if Deepa wanted a photo shoot. After we got to our room at the India International Centre, I gave that card to Deepa, saying that some guy offered to do a photo shoot. One look at it, and Deepa exclaimed, "'Some guy'? He is Avinash Pasricha, the most renowned photographer of dancers!" And so we took an appointment and went to his studio the next day, and it was like a gallery of portraits of all the renowned classical dancers in the country. Over the years, Avinash and his wife Santosh became close family friends of Deepa and Shyam. Another significant outcome of the show was the review of the performance by Subbudu, a highly-regarded dance critic based in Delhi. He was himself an accomplished violinist with a profound knowledge of classical Carnatic music and dance forms of the south. He was particularly known for his brilliant reviews, reflecting a deep insight into the nuances of the dancer's performance. I had no knowledge of Subbudu or his reputation. His review came to Deepa's notice; I think it was in the *Statesman*. Not only was the review highly complimentary, but more significantly he put this budding artiste on the radar of the Indian Council for Cultural Relations (ICCR). Thus it was that Deepika came to be noticed by the aficionados of dance and culture in Delhi.

In Delhi, the flag of Kuchipudi as a classical dance form was, I think, unfurled in a significant way by the iconic Yamini Krishnamurthy. The introduction and explanation of each of the items in her repertoire by her father Krishnamurthy made her performances highly enjoyable even to the uninitiated. Then we had Swapna Sundari, who held the field for long as a premier Kuchipudi artiste and travelled widely, representing the country in many cultural events globally. When we were in Delhi, there were two dance duos successfully propagating Kuchipudi: Raja and Radha Reddy, and Vanashri and Rama Rao. We used to meet Radha and Raja Reddy, who were excellent hosts and used to have friends over often. Raja Reddy hailed from an agricultural family of a remote village in Adilabad district (now a part of Telangana state). I was always amazed at how he—without any mentor and without any Kuchipudi background in the family, or in the environment he grew up in, for inspiration and encouragement—had, out of the sheer passion he developed for this classical dance form, risen to great heights by dint of relentless *sadhana*. His enthusiasm and dedication obviously rubbed off on his devoted wife Radha Reddy, an accomplished dancer herself who could match him step for step. The other duo, Vanashri and Rama Rao have also been in Delhi for long, and by their dedication and hard work, have created a niche for themselves in the cultural space of Delhi. Only one close to artistes at that level can get to see the depth of commitment and dedication with which they tirelessly pursue the art to justify their recognition as a performer or guru. That said, Radha and I as parents can claim such insight, seeing Deepa's total devotion and sadhana.

Deepa would fulfil her ambition of learning under the legendary guru of Kuchipudi in recent times, Dr Vempati Chinna Satyam. As she would often recount later, while she was pursuing dance and presenting solo performances, she had seen '*Sreenivasa Kalyanam*', the great Kuchipudi ballet produced by Dr Vempati, and decided to have her skills fine-tuned by him. It was not going to be an easy task, since Dr Vempati had established an institute in Chennai, and anyone wanting to learn from him had to go there. It was a typically *gurukula* environment, with all the young women learners coming from outside being put up in thatched cottages, and Dr Vempati's wife and family ensuring a boarding facility for them; the classes would go on from morning till evening. Deepa may have spent almost a year there, frequently travelling back and forth from Hyderabad. All this trouble of commuting to Chennai and the effort of constant practice even after marriage only reflect how passionate she had become about Kuchipudi, which had begun as a hobby. The great learning experience while she was there, besides exposure to a traditional rural lifestyle involving drawing of water from a well for bath, etc., is something Deepa cherishes most fondly and she never tires of acknowledging her deep sense of gratitude for the opportunity she had to learn the finer aspects of this classical art under guru Dr Chinna Satyam.

As for Siddharth, after completing his twelfth, he wanted to join engineering and so appeared for the Common Entrance Test [CET] in the state. Before the results were out, I had this offer to admit him in the Muffakam Jha College run by one of the Nizam's Trusts, since the trustees were known to me closely. In fact, they were prepared to admit him in the computer science course, which was the most sought after then. Siddharth was, however, keen on doing mechanical engineering before pursuing an MBA abroad, and was also hopeful of securing admission through the CET. He did get admission into the Chaitanya Bharathi Institute of Technology, in the mechanical wing he wanted. He insisted on buying a motorcycle to go to college, rejecting our offer to use the Maruti 800 which was available as a second car. After we left for Delhi, Bharathi Aunty took the responsibility of taking care of her grandson quite seriously, causing some mild friction between them, since the young man, with his innumerable friends, would not be back home till late. Can't blame him, though his grandmother couldn't quite understand his extra-curricular activities. Besides badminton, he was very much involved with activities of AIESEC (originally, an acronym for Association Internationale des Étudiants en Sciences Économiques et Commerciales), an international students' organisation, initially as a member and later as president of its Hyderabad chapter. Two of his close friends, Bashir Babukhan, his schoolmate and Radha Manni, were also actively involved in AIESEC along with him.

Siddharth completed his graduation in engineering well, and was keen to do his MBA in one of the reputed business schools in the USA. Most of the noted business schools gave preference to candidates with work experience for admission into MBA, and so Siddharth started scouting for a job to satisfy the requirement. He had received a job offer as sales executive for one of the Shriram Group of companies in Calcutta. When he said he had accepted it, during one of our visits to Hyderabad, I was quite annoyed that he did not choose to consult us. The executive who interviewed him was apparently keen to have him and played this mind game of tickling his ego by saying, "Surely you don't need to consult your parents for this", and our friend fell into the trap. I had to put my foot down, saying no to his joining as sales executive, running around Calcutta on a motorcycle. He was then offered a suitable job in their manufacturing unit in Uttaranchal. From there, he moved back to Hyderabad to join Shriram Refrigeration as executive assistant to the CEO, who incidentally at that time was Mohan Guruswamy. With a couple of years of work experience added to his CV in his application, Siddharth was offered admission at Columbia University and University of Michigan, Ann Arbor, for MBA. He called me in Delhi for my opinion, and I had none to offer, since it was an unfamiliar field. While the former was an Ivy League university, the latter was a business school which had for years figured in the top four business schools in the US. He chose Michigan Business School, Ann Arbor, and perhaps did the right thing; apart from recognition in the corporate world, the school was also known for its idyllic campus.

After his MBA, Siddharth got an offer from Merrill Lynch Investment Managers, and joined them as director and associate portfolio manager. He was in Princeton, New Jersey, USA, living a happy life, finishing his work early and returning home late after playing racket ball. Presumably not satisfied with the relaxed schedule and lack of excitement, he moved to California to try his hand in some start-up and eventually joined Indus Capital, an investment management firm; for the last few years he has been in Hong Kong, managing its affairs as a partner and managing director. In practical terms, his job responsibility appears to be managing some large hedge funds. It took me a long time to gain insight into what his work really involves, though I knew that he travelled a lot, meeting corporate honchos across India and countries in South East Asia, which constitute his area of operation. I have also come to learn of his being invited to attend meetings with ministers, central banks and policy makers across the region, which he must find exciting, and expanding his vistas of knowledge in the area of global financial management. Closer home, after attending many meetings, where then finance minister of India, the late Arun Jaitley was also present, Siddharth, at my instance, introduced himself to Jaitley—whom I had known well as an esteemed colleague at the bar—only few months before Jaitley's sad demise, and I was happy that he remembered me and our family fondly. Regardless of his accomplishments in the political arena, Arun never ceased to maintain bonhomie with his lawyer friends. In fact, when he joined the cabinet for the first time, with the late A. B. Vajpayee as prime minister, on his visit to Hyderabad, Arun accepted our hospitality at dinner, ignoring pressures from political leaders and others. His passing away deeply saddened me and Radha, who had known him and Mrs Jaitley for long.

Siddharth chose his bride-to-be, Aditi, before he left for his MBA to the US; and the marriage was performed in Hyderabad in December 1994, to be followed by a reception in Delhi, where we were then living. Aditi is the daughter of Dr Amulya and M. Prabhakar Reddy. Amulya and Radha were together in college, and close friends; besides, Amulya's father Dharma Reddy, who was director of industries in the AP Government, was with Nukala in college, and thus the family was closely known to us for long. Aditi did her MBA in Hyderabad and after marriage, while in the US, she joined Lehman Brothers—the operations of which supposedly caused a global financial meltdown in 2008. She later moved to Nomura, which bought over part of Lehman's operations, and from there to Credit Suisse, where she is presently a managing director. Her phenomenal rise in the global financial sector, overcoming the generally perceived dog-eat-dog syndrome of Wall Street and elsewhere, should be an inspiration for aspiring young women pursuing their professional ambitions. When Siddharth, who was naturally excited and happy for his wife on her appointment as a managing director in Credit Suisse, shared the good news with the family, I recall texting an anecdote by way of response, conveying in a subtle and witty way my appreciation of her accomplishment, which reads thus:

There was this successful couple who one day had a serious argument. The wife, who noticed a touch of patriarchy in the talk and actions of her husband, braced herself and said to him: "Hey, don't forget that I have done better than you all through, with better grades in college, better start as executive and, now, in a more responsible position."

The husband's comment: "Forget all that—overall I have done better" raised hackles with her, who retorted and said: "Don't be an MCP as always. How dare you say that you have done better! I demand an explanation." The husband, without losing his cool, said: "Dear wife, don't you realise that I married better than you!"

It is time now to revert to the marriage of Deepika with Shyam Gopal (Shyam) on 15 August 1985. Shyam is the son of the late Nallapureddy Guruwa Reddy (N. G. Reddy) and Sudarshanamma. Shyam had his schooling in Hyderabad Public School and graduated in electronics and electrical engineering from Andhra University at Vizag. The family ran an engineering firm, Instrumentation Engineers Private Ltd., which had collaboration with an American company. Shyam, after graduation, had trained with the American company for some time before he started managing his family firm. N. G. Reddy, though not a qualified engineer, had a sharp mind with a flair for technology, and their family house in Banjara Hills was one of the earliest with central air-cooling and other modern facilities. Sudarshanamma is known for her knowledge of mythology and philosophical thought. I had aptly coined a mode of address for her as "Sudarshananandamayee". She conducted *satsang* sessions which were popular amongst ladies from known families. She was apparently taken by Deepa's dancing prowess and potential at her debut. Over the years, Shyam has become the cornerstone for the functioning of Deepanjali—an institute for excellence in Kuchipudi dance founded by Deepa, providing managerial and logistical support. As far as the family is concerned, I must say that with his boundless affection, Shyam blended in beautifully. With Shyam here in Hyderabad and Siddharth overseas combining as a team, there is a sense of security for the family members.

13 Gen 3

The belated starting of a family, though unintended, may have given Deepa the requisite freedom to spend time in Chennai at the institute and devote her time to the sadhana of her dance. It was undoubtedly a period fraught with disappointment and anticipation for us all in the family. Meanwhile, we had our first grandchild, Nitya, daughter of Siddharth and Aditi, born in 1998 in New Jersey, US. Later, the good news of Deepa's trouble-free pregnancy came as a great relief for us, and all care for proper monitoring (here and abroad) was ensured by Shyam and us all, and on a weekend in December 2000, while I was away in Bangalore to attend a meeting, Deepa was admitted into a maternity home in Hyderabad for her delivery. There, while having lunch with Meena Naru and her parents visiting India, whom I had invited to my hotel, I got the exciting news of Deepa delivering twins, a girl and a boy. Since their arrival was somewhat premature, I was having anxious moments, constantly calling to find out the developments. Dr Swaroop (Nani), being a consultant for paediatrics and neonatology, was with the babies, attending to them and making arrangements to shift them to Apollo Hospitals, where there was proper neonatal care available. I was concerned about the logistics for shifting them, from Somajiguda to Apollo. Nani apparently organised incubators for their journey to Apollo, taking the help of Ms Sangeeta and others, and I was informed that they could be shifted comfortably and that while Shloka—the baby girl, older by a minute or two—was in an incubator in the room, Abhinav, who required breathing support for some time, was in the paediatric ICU. It was a great relief to know that, and I got my return flight advanced to that evening and took Meena to a florist to buy a bouquet for Deepa. As the flight landed in Hyderabad, expectedly, I was the first at the exit, waiting for the door to be opened. As I stood there, the air hostess saw the beautiful bouquet in my hands and said "Nice flowers, sir", and my instant response was that I was carrying them for my daughter who had delivered twins earlier that day.

Having said that, I started wondering why I was saying all that to a stranger. I suppose it was the irresistible urge to share the boundless joy in my heart. Deepa once chided me for speaking about my grandkids incessantly, reminding me that I was not the only one having grandkids. Not that it curbed my tendency to consider the role of grandkids as the brightest spot in life's journey. One day, as I was disembarking from a flight in Hyderabad, I noticed the iconic painter M. F. Hussain, also waiting to disembark. I immediately picked up an airline postcard and approached him for his autograph, saying that it was for my grandkids. He sweetly asked for their names and wrote them down, conveying his best wishes.

From the airport, straight to the hospital to see the divine gift bestowed as two babies, that, too, a girl and a boy, to make my loving daughter's family complete. I saw Shloka in the incubator and then I was taken to the ICU by Nani to see Abhinav. Both were far too tiny, and we had to wait for a couple of weeks before we could carry and cuddle them. Their very sight was a sublime joy and a delight, experienced not too often in one's life.

I used to spend as much time as possible sitting in the room and watching Shloka in the incubator. The first major event, as they grew out of their cribs, was the trip to Tirupati for the traditional tonsuring. As a thanksgiving, I also had my head shaven, and from there we went to Srikalahasti, where my close friend Chenchu Reddy had made arrangements for a special puja by Deepa and Shyam. While there, a small incident is indelibly etched in my memory. We were to go into the main temple from the guest rooms a little before noon, when the sun got hot. I was carrying Shloka and instinctively I was holding my *angavastram* over the tiny child to protect her from the sun. Chenchu Reddy, who was with us all through, would often marvel at the manner in which the two tiny tots stayed put without crying, despite the noise and the stale air in the temple packed with devotees. The manner in which he recalls such small details shows how immersed he was along with the family in what was being carried out. A true friend is there to share your joys as if he were a part of you. After Abhinav grew up and, as a teenager, would go to Srikalahasti to play tennis tournaments there, Chenchu Reddy would be prominently visible and his presence as a VIP of the town used to make Abhinav, mild-mannered and self-effacing by nature, uncomfortable to the extent that he would ask his mother to tell uncle Chenchu Reddy not to trouble himself to attend his matches. Nothing can make my devoted, energetic friend reduce the level of his excitement and *hungama* when it comes to his friends like me.

Abhinav, who became passionate about his tennis, used to travel to various venues in the country like Srikalahasti and also abroad. Playing international tennis tournaments in several countries, he secured a world-ranking high of 1556. While in Chirec International High School here, he was elected sports captain and tennis captain for the school team for four years. Such exposure may have helped him, coupled with his grades and good score in the Scholastic Aptitude Test (SAT), to secure admission into Haverford College in Philadelphia, US—where he is presently pursuing an undergraduate degree in economics. From day one, he has been part of his college tennis team, and it was heartening to know that he won his debut tournament in doubles, which was not quite his forte, since, as I had known him, he is basically a singles player. Radha and I had gone along with his parents—Deepika and Shyam—to get him settled in his college and hostel, in August–September 2019. The facilities for academics and sports were impressive and no wonder it is one of the most sought-after institutions.

While in the US, we visited Nitya and it is perhaps time now to rewind a bit. Though primogeniture as a legal concept has relevance, if at all, for determining *inter se* rights of a succession of siblings, amongst grandchildren its operation can only be on an emotional plane. The arrival of Nitya, daughter of Siddharth and Aditi, heralded the advent of the Gen-3 era in the family. It was on the auspicious day of 11 December 1998 that Nitya arrived, in New Jersey, sealing for her the right to an American passport. I missed all the excitement of being around to welcome the bundle of joy of the first grandchild, the high seas keeping us apart. I had to be content earmarking my earnings of the day to the new-born as commemoration of the joyous event. Needless to say, considering the modest fees I charged, it must have been a meagre amount deposited in her name.

Over the years, Nitya has always had a special place in garnering my love and affection in good measure, making her, sweet and unassuming child that she is, often feel embarrassed, and I would have to explain that she is my first grandchild and shall remain so. This also led to the well thought-out designation of "Captain" being conferred upon her, with the expectation of her leading the Gen-3 team, the strength of which disappointingly remained frozen at 2+2 = 4.

Nitya did her schooling from the International School, Hong Kong, and, with her accomplishments in athletics, swimming and basketball, was one of the prominent and popular students to graduate from there. She has passed on the bat onto her sister Megha, who will be graduating from school shortly. Megha, known in the family for her soft-spoken, affectionate nature, seems to be doing exceedingly well with mind-boggling scores, particularly in the sciences, while being a leader of the 24-hours race club in her school as a competent track athlete. I always found the co-curricular activities promoted by their school, particularly those focusing on service to humanity, remarkable. The ethics and values they instil in the minds of students came to light when Nitya went, as part of a group of students, to Calcutta with the assigned duty of serving destitute, physically and mentally challenged children at the centre run by the Missionaries of Charity founded by Mother Teresa. During the period the students were to spend there, they were to be totally immersed in their humanitarian tasks, without any communication with friends or family. Nitya developed a great passion for rendering such service in a hands-on manner, as was evident from the email I received from her at that time. Megha also had a similar experience at another such institution, I think in Tamil Nadu, and both of them, when they are here in Hyderabad even for a few days, love to spend time at Spandana—an institution for destitute children. How I wish elite schools and educational institutions in India could also emulate such admirable practices to make their students grow into enlightened citizens with an awareness of their duties towards the underprivileged in their society.

Reverting to Nitya's present student life at Brown University—an Ivy League school in the US with an excellent liberal arts curriculum—she is pursuing a double major in economics and creative writing. She is president of the Economics Department undergraduate group, and chief development officer of their Smart Women's Investment Club. She is also a sector analyst at Brown, a socially responsible investment fund that manages a portion of the Brown University endowment. In keeping with these economics and finance-related accomplishments, as I learn, she is due to intern as an investment banker shortly in a reputed firm. We have all had a taste of Nitya's flair for creative writing as well when she mailed her pieces in Brown's *Vagabond* magazine.

In the recent past, one of my favourite activities for brushing the rust off the brain has been exchanging emails with Nitya. In some context, Krishnayan happened to see a couple of emails I had sent her, and suggested that we might include some in this memoir. When she was to leave home in Hong Kong, understandably with a heavy heart, to join Brown University, she expressed her feelings in her email to me, and my response was as below:

> Nitya dearest,
>
> I'm glad you could open out to me. Good to do that to the ones you believe in, whether you benefit by their response and advice or not, it helps in making you identify thoughts and anxieties troubling you, making it easier in meeting them with gusto as you move forward. You tried to extract info on my childhood, possibly for making a biopic in your mind on my life at that time. Well, my childhood was so uneventful that it may not be worthwhile to recount the same. Not complaining though, no dearth of care, concern and love from parents, just that the times were so different that it will be difficult for you guys to relate and view in proper perspective.
>
> Coming to your anxiety about leaving home, would say it's only natural. It's only a reflection of the blessings of a very happy childhood you have had. You can't have it for all time, since it will be going against evolution, which is the order of nature. Might interest you to know that parent eagles are known to destroy their nest once the eaglets learn to fly and pick their prey. Their mindset is obviously predetermined to facilitate evolutionary process.
>
> That said, remember that the loss of your company will be felt equally by your loving family. Whenever you try to draw upon frozen pictures of a happy family soaked in love to pep up your mood. I know you are far too bright and mature to

have any such issues. Start telling your mind that you are going to like it and make the best of it from now on.

There was another occasion when Nitya had shared her thoughts, at a time when she was veering towards writing as a career. And I had to apply my mind to articulate my thoughts carefully in response, without in any way imposing my views, and my email, reflecting the balancing act, read thus:

> ... Aditi was here a while ago and told us about your 2020 internship in HK. Being excited about the area you are to work in as an intern, it's time, I think, for you to gradually focus on what next, career-wise. I took serious note of your flair and fascination for writing. Fascination for any creative activity is bound to be overwhelming.
>
> I just pulled out two books of Indian English authors and they are Amish Tripathi's *Boring Banker Turned Happy Writer*. Success of his debut novel encouraged him to give up fourteen years of service in financial services and focus on writing.
>
> Chetan Bhagat, the rockstar of Indian publishing and the bestselling English language novelist in Indian history, quit his international investment banking career, to devote his entire time to writing. You can see his in-depth knowledge of that field in his novel *One Indian Girl*.
>
> Now let me refer to my practical experience. This young law student from National Law School Bangalore interned with me while I was in Delhi. Being on their executive, I had gone to the school for their convocation, and there this guy, who was also to receive his degree, came up to me for advice. While doing his law he had appeared and succeeded in both the prelim and final exams for selection to the Indian Administrative Service and, being a sharp guy, cleared those exams and was to appear for interview. He wanted to know what his choice should be: law or administrative service. Knowing my opinion would impact his decision-making, I had to bestow serious thought. For one thing, sharp that he is, he would do well in either of them. I suggested that he might consider taking the Service, the logic simply being that if he missed it out, he cannot get into it with similar advantages at a later stage, while law he could switch to

whenever he chooses and the exposure he had, meanwhile, would only be of help in his legal career. He did just that, and he worked with Nandan Nilekani in the creation of UIDAI-ID (AADHAAR) card, and is now considered to be one of the highly regarded young officers in Karnataka. Well, my advice was not unsolicited and I only hope he will not regret his decision. These are merely rambling thoughts, nothing more. Shall sign off repeating what your Professor said: "Nitya, I shall look forward to seeing with great interest and anticipation what you do in future."

Pausing here, I must say one feels most elated to learn about the accomplishments of one's grandchildren in far-off countries. But it is never the same as having them here amidst us. So we felt most heartened when Shloka made known her disinclination to go abroad for her undergraduate programme and decided instead to be rooted firmly in Hyderabad. She joined St. Francis Women's College to pursue a Bachelor of Arts, majoring in Mass Communications, Social Management and English Literature. Considering her co-curricular achievements in school, including as founder of AT-RISE, an initiative aiming towards rural independence, her choice of subjects seemed appropriate. Though I was not excited about Shloka pursuing classical dance, perhaps with the thought that one such in the family was enough, today this passion of hers seems to have, to a great extent, influenced her decision to stay back in Hyderabad. Though in the field of politics, lineage is referred to in uncomplimentary terms for the offspring's success, in the field of performing arts, be it classical musicians or dancers, lineage is seen to be a natural contributing factor impacting the successor's accomplishments. So it is small wonder that Shloka, besides being seen by knowledgeable critics as a dancer of great promise, has developed the flair to not only guide her co-learners but also help her guru and mother with ideas for choreography. Shloka is the recipient of the Bala Chaitanya Award, the International Children's Film Festival 'Child Prodigy' award, and currently holds a National Cultural Talent Search scholarship for Kuchipudi dance.

14   Deepika, the Guru

The tipping point for Deepika's transformation into a teacher and guru came when Sravya—sister Saraswathi's granddaughter and daughter of Sai and Manasa—who was learning dance from some institute, turned to Deepa for a few sessions of learning. Pleased with her improvement, Sravya then brought her friend Mihira along, and so the number grew for informal training under a dancer who was yet to don the role of guru. This had its natural culmination in Deepa formally starting her own institute, 'Deepanjali', utilising the space in her house in Jubilee Hills, the plot bearing the number 123, a reflection of progression in life. I think despite her efforts to limit the number, there might be more than 150 students and teaching assistants in Deepanjali. It is indeed a pleasant sight to see these enthusiastic young students, mostly girls, with their equally enthusiastic parents or family members accompanying them, flocking to Deepanjali in the evenings. Deepa is blessed to find a sense of fulfilment in grooming all those young learners, besides choreographing dance ballets and innovative repertoire for presentations along with her students.

Deepika performed for one or more *sabha*s in Chennai during the December–January season for a number of years, and is the recipient of many awards from reputed sabhas in Chennai. In 2007 she was awarded the title Kala Ratna by the then composite state of Andhra Pradesh and lately by the Telangana State. Temperamentally, she never really considered receiving awards as the ultimate reward for her effort and contribution. When some award did not fructify, despite proposals by successive state governments, she took it in her stride, and would tell me not to feel disappointed. I cannot but admire such a philosophical mindset. But then, due recognition accorded to artists and gurus like her is not merely something personal—it also provides inspiration to the associates who work with them and, more importantly, to the young learners who are their disciples.

Deepika, the Guru

Deepika was immensely happy when the Sangeet Natak Akademi, Delhi, chose her for the Akademi Award 2017 for Kuchipudi, and so were all in her Deepanjali family. It was a proud moment for us to be present at Rashtrapati Bhavan, New Delhi, for the presentation of the National Award by the President of India on 6 February 2019. I would tell friends and well-wishers who called to congratulate on the occasion that artistes like Deepika are *karmayogis* for whom awards are not the goal but a source of inspiration to promote and propagate their art with greater zeal and commitment.

In passing I may mention the inclusion of my name for consideration for one such award. It was after I moved to Hyderabad as a retiree. Kiran Kumar Reddy, an amiable young political leader, was then Chief Minister of AP, unfortunately at a time when the state was embroiled in the process of bifurcation. He had known me for long and, presumably in recognition of my services as a law officer in the state and Centre and my contributions as chairman, BCI, he seems to have included my name, without reference to me, for, I believe, the Padma Bhushan. I had absolutely no knowledge of it and I would have felt embarrassed if it had become public, though it was not uncommon for senior advocates and law officers to be conferred such awards. What is most gratifying in Deepika's case is that she is totally immersed in dance and enjoys her chosen art form, and has great commitment to pass on the cultural legacy to her students.

15 Collateral Activities

Reverting to the time I was in office as a government pleader, when the handling of work, both in the chambers and in courts, was getting systematised, I felt the need for some recreational activity. Though I had become a member of the Secunderabad Club a few years earlier, distance was a deterrent for regular visits. I played tennis in the evenings at the club on and off, till I developed 'tennis shoulder', and tried my hand at squash, only to find that it was not suited for me. I then took to golf, along with Vikram, Jagadish and Ramesh, cousins of Radha, with whom I could bond well as friends. The golf course was in Bolarum and was an annexe to the Secunderabad Club in those days. But then I could manage to play barely a round once a week.

Then, one day in 1977, I decided on a whim to contest for membership of the managing committee of the club, and shot out letters seeking support from members. Since from the legal circle there were hardly any members, I had to count on friends and relatives. I think my being a professional holding a position of responsibility as government pleader seems to have swung many uncommitted voters to support my candidature, and I stood second in the tally of votes polled. Pradeepak, a noted sailor, sportsman and active participant in club activities, stood first as expected, and immediately after me was Dr Ram K. Vepa, a senior IAS officer who, after his stint in the Central government, moved back and was heading the Andhra Pradesh Industrial Development Corporation (APIDC). In the first meeting after the election, presided over by Ranga Rao who was then the president, the newly-elected members had to choose the subcommittee of which they would be the chairman. Pradeepak naturally opted for the house committee and, being next, I made my preference for the library subcommittee known. Curiously, I found the president trying to persuade me to opt for the sports subcommittee, which was normally in higher demand after the house committee. I said no, and insisted on the library. When Dr Vepa opted to become a member of the library subcommittee, I could guess why Ranga Rao was persuading me to opt for the other. The main task of the subcommittee, besides overseeing the functioning of the library, was to select new publications, fiction and nonfiction, which the book sellers would bring and spread out before us during the meeting. Managing committee meetings used to be fun, with all the balloting of applicants for membership and other administrative issues. It was a matter of satisfaction to me that I could successfully prevail upon a particular member who had a tendency to be judgmental and an obstinate dissenter on many matters.

Two significant events during my two-year term are worth recalling. The first was the decision to receive new applications for membership after a long pause. The Secunderabad Club being highly prestigious in the city, hundreds of applications had piled up and an earlier committee had decided to stop receiving any fresh applications. When the backlog was almost about to be cleared, we had to decide upon receiving fresh applications. But then, since we knew prospective applicants in hundreds were waiting to put in their applications, the knotty question was how we were to go about it, since the order of priority used to be on a first-come-first-served basis. One fetter in place to limit the number was that an eligible member could propose or second two applicants in all, and this, to our knowledge, made the interested applicants approach members, wherever they were, to propose or second an application. The dilemma really for us was that if we started receiving the applications from a designated time on a given day, we could foresee the unseemly situation of prospective applicants lining up from the previous day itself. We averted any such undesirable outcome by deciding to receive applications for a week, at the end of which they were to be pooled, and lots drawn for seniority in a transparent manner.

The other significant event was the club's centenary celebrations. Planned on a large scale, there were diverse events, including concerts by reputed artistes. The library committee had organised an exhibition of rare and priceless books, which were aplenty in the storerooms. When we were to have an evening get-together, the employees' association decided to go on strike to press their demands, smartly figuring it to be the best time for arm-twisting. So at our instance the members pitched in as bearers and other staff, with some of the ladies and spouses taking charge of the kitchen to ensure that the programme went as scheduled. On the valedictory evening, we had slated recitals by Bharat Ratna awardee, Ustad Bismillah Khan, eminent flutist Pandit Hariprasad Chaurasia and santoor by Pandit Shiv Kumar Sharma, with Ustad Zakir Hussain accompanying all of them on tabla. Zakir Hussain's flight got delayed, and we were keen to get started with one of the maestros. But then who would play without the accompanying tabla? To our great relief, heeding our request, Pandit Chaurasia agreed to commence his recital, and with that, the evening's programme began; the celebrations ended on a happy note with my concluding remarks.

By the time my term as member of the managing committee of Secunderabad Club ended, I had come to be recognised as an active member of the Hyderabad Race Club (HRC), of which I became a member in about 1972. Not that I was a racing fan or an avid punter. I had visited the racecourse at Madras once while in college in the company of C. V. Rao's friends, and the Royal Ascot while in London with Prabha and N. R. C. Reddi (NRC). My friend Muddappa used to lay small bets in the betting shops in London and once I had a fling, making him place a bet for me in the Grand National, a steeple chase race, on a horse with the name of a tennis player I was familiar with, 'Ayala', and made some money, despite being a rank outsider. I became a member of HRC along with Jagadish, Vikram and Ramesh on the suggestion of Narayan (late A. V. Narayan Reddy) since a new racecourse in Malakpet was coming up. Horse racing in Hyderabad, which used to take place at the Secunderabad Gymkhana grounds on a minor scale, got shifted to its present location in Malakpet at about that time. It was the good fortune of racing enthusiasts of the twin cities that we had Surender (R. Surender Reddy) as chairman and N. Narender Reddy (NN), an acknowledged racing expert at the international level, as secretary of HRC. Their initiatives, aided by the support of enthusiasts like Hyderabad sports icon Ghulam Ahmed, who headed the committee as chairman in the initial period, and many others, resulted in Hyderabad becoming a reputed racing centre with excellent infrastructure and a reputation for clean and transparent professional racing.

When HRC was newly formed, I became a member along with cousins in the family and friends, and as a group of youthful members we used to question the managing committee during meetings, raising various issues. We used to be a highly vocal element and often a thorn in the flesh for the administrators. HRC, in its nascent years, not being an independent Turf Authority, used to race under the aegis of the Madras Race Club (MRC) and had to depend on horses from various centres. When HRC started encouraging local ownership of horses by providing loans, to make racing more competitive and less dependent on horses brought from other centres, Jagadish and I jointly bought a horse, 'Cosmic Fury', which raced without much success. When Jagadish gave up ownership of horses, I bought a colt myself and named him 'Mandamus', which proved a dud as well. Looking back, we treated it as an investment, and for the excitement associated with owning a racehorse.

All such involvement led to my contesting the election and becoming a steward, that is, member, managing committee, HRC. This required attending meetings of the Board of Stewards, besides being present on race day to oversee the races along with the officials. Besides, the scale of financial operations, running into crores, had to be assiduously administered since it is the money of the racing public. There were many responsibilities, like inquiries into infraction of racing rules besides allegations of malpractices by bookies, punters and racing professionals. Many a time an inquiry had to be concluded before the result of the race was formally announced if there was a complaint against the rider of a horse for causing obstruction or any other violation of racing rules. The stewards had to meet and take a decision after an inquiry. Though in the initial years this exercise was based solely on visual observations of the stewards and racing officials, later, with the advent of video recording of races and other aids of technology, the task became considerably easier and more transparent. Rules provide for an appellate body to consider the validity of decisions and penalties imposed by the inquiry committee by way of fine, suspension or withdrawal of license of professionals like jockeys, trainers, etc. One of the early decisions of the Privy Council on principles of natural justice interestingly related to action against a jockey in England.

An inquiry of far less significance verging on triviality, during my time on the committee, was the one relating to stale biryani served at a banquet. After the Derby race, held every year on 2 October, the HRC traditionally used to host cocktails and dinner for all the outstation guests from other centres, besides owners of participant horses. On one such occasion, the biryani laid on the table was found to be stale, and this was taken seriously by the Board of Stewards, which instituted an inquiry committee of two of its members—D. Pratap Reddy, IAS, Home Secretary, who was a government nominee on the board, and myself—to inquire into the lapse and submit a report. We went about the task seriously and examined all concerned in the food and beverage (F&B) department, including Rohini Dhar, the then F&B manager. It came to light that one of the board members, Dr Harishchander, a noted paediatric consultant who was a connoisseur of Hyderabadi cuisine, had sometime earlier recommended a butcher's shop in Secunderabad for procuring meat for the club's needs, and so Dhar shifted the procurement source to Secunderabad from Hyderabad. This led to the meat having to be bought the previous day itself, and the lamb for biryani was stored on the top in the freezer box—which was already almost full—and, according to Dhar, the lid may not have closed properly, causing the items stored on top to become stale. Well, for the time spent, my knowledge of culinary techniques improved to an extent that I would on occasion quiz people on the number of pieces a kilo of lamb is to be cut into for proper Mughlai style *dum* biryani. It was indeed fun, particularly with all friends as colleagues on the board, like Vijay (B. Vijay Reddy), Sudhakar (Sudhakar Reddy), Marideshwar (Marideshwar Rao), Chandrashekhar (T. Chandrashekhar Reddy), Dr Harishchander, Vikram (J. Vikram Dev Rao), besides the leaders Ghulam Ahmed and Surender and the government nominees. We used to visit other centres on invitation for important races, and I had an opportunity to attend the Asian Racing Conference at Seoul, Korea as part of the delegation in the year 1980.

As part of the trip we visited Hong Kong and were amazed to see the computerised totalisator system. The betting system most of the racecourses have at the venue is broadly of two types. One is the system of bookies licensed by the club, offering odds for the runners of each race, based on which punters are drawn to place their bets, with the winners getting paid by the bookie as per the odds offered when the bet was placed. In this the bookmaker's expertise comes to the fore, in balancing the books to ensure that he doesn't stand to lose. Many big-time punters have running accounts with the bookies to place bets and receiving winnings without cash changing hands. On all the bets, betting tax has to be collected to be remitted to the state exchequer. Totalisator or tote betting is run by the club, where all the bets for each of the different wagers like win, place, forecast, jackpot, etc. are pooled and divided amongst the winning tickets after the results are out. In this system no one can foretell precisely the amount receivable on a winning ticket till the results are announced and calculation made. This fundamental difference of the punter knowing the precise amount by way of winnings as he places a bet attracted most of the bookies, with very few placing bets at the tote. The computerised totalisator, such as the one seen in Hong Kong, had the advantage of giving a fair idea to the better of the returns in the event of his choice becoming a winner, since, as the bets are placed, calculation is made by the computer for the possible returns on each horse or combination before the race and displayed on the digital boards.

Though we were all aware of the existence of such a system, to install one in HRC, the high cost involved was a dampener. The then chairman, Ghulam Ahmed was not quite convinced of the desirability of such an investment, taking into account the cost–benefit ratio and as such, Narender, the secretary, and other votaries were not successful in getting a favourable decision from the board. When we saw how the system was working in Hong Kong, junior members of the board Vikram and I were sold on the idea. On our return, before the board meeting, I hurriedly got a letter addressed to the chairman and gave it to him at the meeting. As I can recall, I highlighted the demand by many legislators and others for a total ban on horse racing. With the demand becoming more vocal, after the relative of a close associate of then CM Anjaiah committed suicide reportedly owing to heavy losses in horse betting, I proceeded to analyse the difference between the two systems of betting. While bookies run the show with profit motive, in the tote system the beneficiary is the government, which receives the tax amount without any evasion, and the club, which is a non-profit making body and spends the surplus if any on charitable public causes. Finally, I concluded saying that the only way the club could wean away vulnerable punters from the bookies to the tote, is by making the tote also provide information to the prospective bettors of the possible odds for different runners, and this would be possible only if the system is computerised. The repeated demand for the abolition of racing, saying many families are getting ruined, in the assembly and political circles generally, and the passionate plea of some members made chairman Ghulam Ahmed soften his attitude and agree in principle to computerisation. Indication of this came with Ghulam asking NN to look into the costs and other aspects. The rest is history, with HRC becoming one of the foremost clubs in India to successfully computerise its tote system. NN, with his wide experience and keenness to make it a success, left no stone unturned. On one of our recent visits to the racecourse, Vikram and I recalled sitting at different levels of the gallery to help decide upon the ideal height for the display board of tote odds in front of the members' stand.

After a term I didn't seek re-election as steward, despite considerable goodwill enjoyed amongst members of the club, since I had meanwhile become a member of the BCI, which involved frequent travel to Delhi and other places, mostly during weekends when racing activity was also on. I can recall Deepika's admonition, that as a kid she used to detest Sundays, instead of looking forward to a day away from school, since Radha and I used to head for the race club at noon. This was even before I became a steward. Racing in Hyderabad, which back then was held only during the monsoon for two months or so, was considered a highly-regarded social event, with families of members spending an afternoon together enjoying racing. Demand for guest badges to the members' enclosure was such that stewards and officials used to find it embarrassing to deal with requests from friends. Amongst the members, clamour for a box (exclusive seating) used to be intense and lots had to be drawn since there were not enough for all the interested members.

Lately I have stopped visiting the racecourse, except for special events like the Invitation Cup, and what we see now on normal days of racing is a far cry from what it used to be back then. Now there is an obvious overdose of it, with an extended monsoon besides winter season racing and inter-venue betting. It is indeed heartening to see how HRC has grown to be a premium Turf Authority, with first-class infrastructure and, more importantly, professionalism with transparency in management of racing activity. Such continued growth and garnering of prestige without doubt takes committed and credible leadership, which HRC fortunately has had over the years, with Surender Reddy being at the helm of affairs. I can recall Surender successfully convincing NTR, who was particularly known for being a tight-fisted CM, to reduce the betting tax considerably, the logic being lesser betting tax would reduce illegal betting evading tax altogether. The credibility of the leadership is, I imagine, what makes a difference, and Surender enjoyed it across diverse fields. To recall his political career, he was elected to Parliament five times and as MLA six times, having forayed into politics as president of the Maripeda Samithi in 1959. He had a long and prominent association with the Hyderabad Cricket Association, and is the founder president of the Hyderabad Golf Association. No exaggeration to say that he has been a multifaceted genius, on whose shoulders any responsibility in the public sphere would rest lightly.

16 Warmth of Friendship and Rajampet Gallantry

In the context of the desirability of permitting horse racing, I fondly recall the signal contribution of A. Chengal Reddy, member of a legislative council, with whom I had the privilege of close association. Participating in the debate on racing, he made out a strong case with his rational thinking and effective articulation against any move to ban horse racing, leading many in the political circles to presume that he was an avid race-goer, while the truth of the matter is that he had never visited a racecourse in his life. Such individuals, particularly in the political circle, should be remembered for their objectivity in public life. Besides fair thinking, Chengal Reddy's career in public life was marked by his unostentatious nature. As chairman of Tirumala Tirupati Devasthanams (TTD), he gave up the luxurious bungalow of the chairman to settle for smaller premises so that it could be used for the benefit of pilgrims. When he mentioned to me that he was proposing to do this soon after he assumed office, I disapproved of the move, saying that though I appreciate his gesture and sentiment, his successors might seek to rebuild one later at a much higher cost.

His incredible humility, unassuming nature and affection made him stand the tallest (despite his short physical stature) amongst the noted seniors of his time in Rajampet. The affinity and mutual respect between him and Father were such that one was reminded of the saying that the best of friends are those that sit together for a period of time without exchanging a word, and leave with the satisfaction of having had a good conversation. Every evening, rain or shine, Chenganna used to visit Father and both would sit—one with the morning's *Hindu*, the other with *Bhavan's Journal* in hand—and have half cups of coffee before parting. In my case, no visit to Rajampet, whether from Hyderabad or Delhi, would be complete without spending one whole morning with Chenganna in his house, sitting in the front veranda with newspapers spread out, exchanging notes on our experiences. I acknowledge with gratitude the affection and regard bestowed on me by him, and by advocates like V. Lakshman, P. Venkat Reddy and Rama Raju, and by headmaster Venkat Seshaiah; I used to feel embarrassed when they would come to the railway station to see me off every time I left for Hyderabad. Well, such is the warmth of feeling and affection you can receive only from senior well-wishers of your hometown.

While I'm at it, I must also recall my association with this young man, Balaram Reddy, son of Kasireddy Narasa Reddy, related through my grandmother, who used to spend evenings with me whenever we were both in Rajampet during vacations from college, he from Tirupati and I from Madras. An ardent patriot, he joined the army during emergency commissioning to fulfil his passion to serve his country. He was at the war front in the 1965 war with Pakistan, and I have reverentially preserved what was presumably his last letter, written from a bunker, received by me after his martyrdom. When in Rajampet, I maintain close contact with Balaram's nephew (his sister's son), Diwakar Reddy, and his younger brother Manohar Reddy.

17 Foray into Bar Bodies—Bar Council of India

The next phase is something that provided a sense of fulfilment in my career. After I quit as GP there was, understandably, a bit of lull in court work since, having given up all private briefs on becoming GP, I had to necessarily wait for work to pile up. About that time there was to be this election to the State Bar Council. In the normal course this may not have come to my notice since I hardly spent much time in the Bar Association hall, except briefly to hear political gossip from knowledgeable friends like G. Veera Reddy who used to follow national politics, reading Delhi newspapers like *Hindustan Times*. Luckily, I got to know of the impending elections to the State Bar Council. Though becoming a member of the State Bar Council by itself was not an exciting proposition, I could see in it the prospect of getting elected to the Bar Council of India (BCI) since K. Seetaram Reddy, a member of BCI from AP Bar Council, had become a judge and in the vacancy of few months of his term, a lawyer from the Secunderabad Bar, Veerabhadra Rao, was elected. In that situation, I could foresee fair prospects of my getting elected to the BCI.

Actually, I had never evinced interest in the elections of the Bar Association or any other bar organisations till then. So when I got into the fray it must have come as a surprise to many. Having got into it, I went right ahead, sending printed letters to various bar associations in the state. In that election, the number of members to be elected to the State Council, which under the rules depends on the strength of the lawyers on the rolls in the state, was twenty and election was by the system of proportional representation through single transferable vote. I found the response from the bar members of subordinate courts even in small towns of remote areas highly encouraging. Nevertheless, I decided to visit a few centres and meet the bar members, as advised by friends. I am told that in recent times, campaigning has reached high intensity, with candidates touring the state with friends for weeks on end in cars loaded with goodies. Back then it was more subdued, and I

PLATE 33 Family photograph at 40th anniversary celebrations of VRR and Radha in Hyderabad.

PLATE 34 Chilling with the grandchildren in Coonoor.

PLATE 35 VRR with close friends Sreedharan, Sreekumar and family in Coonoor.

Plate 36 VRR's family performing puja for the *punah pratishthan* (reinstallation) of the temple deity at Hatyarala, Rajampet.

Plate 37 VRR with A. Changal Reddy, former TTD chairman, and P. Venkat Reddy.

Plate 38 VRR with Dr Madan Mohan Reddy and J. C. Diwakar Reddy.

Plate 39 VRR with priests and Nagaraja Gupta, Sudhakar, Raghu, Penchallaiyya, Subba Reddy, Mani, Narayana, Subbayya.

PLATE 40 VRR's daughter Deepika's *rangapravesham*, with her Guru, Sumathi Kaushal, former CM Vengal Rao, former CJ A. Sambashiva Rao and Akkineni Nageshwara Rao.

PLATE 41 VRR speaking at the inauguration of Deepanjali; (L to R) Geeta Reddy, Jaipal Reddy, M.M.P. Raju and Deepika.

PLATE 42 VRR with Pandit Birju Maharaj, after presentation of his production *Ritu Samhar*, in which Deepika was chosen to choreograph and present the Kuchipudi segment.

PLATE 43 Deepika being felicitated by P. V. Narasimha Rao after her performance at Habitat Centre, Delhi.

PLATE 44 Dignitaries present for the Gajjapuja performance by Shloka and Abhinav; (L to R) VRR, R. Surender Reddy, Dr Y. V. Reddy, Jagdish Mittal, Deepika, Shyam, Uttam Kumar Reddy.

Plate 45 Radha lighting the lamp on commencement of Deepika's ballet *Rukmini Krishna*; (L to R) lyricist Sirivennela Seetharama Sastry, former Union home secretary K. Padmanabhaiah, Kavita Kalvakuntla, president Telangana Jagruthi, Dr Jupally Rameswar Rao, chairman My Home Group.

Plate 46 After the ballet, Deepika with the sponsors Vasantha and Varaprasad Reddy, dignitaries Vachaspathi Brahmasri Chaganti Koteswara Rao, Ramanachary, advisor to Govt. of Telangana, singer S. P. Balasubramanyam, music composer and vocalist D. S. V. Sastry.

Plate 47 Deepika receiving the Andhra Pradesh State Award 'Kalaratna' from CM Dr Y. S. Rajasekhara Reddy in 2007, in the presence of K. R. Suresh Reddy, speaker AP Legislative Assembly.

Plate 48 Deepika receiving the Telangana State Award, 2016, from Governor E. S. L. Narasimhan and CM K. Chandrasekhara Rao.

Plate 49 President of India, Ram Nath Kovind, conferring Deepika with the National Sangeet Natak Akademi Award 2017, for her contribution to the Kuchipudi dance form.

PLATE 50 VRR at Rashtrapati Bhavan, with Deepika and family on the occasion.

PLATE 51 Radha being felicitated by CM K. Rosaiah, in the presence of Dr Geeta Reddy, Minister of Tourism and Culture on the occasion of golden jubilee celebrations of Ravindra Bharati in 2010, in recognition of her "dedicated contribution for the development of Ravindra Bharati"; Radha was the prime artiste in the ballet presented on the auditorium's inauguration in 1961.

Plate 52 VRR with Dr M. Veeraraghava Reddy and K. Jayabharath Reddy.

Plate 53 VRR with Vinod Poddar on his 70th birthday.

Plate 54 Post-retirement, VRR on a holiday with family to Kenya.

Plate 55 High school graduation of Nitya, with both grandparents.

Plate 56 In Pune for the launch of a book on the Raste family, with Dinesh and Purnima.

Plate 57 Siva with bouquets received after the 40th anniversary celebrations of VRR and Radha in Hyderabad.

PLATE 58 Family get together at Deepika's house, December 2018.

PLATE 59 Radha on her 75th birthday, with Srilatha Bhupal, Surender Reddy, Jayamala and Dr Indira.

PLATE 60 General Sebastin and wife with VRR's family.

made random visits to a few places, particularly if local friends invited me to meet members of their association. On the day of counting, it may have surprised many regulars in the field to see that I had polled the maximum number of first-preference votes and was the only one to be declared elected after the first count. The most heartening feature, however, was that I had polled votes from practically all the places—Srikakulam to Sangareddy, Anantapur to Adilabad—with en bloc support from associations of a few smaller courts.

Must say, I thoroughly enjoyed meeting with members of the bar at different levels of trial courts, which itself was an educative experience to gain knowledge of the functioning of the bar and courts at different levels. We used to hear interesting stories about 'bullock cart chasing', which was an indigenous version of 'ambulance chasing'. In accident cases the victim was usually taken to hospital in a bullock cart—the readily available transportation in most cases—accompanied by enterprising young lawyers showing 'deep concern' to the victim's family with the covert objective of securing signatures on the *vakalat*, a document authorising a lawyer to represent the victim in the claim petition to be filed for a fanciful amount, in most cases, based on an arrangement for sharing the amount granted by courts. It was disappointing to see the poor state of bar association premises, with hardly any library and furniture. Getting to know many senior members of the bar in the districts made me immensely happy, indeed, more than securing votes. Few of the new acquaintances made readily coming to mind are Ranganatham, Krishnamurthy, Obul Reddy, C. V. Subba Reddy, Raghava Reddy in Cuddapah; Jangam Reddy, Nagendranath Reddy in Kurnool; Konda Reddy in Anantapur; Dharma Reddy, Chandrasekhar, Dwarakanath Reddy, Raghavan in Chittoor; Keshav Reddy, Janardhan Reddy, Venkateshwara Rao in Warangal; Anant Reddy, Ganga Reddy in Nizamabad. In Sangareddy, practically every lawyer was known to me, thanks to my close association with the late P. Ramachandra Reddy and his juniors. It was indeed a fascinating experience, since lawyers confined to the high courts and Supreme Court assume certain things about lawyers and legal work in trial courts in districts, small towns and suburbs, which may not reflect the reality.

Digressing here a bit, to deal with my significant exposure to trial court work involving the examination of witnesses, etc. by recounting my presence in Cuddapah following a criminal trial in the court of the additional sessions judge for one whole week. When I returned from the UK and was about to start practicing at the AP High Court, Naru Ranga Reddy, a noted criminal lawyer sought after for conducting trials as defence counsel, particularly in murder cases, invited me to stay with him for a week and follow a criminal trial he was conducting in Cuddapah. He had, by then, ceased to be active in politics, having earlier been a legislator and cabinet minister in the erstwhile Madras State. It was indeed a god-sent opportunity for me, and I learned a great deal about the art of cross-examination and the strategy of laying the foundation for an alternate defence theory that could be presented to the trial court, and later in the appeals if need be. Ranga Reddy, an anglophile, was meticulous in his preparation and would thoroughly go through the case diary and other documents made available by the prosecution, such as post-mortem report, site plan of the scene of offense, and I would accompany him when he went to inspect the scene of offense before the trial. His reputation for uprightness was such that the lawyers briefing him would never seek his advice on matters like what a prosecution witness willing to help should be made to say. As I later observed, while dealing with appeals, appellate court lawyers are often prone to think that the trial court lawyer failed to pursue a particular line of cross-examination. Such views only reflect an ignorance of the basic principle—that if there is an answer from the witness even remotely helpful to you to develop further by way of argument, it is best that you be content with it and move on, as any further probing would only make the witness wiser and give him the opportunity to improve upon what he said. This is particularly true in criminal trials where a defence counsel could ruin his case by an unwarranted additional question in cross-examination.

Though there were not many opportunities to use the knowledge gained through my exposure to that one trial, on the few occasions when I had to cross-examine a witness, I, without fail, drew upon it. A few years into my practice, there was this call from Venkataiah, the judge presiding over a criminal court at Secunderabad, seeking to appoint me as state counsel to defend an accused who couldn't afford to have his own lawyer. Apparently, the lawyer from the panel to whom the brief was assigned returned it at the last minute, and the judge did not want to put off the trial. So, Venkataiah, whom I had met briefly earlier in the company of Ranga Reddy, decided to ask me to take up the brief, with the trial to commence on the third day. I certainly did not wish to decline, though it seemed a challenge, being my first appearance as a counsel in a criminal trial. The case was the prosecution of a village youth for rape under Sec. 375, 376 IPC. The alleged victim was an equally young girl of the same village, and they had apparently known one another. Her deposition was parrot-like, giving no scope to shake her by way of cross-examination. Matter got posted to the following day for cross-examination of the doctor who examined the victim. This gave me opportunity to burn the midnight oil to pour over texts on medical jurisprudence and forensic science. Mody's is usually the standard text on the subject, but I also managed to get one authored by Cox from someone's library. The next day the lady doctor who examined the girl was to get into the witness box after lunch, and during lunch recess, someone came and borrowed my copy of Mody for use by her. When she stepped into the box nervously, it could be seen that this young lady doctor, who had joined service as medical officer only a couple of years before, could only reel out what she had seen in Mody's text rather than her own examination report. When it was my turn, I proceeded to quiz her on some aspects that I picked up from the other book, and she started looking blank and after a while tears started rolling from her eyes, embarrassing me, and more so the judge, who tried in vain to put her at ease. Then, in sheer exasperation, the judge looked at me and said in admonishing tones that I had complicated matters beyond the witness's comprehension, adding that this was an unusual experience for him despite having presided over so many trials. The day ended on that note, and the male doctor was noticeably solicitous when we were having tea along with the public prosecutor (PP); I think the PP was Mr Manohar.

Another occasion that I had to attend a trial court in a criminal case was when I was assigned a brief in a referred trial as a panel counsel in the AP High Court. The sensational case, of a young schoolgirl killed by a schoolteacher's husband for gain, was reported widely in the press. The main accused, Ram Reddy, an ex-army retiree, was charged with the murder of the girl, enticed to his house by his teacher wife, for some trinkets of gold she had on her, and for burying her body. He was sentenced to death by the trial court, and the matter came to the high court for confirmation. The printed brief was a mere thirty-forty pages. Though I passionately argued the matter for about a week before a Bench of Justices H. A. Iyer and Venkatesam—neither of whom was known for any exposure to criminal work—Additional PP for the prosecution, Gangadhar Rao, at some stage pulled out a photograph of the victim from the case diary and showed it to the judges, who were appalled beyond words to imagine the life of such an innocent young girl rudely extinguished by the accused, leading to strong protest from me. The accused sent a request from jail to the court, wanting to meet the counsel arguing his matter, and the learned judges politely suggested that I meet him. I complied and visited the convict, who was in solitary confinement, awaiting possible execution. During the course of arguments, I raised an issue warranting further examination of a panch witness, whose evidence was sought to be relied on to prove some recoveries made by the police. There being no direct evidence for prosecution, the case had to rest on the statement of the accused as recorded by police, leading to recoveries of material objects, etc. The Bench, while agreeing to re-examine the said panch witness, wanted me to go to the trial court and complete the process. It was the sessions court presided over by Judge Ramlal Krishan. I went there on the fixed day along with my colleague and friend Vasu, and the accused also had an outing since he had to be present in court. After the brief cross-examination to overcome the lacuna, the panch witness, who was evidently a stooge of the police, stepped out of the witness box and started walking past the box where the accused stood, when, in a dramatic moment, Ram Reddy reached out and hit him with a massive boxer's punch. Naturally, there was commotion in the court, before the escorts overpowered Reddy. The judge—I believe a barrister by qualification—was heard screaming at me, asking me to control my client and make him behave, reflecting scorn at this state panel lawyer being sent by the high court to cross-examine a panch witness, and, more importantly, the lawyer going about his task confidently, perceived as unbecoming of a junior advocate.

Going back to the criminal trial followed in Cuddapah, must say that even that brief experience was immensely helpful in appreciating the evidence in cold print while dealing with criminal appeals in the AP High Court and also few such matters that I handled in the Supreme Court. In fact, with that experience, I was so convinced of its beneficial nature that whenever occasion arose, I would advise new entrants into the profession to attend the trial courts before thinking of starting practice in the appellate courts. Equally important is exposure to drafting of pleadings in civil suits. I had occasion to engage Shankara Sastry, an advocate who had shifted to the High Court after long years of practice in district courts. He took his time, and it was highly educative to see how he weighed each averment while drafting a plaint. He would foresee the possible defence and also the evidence likely to be forthcoming from the defendants.

I found the cross-examination of witnesses fascinating. When I had opportunities in arbitration proceedings involving examination of witnesses, I used to sit and figure out the course to lead the witness to the answer or the admission desired. Three major arbitrations involving examination of witnesses in the last few years of my practice in Delhi are worth recounting. During 1997–98, there was this arbitration of disputes between Krishna Commercial Products (KCP Ltd) and Cement Corporation of India (CCI), involving claims and counterclaims arising out of a contract for setting up a cement plant. The two arbitrators were Justice Natarajan (former judge, Supreme Court) and Justice Rajender Sachar (former chief justice, Delhi High Court). The matter went on interminably for more than hundred sittings. I was the counsel for CCI and Kalyana Sundaram, a senior advocate from Chennai, was representing KCP. Since Narasimha, who continued to be in my office then, couldn't spare time, I started looking for a competent junior. Muralidhar, who is now a highly regarded senior judge in the Delhi High Court, came to mind. Though Murali was considerate in accepting my offer, in a couple of weeks we both realised that it would not work, with Murali having substantial work of his own to handle. Then Narasimha suggested that we contact D. Prakash Reddy, who was associated with Madhava Reddy, who had set up practice as a senior advocate in the Supreme Court after retiring as chief justice, and later as chairman of the Central Administrative Tribunal. Madhav Reddy had passed away sometime earlier, and Prakash agreed to assist me. He used to come and sit for hours with the engineers and officers of CCI to pour over all the technical details for briefing me. In fact, the conference room in my office would be cluttered with volumes of documents relating to the case. After the matter ended, the CCI officers were so very impressed by Prakash's grasp and hard work that when they had an arbitration matter in Hyderabad against Andhra Pradesh Gas Power Corporation Limited (APGPCL), they straightaway went and engaged him, while the opposite party came to me through their counsel Prashanth. I often speak about this to junior members of the bar to highlight how hard work and commitment gets recognised. I was immensely happy about the development. Conversely, I was the counsel for KCP in their arbitration proceedings against another party in a similar case, an arbitration before a retired judge of Punjab High Court.

To recall my experience in examination and cross-examination of witnesses, one arbitration proceeding particularly comes to mind. It arose from claims by M/s Ansals, real estate developers, against the Delhi Development Authority (DDA), from whom they bought the property where Ansal Plaza, in New Delhi, now stands, including the right to build over the already constructed basement. The Ansals had evidently paid a fancy price, as later developments would reveal, and disappointingly for them there were no takers for the shops and commercial premises at a corresponding high price. Besides many smaller technical issues relating to the constructed portion, we raised the issue of DDA not completing the convention centre, five-star hotel and other buildings in the area, as shown in the master plan when the property was put to sale. The case was listed before Justice B. P. Jeevan Reddy. While we were cross-examining the witnesses of DDA who filed affidavits, the legal team of Ansals told me that one of the key witnesses, an officer of DDA, would be a tough nut to crack; that made me take it as a challenge and as cross-examination proceeded, I was quite thrilled to see the witness's discomfiture and obvious lack of candour in his responses. Sunil Murarka, the junior assisting me, later told me that Mr Mukhopadhyaya from the office of Shardul Shroff, representing DDA, had asked him whether I had practiced for long in trial courts. In conclusion, I would urge budding lawyers to get some trial court experience, or at least good exposure to the work there, before thinking of starting practice in a high court or the Supreme Court; it will give them valuable knowledge of how the record dealt with in the appellate court was built.

I think that it is equally beneficial for a junior lawyer practicing in the lower courts to have some exposure to appellate work in higher courts. They shouldn't miss out any opportunity of briefing an arguing counsel in a high court or the Supreme Court and if possible, following the proceedings. Normally the focus of a junior lawyer in the subordinate courts tends to be at micro level, without visualising the bigger picture that may have to be presented in the higher appellate courts at a macro level. That requires an ability to take a broad and comprehensive overview, before developing a plausible hypothesis in support of one's version of the case.

Reverting to the Bar Council election, after the day of polling, friends from various places called to say that the response was positive and far beyond their expectations. Counting could start in the Bar Council office in Hyderabad only after the ballots are received from all the polling centres at different courts in the state. Though the entire counting process took days to complete, as is normally the case, the first count, that is, of the first-preference votes, concluded on day one, and I was declared elected.

Immediately after the counting was over, I made known my intention to seek election to the BCI. The composition of the newly-elected State Bar Council was such that more than half of its members were those who had been re-elected. One such, and a veteran in the State Bar Council, G. Narayan Rao, also made known his keenness to seek election to the BCI. Narayan Rao was the president of the City Civil Court Bar Association, and was in the forefront during the agitation for a separate Telangana state. He later gravitated to full-time politics and, after getting elected to the Legislative Assembly, was also elected as its speaker. Being a senior member of the newly-elected State Council, which had about thirteen re-elected members, Rao was expected to have a positive head start. Being aware of it, I immediately got on to contacting members new and old, and was fortunate to get a positive response from many. Since most were from the districts, they were not known to me and I had to briskly make contact with them to introduce myself and seek their support. There were senior members of the bar from the districts whom I met, like E. Vasudeva Rao, former PP Vizag, P. H. V. Somayajulu (Eluru), Karavadi Venkateshwarulu (Ongole), Veeraswamy Naidu (Chittoor), M. D. Y. Ramamurthy (Kurnool), who not only promised me their support but also stood by their word. Particularly, the first three remained steadfast as my friends and well-wishers all through my tenure in the Bar Council. Besides those from the districts, there were about eight from Hyderabad and Secunderabad amongst the elected members.

Elections for the posts of chairman, vice chairman, and member BCI were to be held at the first meeting presided over by the advocate general who is, under the rules, an ex-officio member of the Council. During the run-up to the meeting and elections, I suggested to common friends that if Rao was willing to be vice chairman of the State Council, leaving the post of member of the BCI, we could avert a contest and election, but Rao apparently was not willing to consider the proposal. K. Raghava Rao was a candidate for chairmanship, and I was supporting the candidature of P. H. V. Somayajulu, a highly respected senior lawyer from Eluru, whom most of my supporters were also ready to support. There was a bit of a drama at the meeting. Raghava Rao was elected chairman, beating Somayajulu by about three votes. K. Raja Reddy was elected vice chairman without contest, having arrived at some arrangement with Rama Rao, who was also aspiring for the said post. Seeing Somayajulu, whom I had proposed and supported, losing, with its demoralising effect on myself and my supporters, Rao understandably was hopeful of a compromise; and so in the short break, Harisesha Reddy, my friend from college days and an elected member, carried word from Rao, suggesting that we share the period by way of compromise. I off-hand rejected the proposal since it didn't make sense to me, though it must be said that it was a common practice for rival candidates to agree to share the period, but hardly anyone who got the first half kept to his word and left the post to the other. So, there was voting, and I was elected to be member of the BCI.

18 Bar Council of India—Path for Fulfilment

If there was a tipping point in my professional career leading to a sense of fulfilment, it was undoubtedly the opportunity provided by that success in getting elected to the Bar Council of India, the highest elected body governing the legal profession and legal education in the country. I felt most gratified and deeply thankful to my colleagues for supporting me, despite it being the first time that I became member of the State Bar Council and, for that matter, forayed into any elected body of the bar. I only hope I could live up to their expectations as their chosen representative in the BCI.

Attending the first meeting of the BCI was an incredible experience. Ram Jethmalani—Ram, as he liked to be addressed by young and old, friends and acquaintances—was the chairman, with B. N. Bajpayee from Calcutta sitting next to him as vice chairman. There were other stalwarts: Rajendra Singh (Madhya Pradesh), Mr Rajaram (Uttar Pradesh), Ranjit Mahanti (Orissa), K. G. Vakhariah (Gujarat). Closer home there were Mr Seshadri (Karnataka), Mr Rangaraj (Tamil Nadu), Mr Pillai (Kerala). I vividly recollect an item on the agenda relating to the proposal for a national law school in Bangalore, and many expressed reservations about the project; when the minutes of the meeting were received, I was shown to have supported the proposal unconditionally. I then addressed a letter to the chairman stating that my support was preceded by the statement that in my State Council's view, the focus should be more on welfare schemes for lawyers, which was not shown in the minutes. At that time my stand was quite clear viz., that after taking into consideration views such as that of my Council, if the decision of the BCI is to establish the school, I would rather see that efforts are made to briskly make it a reality. Ram, as chairman, promptly responded saying that he had no clear memory of what each member had said, and that I should take it up with the vice chairman. I mention this only to highlight that paradoxically, over the years, I turned out to be the most prominent protagonist who relentlessly strived to bring the project to fruition.

With different state councils holding elections at different times, the composition of the BCI keeps changing from time to time, with some members retiring and new ones replacing them. One such significant change in the first or second year of my becoming a member of the BCI was V. C. Mishra (VC) becoming a member in place of Rajaram from UP. It did not take long for an astute senior member, K. G. Vakharia, to gauge its possible impact, particularly on the long-term functioning of the BCI, which hitherto had been harmonious, without any groupism or politics in the decision-making. This was despite the two senior members, Ram and Rajendra Singh (Raj), being polar opposites politically, with Raj being a staunch Congress supporter, and Ram being quite the opposite. In fact, Raj was the leading senior counsel defending Sanjay Gandhi in the 'Kissa Kursi case', and was made a Rajya Sabha member by the Congress. Ram was, on the other hand, a bitter critic of Indira Gandhi. Ranjit also had his own political proclivities and was close to Biju Patnaik, then Chief Minister of Orissa. Such diverse political leanings did not in any manner vitiate the atmosphere in the BCI, and proceedings at the meetings were generally smooth and dignified. VC, by then a leading light in bar politics in Allahabad, had his own no-holds-barred style. Vakharia, who was himself into politics in Ahmedabad, though not actively, could recognise this special trait of VC, and foresee its impact on the BCI. Vakharia's commitment to serve the cause of the fraternity is what led him to command the respect of his colleagues. He was the managing trustee of the BCI Trust—created as a measure of tax planning—which had become the repository of many powers of the Council, and organised most of its educational activities like publications, seminars, and workshops. Vakharia, whose term as member BCI was expiring in the initial period of my term, had decided not to seek re-election to his State Council. Keen to ensure smooth functioning of the Trust even after his exit, he resigned as trustee and managing trustee, and, in the subsequent vacancy, ensured that I got elected. Thus, I came to be elected as one of the five trustees in the very first year of my Council membership, and the other trustees were kind enough to elect me as the managing trustee.

The BCI Trust, constituted in 1974, was essentially a legal and research foundation which, pursuant to its objectives, had initiated programmes for promoting legal education, developing law libraries, welfare schemes for members of the profession, and placement of junior advocates. Prof. N. R. Madhava Menon (MM) from Delhi University was the secretary of the Trust, and credit should go to him for the various publications, including the *Journal of the Bar Council of India*, and initiatives in organising seminars and workshops under the 'continuing legal education' or CLE programme. The most important achievement of the Trust was establishing the National Law School of India (NLS), conceived by the BCI's legal education committee and approved by the Council in Bangalore. Without dilating much upon various activities of the Trust, I shall touch upon the ones close to my heart.

The foremost are the schemes for placement of junior advocates, and providing assistance to law libraries of bar associations. The first one was the outcome of my out-of-the-box thinking, readily approved by my colleagues on the Trust. With the advent of many private law colleges, particularly in semi-urban areas, the strength of the junior members of the bar had increased manifold, with most being the first lawyers in their families. If any of them desired to set up practice in high court or the Supreme Court, it would be extremely difficult for them to find an opening in a senior's office for the requisite experience and mentoring. So, being conscious of the above, I took the initiative to formulate a scheme funded and operated by the Trust. Under this a junior lawyer could apply, seeking placement in a senior's office of the higher court desired, provided he satisfied the requirement of not having a senior member of his family in the profession. After the applications were scrutinised on the touchstone of need and potential to cope with the demands of the practice in higher courts, the eligible candidates were invited for interviews, held in different centres. The selected candidates would be placed in the offices of seniors practicing in the court of their choice. No senior whom we approached in this regard had declined to take on the responsibility. The Trust would pay a monthly stipend to the junior under placement for a year. The idea was that given such an opportunity, if the candidate showed promise, the senior concerned or some other senior would take him as a regular junior.

I can vividly recall traveling to different centres to conduct interviews along with a few of my colleagues. I can say with immense satisfaction that most of those chosen by us under the scheme have done extremely well, and it used to be gratifying to see a couple of them active in the Supreme Court; one such might hopefully be designated a senior advocate by the Supreme Court shortly. The other, similarly selected and placed in the office of Fali S. Nariman, continues with him even now. The scheme for developing law libraries in bar associations of mufassil courts was also very popular, with many from different parts of the country seeking assistance.

The most significant task, the profound impact of which is noticeable even today in the field of legal education, was the setting up of NLS in Bangalore. At about that time there was this decision of the legal education committee to dispense with the three-year course in law and instead have a five-year integrated course from plus-two level. The backdrop against which these decisions were taken, and the impediments faced in implementing the same, were dealt with by me in my 'Goa article' (see Appendix 4). It may be useful to extract the same here for ease of reference.

> In this scenario of a dismal state of legal education, it must be said to the credit of the Bar Council of India that it took the necessary initiative as a body charged with the responsibility of laying down and ensuring compliance with standards of legal education under the statute. The Legal Education Committee of the Bar Council, headed by Justice Hidayatullah, after wide-ranging consultations with the universities, the UGC and other concerned, came out with a proposal of restructuring legal education, by introducing a five-year course from the 10+2 stage. More or less simultaneously, the Bar Council of India decided to establish an autonomous institution dedicated solely to law, namely the 'National Law School of India'. This unique national-level institution was intended to act as a 'pace setter and a testing ground for bold experiments in legal education.' The simultaneous ushering in of these two schemes had led one to believe that one depended on the other. Despite wide-ranging consultations over a long period of time by the Legal Education Committee, presided over by Justice Hidayatullah, who was not only gracious enough but enthusiastic to continue his association

with the committee even after assuming the august office of the Vice President of India, the decision regarding a five-year course evoked strong opposition. Many of us have fond memories of the hospitality of the Vice President's house and the dignity and stature enjoyed by the committee which had as its members stalwarts like Ram Jethmalani, Rajendra Singh, Ranjit Mohanty from the legal profession, besides those from the academic world, prominent of whom being Prof. Upendra Baxi. It is a different matter that the decision to switch over to a five-year course with a cut-off date could not be implemented owing to vociferous objections, particularly from the lobby of the private law colleges and a section of law teachers. There was also a genuinely felt apprehension regarding the desirability of making a student decide upon law as a course of study soon after completing 10+2. There was yet another misgiving that such a switch over to a five-year full-term course would disable those who wish to pursue law as a part-time course with a view to improve their prospects in the employment held by them or to facilitate meeting of expenses from the earnings from such employment. So intense and acrimonious was the debate that some started characterising the five-year degree programme as anti-poor.

The problems with regard to the National Law School were far more formidable. The Bar Council of India, with its changing composition, did not continue to subscribe to the idea with conviction and commitment. Many State Bar Councils had serious reservations. Amongst the members of the Bar Council of India the vocal proponents were very few, with the others either strongly opposing the project or being indifferent to the proposal. In such a scenario it is not perhaps surprising that a newly elected member of the Bar Council of India, when approached for support for my candidature of chairmanship of the council, said with candour and aplomb that I can expect his support only if I was prepared to join the opposition to the five-year course and the National Law School, since such was the commitment made by him to his colleagues in his State Bar Council when he was elected as member of the Bar Council of India. Needless to say that I neither could secure his support nor succeed in the election on that occasion.

> To compound the problems was this reluctance of the UGC to confer deemed university status upon the institution. This could be eventually overcome by the unique piece of legislation of the Legislature of Karnataka, viz., 'The National Law School of India Act, 1986 (Karnataka Act 22 of 1986)' by which the National Law School of India University came to be formally established on 29 August 1987. At its infancy, the institution had to face multi-fold problems without any infrastructure and financial resources. The apathy and indifference with which our approaches for financial support were met with are still etched in my memory. Thanks to the innovative methods that Dr Madhava Menon, the first Director of the School, and his team of committed academics could evolve, the school was able to overcome the severe financial crunch felt in the initial years. It is a different matter that once the institution gained recognition, one had to become selective in accepting offers of support.

Though it was assumed that the integrated five-year course was conceived by the BCI's legal education committee, I noticed from a boxed item in the *Deccan Chronicle* that Justice Gajendra Ghadkar, the then CJI, had suggested introduction of such a course while addressing a conference. That, of course, does not detract from the intense debate and discussion by the experts in the legal education committee, which ultimately resulted in the BCI approving of the five-year course, and deciding to discontinue the three-year course on a time-bound basis. It is a different matter that the three-year course continues to be in vogue and a substantial number of new entrants happen to secure enrolment with such qualification.

I clearly recall the apathy with which our initial requests for funds were met. I made a visit to Bombay as suggested by Ram Jethmalani, who secured an appointment with Nani Palkiwala, a legend and doyen of the Indian Bar. We were warmly received by him, and when we explained the NLS project and sought assistance from the major trusts he was associated with, Palkiwala didn't sound optimistic, expressing his doubt if those trusts would be inclined to fund a law university. I had pleaded with colleagues in BCI to see if any assistance from their state governments would be forthcoming, to no avail. About that time N. T. Rama Rao had become the Chief Minister of Andhra Pradesh, and Jethmalani had close relations with him as a lawyer and as a political activist. There was this call from Ram one evening, saying that he had landed in Hyderabad since the CM had given an appointment to see him early next morning at 5.00 a.m. The idea was for the two of us to call on the CM and request for funds for NLS, though I told Ram it would be a futile effort, knowing how frugal the CM was in parting with state finances. However, since Ram was enthusiastic, I religiously picked him up and we went to the CM's residence. We were no doubt very warmly received and, when the purpose of our visit was made known, the CM's instant response was that he had advised institutions in his state to mobilise resources and be self-reliant. There was this delectable breakfast spread of *upma* with ghee floating, besides other goodies, and after a bit of political tête-à-tête between Ram and NTR, we departed. Later when N. Janardhan Reddy became the CM and I was the Advocate General of Andhra Pradesh, I prevailed upon him to make the government contribute some amount, which incidentally made AP the only other state government apart from Karnataka that provided some financial assistance to NLS.

More disappointing was my trip to Calcutta, when the then CJI, Justice Sabyasachi Mukherjee was visiting the city. It was a hurried trip for a meeting with prominent members of the legal fraternity availing the CJI's presence there; however, no offer of assistance was forthcoming from the heads of prominent law firms present there besides others. Interestingly, funds started flowing in from these very sources for instituting medals and awards when the NLS finally got going, to the extent that we had to consider discouraging the trend. I had initiated a scheme to admit members of the bar as members of NLSI Society on paying Rs 5,000, with the object of generating funds, besides creating a sense of participation amongst sections of the profession.

The NLSI Society was formed and registered, with me as president, to satisfy the requirement of the University Grant Commission (UGC) that NLS be a truly autonomous entity before it could be considered for deemed university status. The creation of the Society was also a move to distance NLS as an entity from BCI, though members of the BCI were ipso facto members of the Society and its managing committee. The Society formulated rules for the functioning of the school; however, despite thus crossing the initial hurdle, recognition as deemed university was not forthcoming. Our understanding was that NLS, as an institution for the teaching and research of the single discipline of law, was, in a sense, unique. The UGC secretary and some others found this difficult to accept. I can recall meeting successive UGC chairpersons—including Dr Manmohan Singh, Prof. Yashpal, and Dr Madhuri R. Shah—along with Prof. Madhava Menon, to explain our position, without success. After all our efforts, the UGC came out with this suggestion that NLS should start functioning as an affiliate of the Bangalore University, so that the Commission could evaluate it and take a decision after some time. But then we all thought that it would be self-defeating, since the whole purpose was to have the autonomy to formulate courses and curriculum departing from the beaten track. Thus, despite our best efforts, this knotty issue remained unresolved, and the delay provided greater fillip to the antagonists of the five-year course who erroneously perceived NLS as part of the endeavour to implement the course.

Its most vocal opponent was this large group of part-time lecturers teaching the three-year course in part-time law colleges. Many such colleges that had mushroomed were apparently functioning from premises which could be used for those few hours in the evenings. There were many members of the local bar engaged as part-time lecturers, drawing salaries at the UGC scale of pay, and others who organised these part-time colleges for the three-year course. Their strong lobby could prevail upon the then union law minister S. N. Kakkar to have the Advocates Act amended to ensure that those teaching for three hours or less are not legally disabled from the right to practice law. This, in a way, assumed the hue of a semi-political movement in states such as Uttar Pradesh, characterising the new course as 'anti-poor'.

I can recall this conference of 'Bar Councillors' convened in Pune by Kholse Patil, an activist lawyer-cum-politician and former parliamentarian. He had the then CJI, Justice Y. V. Chandrachud, deliver the inaugural address and Justice P. N. Bhagawathi preside over the valedictory session. Since Bar Councils, including BCI, as such were not involved in organising the conference, I took the view that the BCI should stay away from it. But then Jethmalani, as BCI chairman, had different views on the matter and insisted that

Prof. Menon and I, as secretary and managing trustee of the Trust respectively, should attend and put forth our point of view. So we both rushed to Bombay by the evening flight and reached Pune by road, late on the night before the conference. First thing the next morning, before the inaugural address of the conference, I called on the CJI, who wanted to know why law colleges were not permitted beyond a specified distance from the seat of a district court. Though I clarified that this was not in any way related to the introduction of the five-year course, and also the rationale for that distance rule, I left with the feeling that the organisers had not briefed the CJI on the core issues relating to the new course. Well, there was acrimony just short of getting physical when we tried to put forth our point of view.

Reverting to the school project and the continuing impasse relating to clearance from the UGC, must say that the solution came like a flash, with Jethmalani suggesting that we give up pursuing the matter with the UGC—which was persistently stonewalling our proposal—and instead approach the Government of Karnataka for creating the university through a state legislation. Ramakrishna Hegde was then the CM of Karnataka, and the rapport Jethmalani had with him helped in the Government of Karnataka agreeing to this process, not so common back then. To help prepare the bill to be introduced in the legislature, I used to meet up with Mr Chamayya, the law secretary then and one of the finest officers I have known. A gentleman with no trace of ego, he helped our cause with a sense of commitment. Thankfully, the then law minister A. Lakshmisagar, an unusually unassuming gentleman whom I refer to as a true Gandhian, was also equally committed and helpful. When Chamayya and I agreed upon the basic provisions to be incorporated, we had a final meeting with Prof. Baxi, the director designate of NLS in Delhi. Since I was visiting Delhi in connection with a matter of GVK (G. V. Krishna Reddy, chairman, GVK Group) in the Supreme Court, I requested Chamayya and Prof. Baxi to spare time for a meeting. We met in the hotel where I was staying and the draft bill, which eventually was introduced and came to be passed, was finalised. Here I must acknowledge with deep appreciation the exemplary attitude of the Government of Karnataka, which did not seek any quid pro quo and, much less, control over the administration of the entity being brought into existence through their statute. In fact, it was at my instance that a provision was made for the state secretaries of law and finance to be ex-officio members of the executive committee of the proposed university. The autonomy of the institution in all aspects of its functioning was scrupulously protected under the statute, which has become a model for many other state legislations creating such universities.

With this significant development, NLS became National Law School of India University (NLSIU), and a legal entity. Our focus then naturally shifted to making it a tangible reality. The Government of Karnataka had promised us twenty-four acres of land, besides a one-time financial grant. To set the whole process in motion, as a first step, at my insistence, the BCI Trust decided to transfer Rs 25 lakhs from its resources to NLSIU. The financial position of the BCI being quite desperate, if any amount was to be spared, it had to be from the Trust funds. Then there was this issue of land to be transferred to NLS. The Government of Karnataka decided to make land available at Nagarbhavi, which was within the area of the Bangalore University campus, close to its boundary. But then the vice chancellor of Bangalore University couldn't comply, with the syndicate strongly opposing any such move. Prof. Couthinoe, who was then holding a key position in the university and was enthusiastic to help the NLS project, tried his best but without avail. The syndicate, with some elected members, was quite adamant, and my enquiries revealed that they had some issues with the vice chancellor. When the vice chancellor wanted to go by the suggestion of the government, the vocal section of the syndicate opposed him and successfully scuttled the move. I then started lobbying with antagonists in the syndicate, particularly Munivenkat Reddy, a lawyer, and Dr Krishna Reddy, who seemed to be leading the opposition group, and through them the others. The strategy worked, and the university decided to lease out land to us. By then the contiguous land available at the site on one side of the road was only 18 acres. Since that was the area available as one plot, without wasting any time we had the lease deed executed, with myself figuring as the signatory representing NLS. There was verbal assurance given that towards the balance area of 24 acres of the promised land, on the other side of the road, six acres will be given to us. It is a different matter that that piece of land was taken over by an institute for nuclear sciences.

Since the area delivered to us was enough for the basic infrastructure, we decided to go ahead with preparation of plans for the buildings. On the advice of local friends, we pitched upon M/s Karekar Sundaram, architects with experience in designing educational institutions, and engaged them. Their knowledge and experience was a great help since we had no in-house experts to guide us. The architects were quite open to inputs and suggestions from us. I can vividly recall my visit to the women's college of SV University at Tirupati along with a colleague to inspect the facilities, for permitting them to start a women's law college. The vice chancellor, Dr Rajyalakshmi, I think, took us around the university. I was quite impressed by the planning of the hostel rooms for three occupants, with internal division providing each occupant some privacy. I explained this to our architects, who readily agreed to incorporate the suggested design. We engaged Ramakrishna, a builder, who came to be passionately involved in developing infrastructure for the NLS.

While on the one hand earnest efforts were being made for finalising plans and commencing construction, considering the time constraints and the limited resources, we decided to explore the possibility of getting the school started by securing suitable temporary accommodation. The anxiety really was to avert the law of diminishing intent coming into play, particularly with some of my colleagues in the BCI and the Trust being less than enthusiastic about the project. Whatever may have been their reservations, we could successfully overcome them, and here, I must acknowledge with deep appreciation and gratitude the enthusiastic support we had for the project from the Bar Council of Karnataka, its successive members and the legal fraternity of Karnataka. We began scouting for suitable temporary accommodation for starting the NLS. Ranjit Mohanty, who had taken over as chairman of BCI, got a call from Pramila, an activist lawyer and politician in Bangalore who was perhaps also a member of the State Bar Council, saying that she had located a premises lying vacant, possession of which could be secured. She wanted Ranjit or I to immediately visit Bangalore for further steps. Though I was sceptical, as I had no details of the location or a description of the premises, Ranjit made me go to Bangalore post-haste, and there Pramila took me to the Gandhi Memorial, a large meeting place and prayer hall with a dome-like roof, and assured me that she could secure possession of the premises for our use. While appreciating her zeal to help, I had to politely decline the offer, saying it was unsuited for our purpose.

From the state government, Veerappa Moily, then the minister for education, whom I had appraised of our efforts, called me over phone and wanted me to go to Bangalore, saying that he had a suitable place in mind. I rushed to Bangalore, and was shown the Bangalore University union building, which was in disuse for some time. But then it was wholly inadequate and unsuitable. I was deeply grateful to Mr Moily for the interest shown by him. This incident seems to have been etched in his memory; for years later, while delivering a convocation address at NALSAR University of Law in Hyderabad as then minister for law and justice in the Central cabinet, he referred to how he tried to help NLS as a minister in the state cabinet whenever "Mr V. R. Reddy approached him". Coincidentally, Prof. Hajappa, also associated with the NLS in its initial years, was sitting next to me when Moily recalled his help for the NLS project. Yes, there was indeed a lot of goodwill and help forthcoming from this astute and respected political leader.

After the initial futility of our efforts, a suggestion came from one of the university sources that the geology block in the City College of Bangalore University, located in front of the city civil court, was not being used and that it might serve our purpose. The premises comprised one galleried lecture hall and a row of small rooms a little away from the main college building. We were quite satisfied that it would serve our purpose and more importantly, since that block was not in use, the prospect of securing it seemed bright. When approached, Bangalore University was quite cooperative and requested Dr Ramesan, principal of the City College, to make the block available to NLS for starting its teaching programme and operate from there till buildings come up at its own campus. So far so good. But then Dr Ramesan was not one to comply easily, his firm view being that the university cannot meddle with the infrastructure of the college. The resultant impasse went on for some time. I figured that the principal, being no pushover, had to be satisfied of our genuine need for accommodation, and how the school, when it came up, would help enhance Bangalore's recognition as an educational hub. My enquiries revealed that Mr Joshi, an advocate, had some acquaintance with

Dr Ramesan, and managing to secure an appointment through him, Joshi and I visited the principal at his residence one evening. Despite his reputation of being a tough nut, we were warmly received, and on being convinced that occupying a small block away from the main building temporarily with our limited strength of students will in no way hinder or disturb the functioning of his college, he agreed to let us have it. The next meeting of the BCI Trust was convened in Bangalore, to give members an opportunity to see and satisfy themselves of the feasibility of getting the premises ready for use to commence functioning of the school.

Meanwhile, I had Mr Karekar the architect give me details and an estimate of costs for refurbishing the lecture hall, closing the roadside doors and windows to insulate it from the noise of vehicular traffic at the Mysore Bank junction. Approving the proposal and agreeing to release the funds would have been the first financial commitment for the school project. I was therefore quite anxious to ensure that there was no difficulty in ensuring majority support. I recall visiting Rajendra Singh, a senior member and Trustee of the BCI, at Hotel Ashoka the previous evening soon after he reached Bangalore, and explaining to him the significance of the decision to get moving with the project. I remember how he cut me short from a long explanation by saying there should be no problem in releasing funds for refurbishing the premises.

We had a formal inauguration of the NLSIU at the hands of Justice Hidayatullah, then vice president of India. Dignitaries present on the occasion included former CJI Justice Y. V. Chandrachud, Karnataka governor Ashoknath N. Banerji, Chief Minister Ramakrishna Hegde, besides Prof. Baxi and senior members of BCI, Ram Jethmalani, Rajender Singh and Ranjit Mohanty. The function was held on the City College grounds next to our temporary premises. This was followed by the laying of the foundation for the administrative block of NLSIU on the land leased to it at Nagarbhavi by Justice Y. V. Chandrachud. It was a simple function where the chief guest and Mrs Chandrachud were received with the traditional *poornakumbham*, to a *nadaswaram* playing in the background. I counted on Bhujanga Rao, a respected senior lawyer in Bangalore, and his associates to ensure requisite arrangements conforming to the customary regional practices on such auspicious occasions.

Having thus crossed the first milestone for the school to commence operations, we started the process for recruiting teaching staff. There was a good response to our invitation to apply. Prof. Menon, Prof. Hajappa and I constituted the selection committee. Amongst the applicants who came for the interview, Joga Rao I had met earlier as the founder-principal of a private law college in Visakhapatnam, which I had gone to inspect from BCI. I recall asking him if he was sure of settling in the post on offer at NLS, having been principal of a college. The names that readily come to mind of the selected candidates are Mallar, Vijay Kumar, Joga Rao, Muralidharan and Mrs Verghese. I think Babu Mathew and Pillai were not part of that group but came in later. It is indeed most heartening that practically all the appointees proved to be accomplished academics over the years.

During all these stages, Prof. Baxi was the director designate and Prof. Menon was the de facto director. About that time, Prof. Baxi expressed his disinclination to take over the reins, which came as a surprise to us. We learnt about Prof. Baxi's reservations regarding the viability of the school as a full-fledged university. He had a point when he said that he had full faith in the ability of the BCI's then core group in ensuring smooth functioning and mobilising required resources, but, being an elected body, the commitment of its members in the future would be a matter of conjecture. About that time, he also had this offer of appointment as vice chancellor of South Gujarat University at Surat; and in any case Ranjit and I couldn't possibly allay his fears about the distant future. This naturally led to Prof. Menon taking over as director de jure, and the transition was seamless.

The immediate requirement then was to find a suitable person locally for appointment as registrar. I discussed this with Vishwanath Shetty, a colleague in BCI close to me and whose views I valued highly. Shetty, a busy practitioner in Bangalore, was the standing counsel for the agricultural university there and he knew of the availability of Krishnappa, who had superannuated after long service as registrar of that university. Shetty suggested his name and vouched for his efficiency. We then lost no time in inviting Krishnappa to assume office as registrar, and thankfully, he accepted our offer. This was undoubtedly a stroke of luck, since he in all respects suited the requirement for creating systems for administration of a university at its inception.

Krishnappa in turn suggested for appointment as manager finance Ayyanna, who had worked with him in the agricultural university and superannuated. This duo, Krishnappa and Ayyanna, with long years of experience behind them, proved to be a great asset to NLS in its formative years. Ayyanna's trainee Ashwath Reddy succeeded him as manager finance and proved a worthy successor. For that matter the entire NLS staff, teaching and non-teaching, functioned with commitment and cohesion. Though I do not mention them all here by name, I have a vivid recollection of their services to the institution, whether it is the timely refreshments we received during our meetings at the hands of Veerappa, or the efficiency of Ms Savithri (Bhatt got added later), the director's secretary, in helping me with information regarding the chronology of events.

When NLS was all set to start functioning, including teaching, from the City College premises, the immediate problem to be addressed was one of providing hostel accommodation for students coming from different parts of the country. There was no dearth of demand for admissions, and it was gratifying that a plus-two topper from Bangalore in his press interview said that his first preference was the NLS, even though the school was only at the drawing-board stage then. Buoyed by such inspiring response, our resolve to complete the project at the soonest grew even stronger, but then the school being essentially one conceived as a residential facility, organising a hostel became an immediate and imperative task. While I was mulling over it, my friend Shetty floated the idea of approaching Bhant Sangha, a welfare organisation of his community, for lease of a building newly constructed by them for running a women's hostel, which had for some reason not started. We had a look at it and found it suitable for our immediate requirement, and Shetty took me to Sadashiva Shetty, chairman of Vijaya Bank, who was then the president of the Sangha. With the kind of interest Shetty evinced, the chairman couldn't say no. The facility was ideal for us, with the warden's bungalow there used as accommodation for girls and the main hostel building for the boys. Prof. Balachandran and his wife agreed to take charge as wardens. For some of us like Ranjit, Shetty, myself and some of the bar councillors and senior lawyers of Karnataka, it was more like organising something important for the benefit of families at a personal level. I clearly recall how NLS came to own the Bangalore Development Authority (BDA) houses in Bangalore. One day when I was driving past the BDA office, I noticed a big crowd there and my enquiry revealed that they were all making applications for allotment of houses built by BDA. I lost no time in applying for some, which resulted in NLS being allotted one high income group (HIG) house and a couple of middle income group (MIG) houses.

Every time I planned a trip to Bangalore, I would call Tippanna, senior lawyer and chairman, Karnataka Bar Council, and he would without fail make himself available in Bangalore, despite his pressing schedule in Bellary as a busy practitioner in courts and part-time politician. Interestingly, Seshadri and Rajasekhar, who were polar opposites as leaders in the Tumkuru Bar Association, would present themselves in Bangalore even when they were not directly associated with the Bar Councils. B. V. Acharya, who later became Advocate General of Karnataka, is another I would trouble to use his good offices, along with the then Advocate General, Keshava Iyengar, in helping us make the wheels of government move. Nayak at Sankey Road would keep us company when needed as a stress buster. There were many others and the list is long. I acknowledge with gratitude their contribution to the cause of the fraternity in establishing NLSIU.

Of the innovative methods evolved by the first NLS director, Prof. Menon, and his colleagues, the tie-up with Ford Foundation was significant. Back then, for Left-of-centre intellectuals, any aid from the USA was anathema, starting from the time of PL480 assistance. Mercifully, unmindful of that, the school sought, and was happy to accept, research projects and assignments towards which the foundation used to provide funding. Sudarshan, who headed the Ford Foundation in India then, was a very enthusiastic supporter of the NLS, and so was his successor Maya Daruwala.

That said, it might be apt to recount what I had to say during my address at the BAI conference on '40 Years of The Advocates Act, 1961', about the issues and measures to focus attention on, to have the sustained benefit of this magnificent effort and its fruition in the form of the NLSIU.

> It is all well that we have today, besides NLSIU, four other similar institutions, and the general mood is also such that

the five-year law, programmed to the total exclusion of the three-year course, had found acceptability. Though this development augurs well, the magnitude of the problem being what it is, the effect of it can be felt only in a very small measure and that too after a very long period. There are over 400 recognised law colleges in the country. Ensuring that each one of these institutions imparts quality legal education is going to be a stupendous task. Merely providing an agenda or a road map prepared by the NLSIU and other law universities would not suffice. The major problem of acute shortage of competent law teachers has to be addressed immediately. The NLSIU has launched a new scheme in this direction, which is needed to be strengthened and the other law universities also should undertake such a task. Law teaching must be made attractive in terms of remuneration and prestige and avenues for mobility for the academics, be it into legal practice, judicial and governmental assignments on a tenure basis should be seriously explored. Each one of the law universities should take steps for developing requisite infrastructure for adopting the law colleges of the other universities on a limited basis for a specified period and thereby upgrade the standards of academic culture of such colleges. There should be a coordinated synergy in the approach and promotional activity of the law universities in the matter of facilitating upgradation of teaching standards of the various law colleges affiliated to the other universities. For achieving these objectives by coordinated effort the law universities, i.e., the universities dedicated solely to the study and research of law, should have a coordinating body. Adequate resources should be made available to such a body by the Government of India and to the extent possible by the state governments.

In the backdrop of the often-heard cliché that institutions are not made of mere brick and mortar, the faculty of NLSIU—which constitutes the core of the institution for academic excellence—acknowledging the contribution of the 'brick layers' (see the letter below) truly reflects their generosity. Must say, getting to know about it much after the event filled my heart with a sense of fulfilment, and I shall cherish the same with humility.

NATIONAL LAW SCHOOL OF INDIA UNIVERSITY
Nagarbhavi, Post Bag No. 7201
Bangalore -560072

Babu Mathew
Registrar

September 7, 1998

The Chairman,
Bar Council of India
21, Rouse Avenue
Institutional Area,
New Delhi- 110 002

Sir,

The following resolution was unanimously adopted by the Faculty of our University, at its meeting held on 28th August, 1998, with a request that the same be forwarded to the Chairman of the Bar Council of India.

> "The Faculty, at its meeting held on 28th August, 1998, unanimously resolved to request the Bar Council of India to nominate Mr. V. R. Reddy, Former Addl. Solicitor General of India and Senior Advocate to the Executive Council, duly approved by the Chief Justice of India as one of the two nominees of the Bar Council of India. This was in view of the abiding interest of Mr. V. R. Reddy in the development of the National Law School since its genesis and its inception."

We request you kindly to consider the Resolution passed by the Faculty in respect of the nomination of Mr V. R. Reddy to the Executive Council.

Thanking you,

Yours faithfully
Sd/-
REGISTRAR

Readers of this memoir might be perplexed to see the number of pages devoted to NLS (now NLSIU) dealing with its establishment and formative years. Those familiar with the field of law might be aware of the transformational changes in the legal education landscape in the country in the recent past, for which the advent of NLS as a model institution has been, in good measure, instrumental. I consider the opportunity to play a prominent role in the establishment of this prestigious institution a blessing. The success of this institution in terms of its accomplishments may be gauged by the number of Rhodes Scholars, winning teams of international moot court competitions, JESSUPS etc. it produced. The icing on the cake is that the incumbent Vice Chancellor Prof. Sudhir Krishnaswamy is a product of the school, who rose to heights of eminence in the academic world. Special mention must be made in this context of the academics who joined the institution at its inception, leaving their secure assignments and prospects elsewhere, and it is a delight to see many of them making NLS their intellectual home for life while some have left to play prominent roles in developing other institutions. I consider it appropriate to acknowledge with a sense of gratitude all those who helped this iconic institution grow. I mention here by name only those who readily come to mind, while there may be many others who extended their unstinted support in diverse ways, but whose names I have missed out.

The primary object of the NLS is to produce conscientious and competent law graduates of global standards for the legal profession, and its tangible contribution in this respect is widely recognised. The products of this school, and those of similar institutions that followed its basic model, are now considered role models for competence and professionalism globally, and more particularly in our country. Unfortunately, they constitute only a small percentage of all the entrants to the profession, with most others obtaining professional qualification from other university colleges and private institutions. It is time for the organised profession to focus on their development and welfare for all-round enhanced standards of the legal profession in the country, which is on the cusp of reaching heights of recognition for quality and standards.

Generally speaking, the majority of law graduates in India come from non-lawyer families with rural backgrounds, and may have secured poor grades at school and college. They lack training in research methodology, not having been provided any during their course of study in law. The life story of someone, on whom the cap in many respects might fit well, distinguishing himself in his professional career should hopefully be an inspiration and morale booster to them. In my capacity as one among them, I wish to share some thoughts.

Please bear in mind that everyone cannot be a gold-medallist or a high-ranking academic performer, nor are all the rest doomed to be failures in their career. Practical advice: try to hone your analytical skills and use your intellect to its fullest potential in understanding and analysing the issue at hand. As example, I recall here my very first appearance in the High Court. It was a state brief, case assigned to represent and defend an accused who had no lawyer to represent him. Justice Pingle Jaganmohan Reddy, in whose court I was watching the proceedings, asked me if I would like to appear for the accused, and I readily agreed. Justice P. J. Reddy, who on the Bench personified dignity and poise befitting the office, later rose to be the Chief Justice of the High Court and a distinguished Judge of the Supreme Court of India. To watch the proceedings in his court used to be a great learning experience, particularly for the junior members of the bar. His memoirs, *The Judiciary I Served*, is a must read for all interested in knowing the hoary past of the High Court in Hyderabad. It was a criminal appeal against conviction of a postman for forgery and misappropriation; the charge was that he forged a housewife's signature and misappropriated the money order amount meant for her. I spent the previous night trying to figure out a plausible argument. I visualised the scene, using the common sense of a postman coming to the house, and being met by a male family member. The postman might, in all probability, hand over the money order to him and, when he returns with the purported signature of the addressee housewife, the postman hands over the money to him as well. Using some vague suggestions made by the counsel in the trial court, I tried to picturise the scene in a rural setting, and made out a strong plausible defence. The result is immaterial; it is the satisfaction of having done one's best that is most important.

Articulation in the language of the court, presently English, might pose a problem in most cases. Clarity of expression is not a trait dependent merely on language skills. If you develop such clarity in expressing yourself in the language you are familiar with, switching over to the court language over a period of time may not pose a serious problem. I have known successful professionals who would use formal court language even during informal conversation, and that is because their use of English started with their appearances in court. Try not to depend on translation for long, and start thinking in the court language as far as possible. Ultimately, it is your self-esteem and determination to overcome obstacles that matters. Avoid overburdening yourself in trying to match others' capabilities. Always bear in mind that someone else being more competent than you is an inescapable reality for all.

When it comes to the choice of venue for beginning practice, new entrants are prone to consider it fashionable to commence practice in the High Court or the Supreme Court. I would strongly recommend that they should gain some experience in trial courts before thinking of moving to the higher courts. I have earlier dealt with the importance attached to the singular learning experience in trial courts—something I have always strongly believed in. Once, while I was sitting in a hospital waiting lounge, the hospital PR personnel brought this young man, his lawyer, to me. When introduced to me, the lawyer said, "Sir, I had met you years ago when you were practicing in the High Court, wanting to join your office; but you had then advised me to continue my practice in the trial court for some more time, and that is what I am doing." There was evidently a hint of disappointment in what he said. But then, he is in no way a loser, since the option of shifting practice to the higher appellate courts is always open to him, and if he chooses to do so, he will have the additional benefit of trial court work experience which will always stand him in good stead.

Whichever be the court and whatever be the nature of your work, do not make winning a case regardless of the means your primary object. Cutting corners might seem helpful in the short run, but once you cross the line, to quote from John Grisham's *The Rainmaker*, you become a shark in dirty waters. The rationale being, if you muddy the waters, even as a shark you will gain no satisfaction. As we all know, litigation in courts is a contentious business. In our system it is the client who is basically the winner or loser. The counsel is not to involve himself to the extent of casting aspersions on the opponent counsel or the presiding judge. If young lawyers fall prey to the temptation of concocting unjustified excuses whenever a favourable outcome eludes, they will irreparably damage the image of the institution. Do not forget, it is your own self-respect, and the image of the institution of which you are a part, which is at stake, and that compromising either means denying yourself respect and recognition in society.

Going on to the next stage, of dealing with clients, there are certain rules of conduct and norms prescribed by the BCI, but those are not what I propose to deal with here; only some of the ethical norms that are considered relevant and important in the profession. In the early years of practice, a client comes to you on the advice of someone who has known you personally or by reputation. Your foremost duty is to present the truthful and complete picture from your understanding of the case and all its aspects, *prima facie*, favourable or otherwise. This is what is called 'information sharing', which has its relevance and importance even in the medical profession. Try to curb the tendency to present an exaggerated prospect of a possible favourable outcome, with a view to retain the client or to enthuse him to pay the quoted fee, which in most cases clients are prone to find higher than anticipated. I had a friend whose highly exaggerated display of commitment to fight the 'injustice' done to his client used to be quite amusing. After looking into the case documents and listening to his client's tale of woe, he would display his unmitigated anger at the antagonist who had caused such injustice to the client. If a case of cancellation of *patta* for the client's land by some small-time revenue official, he would say, "Who does he think he is? Is it his grandfather's property?" and conclude by saying, "Come and see me in the evening, with the fees, and we will teach him a lesson". The overjoyed client couldn't wait to see him and, as I would add to lend some humour, the case is filed as urgent motion; when it comes up for hearing, the argument is advanced in soft tones from close to the Bench and the judge passes an order, received with a gesture of gratitude by the lawyer. As the lawyer walks out, the client runs out from the visitors' gallery and catches up with him; the lawyer nonchalantly tells him "Okay! Now that fellow who did all this to you has to hear what we have to say."

That in fact is a truthful account of the order made by the judge who, while dismissing the petition, gave the petitioner the liberty to make a fresh representation. The client goes to the station and catches the first train back home, now that 'the work is done', and, the next morning, in a chastened mood, tries to figure out what to report to his wife and family about the outcome of the case, for which he has already spent all the amount he borrowed. Did he win or did he lose?

KYC, the acronym for 'Know Your Client' popular in current usage, might be a good practice to follow for tendering suitable advice regarding advisability for initiating or pursuing litigation. To illustrate again from my experience, there was this High Court judge who was castigated by the High Court while dealing with an appeal against his order for what was perceived as misconduct. He carried the matter to the Supreme Court, without avail. There was much publicity, causing him deep distress. As a last resort he wanted to file a review petition in the Supreme Court, and his long-time friend, a successful Advocate on Record who used to regularly brief me in his matters, brought him over to me to engage me to file the review petition. After patiently hearing him out, I could gauge that he had become an emotional wreck and was keen to avail any opening to salvage matters. Though I could understand his anxiety, I expressed my view that the Supreme Court was very unlikely to entertain his appeal, considering the nature of the case. So I advised him against a review, which in my opinion would only compound his emotional distress with all the attendant publicity, and my sincere advice was that he should learn to live with it and just leave it at that. His elderly lawyer friend was immensely pleased with my counseling. In such instances, KYC might be an appropriate process, but certainly not for determining the fees to charge. In that respect, exercise moderation and go by the norm—the amount must be commensurate with the time and effort involved, taking into account your standing in the profession. Let me enter a caveat and say that I never believed that wealth and prosperity should be anathema to lawyers. In fact, when the Law Commission mooted a proposal to have a ceiling on lawyers' fees, I was opposed to it, expressing my view that if a well-heeled client is keen to have a counsel rated highly in popular perception, let him pay the fees charged by such counsel, and that our concern should only be to ensure the availability of a counsel with reasonable competence and qualification, at a fair fee for a client.

My suggestion is: simplify your task by having a scale of reasonable fees, and do not keep varying it depending on the client's ability to pay and such other factors, which only complicates matters for you, often leading to a questioning of your own judgement with the doubt if you should have charged more.

Lately, I notice young lawyers finding themselves at a crossroads mid-way in their career, doubting if they will ever attain fulfilment in pursuing their practice. As I see it, this is on account of their flawed thinking on the goal and object of their professional pursuit. If I meet someone entering the profession, my advice invariably is to consider the journey in their career as the goal and destination for attaining fulfilment. That is because from what I have seen of lawyers practicing in the High Court here, and perhaps in some other courts, the tendency is to see elevation to the Bench as the primary, if not the sole, object of their legal career. There's nothing really wrong with nursing such an ambition; judgeship is undoubtedly a coveted position. The problem is that achieving it requires one to satisfy many criteria, and lawyers who find themselves not advancing fast enough in that direction are prone to be afflicted by disappointment, self-doubt and frustration. Such clamour for judgeship is to a great extent the cause for unhealthy rivalry, resulting in bad blood amongst members of the bar. I would strongly urge young lawyers to realise that their career as a lawyer and that of the judiciary are two parallel paths, with room for lateral entry from one into the other. As a lawyer, immerse yourself single-mindedly in your work and seek fulfilment as one who performs with absolute integrity and professionalism. Earning such recognition and respect from your clients and peers should be, I think, your true object and goal.

19 Parallel Progress—Professional Career

During all this period of hectic activity involving frequent travel, pursuing the various schemes and activities of the BCI Trust—including the NLS Project—I had to manage my professional work in my office and courts. My office had substantial work in the AP High Court by way of standalone clients approaching for filing writ petitions and appeals, criminal and civil. Besides, I had considerable work from Andhra Bank Ltd., of which I was the standing counsel, and some other entities in the City Civil Courts as well. About that time, there was the nationalisation of Andhra Bank Ltd., and the management wanted to carry on financial business other than banking, utilising the compensation amount, while the minority shareholders wanted to receive the compensation on pro rata basis, winding up the company. So the management issued a notice to adopt the necessary resolutions at the annual general meeting (AGM) to enable the bank to carry on activities other than banking. Two days before the proposed AGM, the minority shareholders formed an association, led by a young activist, and filed a company petition in the AP High Court alleging oppression and mismanagement and also seeking that the company be wound up on the ground that it was denuded of the substratum of its objects. The majority group, headed by K. L. N. Prasad (KLN)—a noted entrepreneur and member of Parliament—had the requisite number of shareholders and proxies to support the resolutions, and so the minority group sought for a direction preventing the conduct of the AGM, together with an application to defer consideration of its proposed special resolutions.

There were many allegations against KLN, chairman of the Board, questioning his bona fides and entrepreneurial competence. The matter came up before Justice Ramanujulu Naidu, the company judge, and it was admitted after hearing the counsel for the petitioners, and the application for interim order was posted for the next day. I was representing the company, and it became evident that the judge was inclined in favour of the petitioners. The situation was that if the stay, as prayed for, was granted the next day, there would normally be no scope for challenging such order by way of appeal; and all efforts of the management in securing the presence or the proxies of majority members would go waste, leading to a snowballing effect of the opposition to the management's proposals. That very evening, even before the interim order was passed, I got a draft appeal ready to file by way of a lunch motion the next day, immediately after the order by the single judge in the morning. But then, even if I managed to get the appeal before a Division Bench, there was this apprehended attempt to filibuster by the other side to ensure non-conclusion of the hearing before the Court rose. The minority petitioners were represented by K. G. Kannabhiram, a competent counsel who advanced arguments with great passion before the judge. Importantly, it was known that the lunch motion, if permitted, would go before a Bench of Madhava Rao and K. Sitaram Reddy JJ., who might take time to decide, not being regular company court judges. I mulled over it and decided that the best way out might be to engage Soli Sorabji, who was seen in the High Court that day having come from Delhi to appear in some matter concerning Ramoji Rao, chairman of the Eenadu Group.

So, after the court, on my way home, I drove straight to KLN's place, though it is not something I would normally do—that is, going to the client's place to discuss his case. KLN always used to come to my office for legal work, and I have visited his place on many occasions on his invitation for social get-togethers. KLN was naturally surprised to see me barge in. I explained the situation and wanted him to fix up an appointment to see Soli through Ramoji Rao for engaging him for the next day. Though initially KLN was insistent that he had full faith and confidence in me and that he saw no reason for engaging anyone else, I explained the complex scenario and convinced him. We both met with Soli at Taj Banjara that evening and Soli said he would be busy in the forenoon, which was not a problem since I wanted his presence only in the afternoon. I am sure he was a bit perplexed since there I was, engaging him without a brief, but there was no order as yet, much less permission for a lunch motion or an appeal brief. But then, it is precisely that scenario which makes me remember every detail even after all this time.

Well, the next day, first thing, the judge passed the order granting the interim relief prayed for. I immediately got the appeal typed and ready with formal applications for interim order and approached the registrar Mr Raju to obtain necessary orders from the Chief Justice for posting the matter before the Bench after lunch. Not being used to such an unusual request, he seemed hesitant and so I requested him to be available at the CJ's chambers during lunch's recess saying that: "I will approach the CJ and seek permission for lunch motion". During lunch recess, the CJ, Hon'ble Justice A. Kuppuswamy—a judge highly regarded by all in the fraternity—permitted me to make my oral request in his chambers and, after I explained the urgency involved, directed the matter to be posted before the Bench. Soli was free by then, appeared and opened the case. After his brief submissions, it was the turn of Mr Kannabhiram, who started taking the judges into minute details of various allegations in the petition and there the clock was ticking away. Soli then intervened to plead that the other counsel should give him five minutes at least before the Court rises, which Kannabhiram agreed to; and in those five minutes, we pleaded that the AGM may be allowed to take place and that the resolution, if passed, would not be implemented till further orders. Bingo, that was a fair solution, and the judges made an order to that effect before the Court rose. The moral of the story, if any, is that management of litigation is not merely your ability to present your case with forensic skill, but much more.

The company petition was heard by Justice P. Chennakesava Reddy; and I had roped in advocate B. V. Subbaiah, a highly-regarded lawyer in the district courts of Krishna and Guntur, who had shifted to Hyderabad to practice in the HC. Considering the need to cross-examine a number of witnesses the petitioner was expected to produce, to speak in support of various allegations in the petition, I thought it best to have someone like Subbaiah with experience in trial court work to handle that part. Evidence was recorded and after arguments, the judge held that on proper construction of the memorandum of association, it is not possible to hold that banking was the main and primary object of the company. On the other petition, the judge held that oppression and mismanagement could not be established by the petitioners and consequently both were dismissed. The petitioners, as expected, filed appeals, and I had engaged my close friend Anil Divan, then senior advocate practicing in the Supreme Court, as our counsel, and the Bench allowed the appeals through the judgement reported as Nagavarapu Krishnaprasad vs. Andhra Bank Ltd.

Anil, who sadly passed away a couple of years ago, was one of my closest senior advocate friends in Delhi. Initially, before he formally shifted to the capital, he used to shuttle between Bombay and Delhi; and while in Delhi, he used to stay at the India International Centre, where I also stayed when visiting the city. We would spend time together at breakfast and dinner. His preparation of cases used to be thorough, and presentation in court always marked by clarity. He used to be punctilious and whenever he had to come to Hyderabad for a hearing, before anything else, his confirmed return air-ticket had to be placed on his desk. KLN, being an influential MP, was not used to any advance bookings and so used to find it odd that Anil should insist on seeing a confirmed return ticket. In the later years, Anil and I had visited Brazil, Peru, etc. extending our travel after attending the Biennial International Bar Association (IBA) conference in Buenos Aires, Argentina. Anil, on learning of my plans to attend the conference, wanted to know if I would be interested in visiting a few places in South America after the conference, and I readily agreed. Anil made meticulous arrangements for our travel and visits to the rainforest in Brazil off Manaus, where we stayed in a tree-top lodge, and Peru to visit Machu Picchu. Looking back, I am beholden to him for the opportunity he created for me. Anil and his loving wife Smita were our close family friends who had attended Siddharth's wedding in Hyderabad, and spending time with them in Ooty during summer used to be a delight. Their son, Shyam Divan, Senior Advocate in Supreme Court, and his wife, Madhavi, also a noted lawyer and presently Additional Solicitor General (ASG) in the Supreme Court, maintain the family tradition of friendship marked by affection and warmth with us as in the past.

Reverting to the Andhra Bank matter, we took it to the Supreme Court, availing the leave granted by the Division Bench of the High Court while suspending operation of the judgment for a period of three months. In the Supreme Court, we went by the words of wisdom: 'Discretion is the better part of valour'. We compromised and agreed to pay an amount, arrived at after much higgle-haggle, for the shares held by the minority shareholders.

Yet another VIP client regularly visiting our office was Raja Rameshwar Rao (Rameshwar) of Wanaparthy. Rameshwar, a person known for his high intellect, was director and chairman of the reputed publishing house Orient Longman (now Orient BlackSwan), and member of Parliament. All through my years of practice in Hyderabad, Rameshwar used to consult me on all legal matters. It was more a matter of discipline for him that he should consult the professional concerned in all matters. I recall telling him that the vetting he wanted done by us was quite unwarranted since his drafts did not actually require any vetting. But no. He would drive his car himself and be the first visitor to my office for a discussion and, though I often thought he was unnecessarily troubling himself, I used to enjoy chatting with him. Rameshwar Rao was the Raja of Wanaparthy, succeeding his father Raja Krishna Dev Rao. He administered the State of Wanaparthy from the age of twenty-one years, and was one of the first to offer accession and merger of his state with the Indian Union after Independence.

Rameshwar Rao graduated with a first class from Nizam's College, then part of Madras University, and later did his Masters and law. He also had the distinction of being appointed first secretary of India's first mission at Nairobi, covering East and Central Africa and Belgian Congo, and was India's youngest head of mission abroad. Later, he was successively elected five times to the Lok Sabha from Wanaparthy. He was part of many Indian delegations at global conferences, besides the UN. Whenever Rameshwar visited me, I would see him carrying journals of international relations.

Board members of his company Orient Longman, which later became an Indian company, were eminent writers and renowned public figures, such as Khushwant Singh and Romila Thapar to name just two. Apart from mundane legal work, I had to appear for the company in Calcutta High Court and Supreme Court in a copyright matter relating to the autobiography of Abul Kalam Azad. Over a period, our association deepened and Rameshwar used to discuss many of his political and private matters to seek my opinion. It was no doubt a matter of immense gratification to have such a senior and accomplished intellectual take me into confidence, and I cherish fond memories of my association with him.

While, at the office, we thus had our hands full, I had this call from Dr Tata Rao (TR), then chairman of Andhra Pradesh State

Electricity Board (APSEB), to inform me that he was proposing to appoint me as standing counsel for the Board. I had known TR when he was on the Board of Directors of Andhra Bank Ltd. I told him I was wary of such governmental assignments after my past experience as government pleader, leading to my resignation. He, however, said that he would not take a no and that the proceedings were ready to be issued. I pleaded with him to hold it up till I saw him at his office the next day on my way back from the court. When I explained to him my disinclination to accept any governmental assignments and that I was happy with my practice as private counsel, he said that neither he nor I had a choice in this case. The background of the matter was that he had called on Chief Minister NTR early that morning and, when he mentioned to him that he wanted to appoint a standing counsel for the Board, in his words, it was the CM who suggested my name, and that TR had not even mentioned that he knew me. TR then made this profound statement in Telugu: "*Peddayana Kavalante nuvvu vaddantava*", meaning—When the elder (may not be so to him, but a respectful reference) wants it, would you say no? That softened my negativity since I had great regard for NTR, and so I looked into the draft proceedings that Dr Rao pushed towards me on the table and instantly found another issue.

Along with me, M. Chandrashekhar Rao, an experienced lawyer, who had moved to Hyderabad after long years of practice in Guntur, was also sought to be appointed. No issue on that. But TR, without realising the implications, had shown M. C. Rao's designation as senior standing counsel, and mine as standing counsel. When I said that this was unacceptable, he was quite surprised. Can't blame him really, since TR's logic presumably was that M. C. Rao, being older to me, may have put in many more years at the bar, and, more importantly, that I was not designated as Junior Standing Counsel. Anyhow, on realising that my taking exception to it was justified, he had it changed, designating both of us as standing counsels. M. C. Rao was assigned services and labour-related work; and I was to handle tariff-related and other matters. The work was quite substantial, and cases involved the enormous resources of the APSEB.

If I have acquitted myself well to the satisfaction of my clients and, most importantly, to my own satisfaction, it is undoubtedly because of the able assistance I had from my juniors, who worked with commitment and competence. Murthy (Sarveshwar Murthy) would take care of all the work in the city civil court without troubling me. He had pleadings settled by me only in a few complicated cases, and I may have gone for arguments in a few involving complex legal issues. Nagarjuna (C. V. Nagarjuna Reddy) would bear the burden of most of the other work, including individual private writ petitions, besides the APSEB's work. While in court, awaiting cases to reach a hearing, we never wasted time in idle gossip in the corridors or the Bar Association hall, but would head to the chambers, where I would dictate petitions or counters to be readied, and Nagarjuna had no hassles writing it down by hand. Since these were the pre-computer/pre-laptop days, dictation and typing normally would be possible only when the stenographer was available in the office or at home during evenings. In the process, a stage came when I had a problem figuring out whether a petition or counter I was reading was one prepared on my dictation, or Nagarjuna's own draft. That is because he had the benefit of following my style of narration and in the process, if I may say so, excelled. We used to have batches of writ petitions challenging tariff notifications periodically issued and we had to follow up matters through to the Supreme Court as well. It was indeed a specialised subject, the nuances of which we had to learn from the engineers and officers briefing us.

Mention must be made particularly of S. B. G. Krishnamoorthy, who dealt with tariffs and was known to be a confidant of TR. His dedication and knowledge of the subject were exemplary. It was often difficult for him to find a counsel with a satisfactory grasp and knowledge of the subject. When matters were to be argued in the Supreme Court, he would look with disdain at the advocates on record (AORs) whom he had to brief, more out of the exasperation of having to explain to them the basics. No wonder TR used to count on Krishnamoorthy in all tariff-related matters, including the framing of tariffs.

TR himself was known for his deep knowledge of power-related matters in the country and this, in fact, was why he did not agree to the tariffs received from the National Thermal Power Corporation (NTPC) project at Ramagundam, while other state electricity boards in the south agreed to it without demur. So, to overcome his strong opposition, a tariff was mutually agreed to on a tentative basis, with the understanding that it was to be finally decided on the basis of actuals, after the plant was operated for a couple of years. When the time came for a decision, there were serious disputes between APSEB and NTPC on the calculation of production costs, and the matter was referred for arbitration. I recall TR's caustic comment—that in the name of coal, muck was being supplied—highlighting the dismal calorific value of the coal supplied, which would naturally boost the cost of inputs. NTPC nominated Justice A. C. Gupta as their nominee arbitrator, and I could persuade Justice O. Chinnappa Reddy (OCR), who had by then retired as a Supreme Court judge, to be the nominee arbitrator for APSEB. The seat of arbitration agreed between the parties was Bangalore.

From the word go, OCR could neither understand nor approve of the typical practices and procedures of arbitration that had come to be in vogue. To mention some, the practice was for the arbitrators to sit only till lunch and to treat a sitting beyond lunch as an additional day's sitting, and there would be a number of such avoidable sittings at the stage of filing pleadings and documents. Justice A. C. Gupta, a much sought-after arbitrator, had to give in to OCR's firm views in this regard. The two of them had to name the third arbitrator as umpire, and on OCR's suggestion, Justice Krishna Iyer—not known for acting as an arbitrator after his retirement—agreed more in deference to the wishes of his close friend OCR, for whom he had deep affection and regard. As I learnt, Justice Iyer had acted as arbitrator only in one matter earlier concerning a university in the north-east, and had made sure that it ended in a compromise without a long-drawn out hearing. Mr Dutta, ASG in Supreme Court, was representing NTPC and the initial arguments went on for a few days.

Presumably the senior counsel and in-house lawyer of NTPC, not being pleased with the trend during the initial hearing, came up with the proposal that the umpire also be requested to join in, purportedly with a view to avoid a de-novo hearing if the matter were to eventually go before him. I was surprised and objected strongly to the proposal on the ground that when the matter has already been heard partly, such a suggestion was unacceptable. The arbitrators were, however, agreeable and so, Justice Iyer, the umpire, was present from the adjourned date of hearing. It hardly took him any time to grasp the whole controversy, and after just two–three days of hearing by the three-member panel, he called the officers of both parties and told them to compromise instead of prolonging the unseemly acrimony between two public-sector undertakings. And that, of course, had the salutary effect of the two sides arriving at a compromise. The preparation preceding the hearing to effectively represent my client—particularly to ensure that TR's firm stand that the tariff rate claimed by the Oil and Natural Gas Corporation (ONGC) was excessive and far above the actual costs was vindicated—turned out to be an educative experience for me in understanding the factors for arriving at costs of generation. Needless to say that the unit price finally agreed to through compromise was less than what ONGC had initially sought and what the other boards had agreed to.

Gaining a firm grip over a subject of litigation gives the counsel concerned great confidence and recognition as a specialist in that field. Nagarjuna, who was assisting me in the case, evidently acquired in-depth knowledge of law relating to electricity, and the functionaries of the Board opted to have him as their standing counsel when I gave up the assignment on my designation as senior advocate. It is gratifying to see him assume office as chairman, AP State Electricity Regulatory Commission (APSERC), after his retirement as judge of High Court of AP and Telangana. I think such subjects should be taught as optionals in the last two years of the five-year course or as subjects for the pre-entry test. I had expressed this view on the advisability of making budding lawyers learn such subjects of specialisation during apprenticeship for making the pre-entry tests more meaningful.

In this context it may be apt to quote from my Goa article (see Appendix 4), reflecting my views based on experience. While dealing with the desirability of apprenticeship and the pre-entry test as a precondition for enrolment, this is what I had to say:

> Further, experience shows that there will normally be neither adequate motivation amongst the candidates nor earnestness amongst those enforcing such rule. An apprentice in the early times when such practice was in vogue was, more often than not, unwelcome appendage in an office with hardly any Senior evincing interest in training the apprentice. In most of the cases apprentices were hardly spending their time in court and the maintenance of diaries was reduced to a shallow formality. Though some State Bar Councils used to

arrange for lectures and were serious about the conduct of tests, in most others, the impression was that the candidates ran the risk of failing in the test only if the invigilator did not know the correct answers. While such was the position earlier, I do not think that there was any noticeable change when recently the Bar Council of India sought to re-introduce the system by framing Bar Council of India Training Rules, 1995. During the period 1997–98, as Chairman of the Committee appointed in the place of Delhi Bar Council, I had the opportunity, along with my esteemed colleagues who were members of the committee, to interview candidates and particularly with reference to the period of apprenticeship that they had spent and diaries maintained by them. Though few of the candidates had made good use of their association with a Senior, most of the others were evidently biding their time, making superficial entries in the diary of the proceedings in courts which were supposedly followed by them. The view that apprenticeship and earmarking of the period of one year for training under a Senior would have major beneficial effect may not be wholly correct. The question therefore would be whether it is desirable to make a candidate spend a one-year period when the benefit from the training can only be marginal in most of the cases.

As far as the pre-enrolment test is concerned, here again no particular purpose will be served if it is to be yet another examination. If the training and tests are to be meaningful and beneficial to the candidates, they should be structured in such a way as to create sufficient impetus and motivation for the candidate concerned to seriously apply himself to the said task. The entrance examination may have to be structured in a way that a candidate has the choice of subjects, or a combination of them, qualifying in which could in the long run help him to claim specialisation in such subjects. This has to be backed by a programme for capsule courses by way of week-long lectures and distance education. This exercise run simultaneously along with the apprenticeship under a Senior, to my mind, might produce better results if recourse to apprenticeship and pre-enrolment tests is found unavoidable.

20 Global Fraternity

The major takeaway I have had during the period of association with BCI was the opportunity to visit various countries and attend international lawyer conferences. But for my association with BCI it may not have been possible, what with the difficulty in securing release of foreign exchange and all the restrictions then in force. Besides the foreign trips, our responsibilities made visits to different parts of the country a matter of routine.

The earliest such trip abroad was to China in 1980–81. Those were the days when China was a forbidden land of sorts, which naturally made one highly inquisitive of what goes on behind the iron/bamboo curtain. So I was struck by the idea to try and manage an official visit to China. I was then the managing trustee of the BCI Trust, and I corresponded with the Chinese embassy, floating this idea of reciprocal visits of lawyers as an exchange programme. The idea was for a small group sponsored by the BCI to visit China at their own cost, with the corresponding Chinese organisation, 'The China Law Society', taking care of hospitality for the group while in China, and later, we here to play hosts for a similar group of Chinese legal workers, inviting them to India. It clicked, and on the invitation of the China Law Society, ten of us made this trip. Apart from some bar councillors, our group included: Rajendra Singh, B. N. Bajpayee, K. G. Vakharia and Rangaraj from the BCI; Mr Tippanna and B. V. Acharya from Karnataka; Mr Garg, chairman Delhi Bar Council and, significantly, two elderly celebrities, Justice R. S. Narula, retired chief justice of Delhi High Court, and Hiralal Sibal, who was for years Advocate General of Punjab or Haryana alternatively; Kapil Sibal is his son.

It was just a few years after the Cultural Revolution, with the Red Guards holding sway, had ended, and China had not yet opened up fully. A few visitors like us had to use special currency meant for visiting foreigners and they had in Beijing a special shopping facility known as Friendship Store meant for foreigner visitors. There were no high-end hotels then, as later came to be seen all over China during my visits in the recent past. We were put up in a high-security state guest house, normally meant for important dignitaries, and the officer from the Indian embassy who came to meet with us was pleasantly surprised that we were accommodated there. Chinese officials, as always, were known for their punctilious nature. Even before we started out, we were asked to indicate our dietary choice, vegetarian or non-vegetarian. Bajpayee, who couldn't make up his mind, I think, had the best of both worlds. Invariably it used to be designated seating on two circular tables, each with an interpreter. On one table their chief host for the evening would be sitting with me, and the other table had their number two and our Mr Rangaraj (Ranga), vice chairman, BCI. I used to enjoy the formal conversations between the two groups before the raising of the toast. Mostly it used to be platitudes, both sides speaking of our common ancient cultural heritage and interaction between the people of the two countries as seen from historical records and accounts of renowned travellers. Each sentence spoken had to be translated for the benefit of others, like we see during interactions between leaders of different linguistic backgrounds.

They had a well-thought-out itinerary for our visits to different places and courts of different levels, with simultaneous translation facility for us to follow the proceedings. After we landed in Beijing, Ranga mentioned to me that he wanted to contact a Press Trust of India (PTI) correspondent posted there from India, who was related to some friend of his in Trichy. He contacted him and since the correspondent couldn't visit us in the guest house, they decided to meet at the Friendship Store which we were to visit later that day. The previous day, one of the first visits organised by our hosts was to a prison in Beijing. It was undoubtedly something like a model detention facility. We were shown the cells, all very neat and clean with a thick mattress, and the food being served, a thick broth. The next day during our visit to the Friendship Store, I quickly finished my purchases of a jade piece and some embroidered wall hangings, etc., and found Ranga missing. I was told that he had been chatting with his PTI contact on the landing of the stairs. They were evidently together for long and so when we were back at the guest house, I was inquisitive to know from Ranga what kept him for so long with the

PTI reporter. Ranga sounded evasive, saying nothing in particular. Knowing the minds of journalists and their quest for news, I quizzed Ranga when he said that the guy wanted to know what all we had seen and that he had told him about our visit to the prison. Then, when egged on, he blurted out that the guy had asked him how the prison was, to which Ranga seems to have made a cryptic statement that our prisons are better. Oh my God! There we were, on the third day of our visit—which in a way was a historic event of the first interaction between legal communities of the two countries—and here was my friend, saying that our prisons were better than what our hosts had shown us, which, presumably, was their model prison. I was livid with Ranga for trying to be an authority on prison facilities in India and for tactlessly making a critical remark. I desperately tried to contact the embassy official who had visited us to see if the news item could be quashed from being reported by the PTI, to no avail. On our return, I got to know that *The Hindu* carried a very small item, reporting the view expressed by Ranga.

Expectedly, when we were to play host to the delegation of the China Law Society, one of the things they particularly asked for was a visit to a prison. When my office informed me, I told them to leave it to their visit to Hyderabad, where I would take care of it. The Chinese team was headed by their Vice Minister for Justice, and after arriving in Delhi they were taken to Bombay, Calcutta and Hyderabad. They were shown different courts in each city, apart from other sites of interest.

In Hyderabad, I arranged for their stay at the Lake View Guest House, managed to get an old convertible car from the Raj Bhavan and engaged an air-conditioned coach for the group to travel. The Chinese delegation visited the AP High Court and from there the Police Academy, and in the evening, I hosted a dinner for them at the Secunderabad Club, inviting some senior lawyers and judges. To give them a glimpse of our cultural activities, I took them to Ravindra Bharathi where there was a debut performance by a budding artiste. My daughter Deepika had organised front seats for the visitors. I vividly recall A. Nageswara Rao, the chief guest for the event, walking in; when I pointed to him and mentioned to the visiting foreign dignitary that he was one of our noted film artistes, even before the interpreter could complete her translation, the visiting dignitary asked if he was the Chief Minister—such was the homework he had done. He also knew that the then CM, N. T. Rama Rao was a famous film artiste. From there, while proceeding for dinner at the club, I suggested to the visiting minister that we travel together in the coach since it was air-conditioned, and he indicated his preference to get into the old convertible with the top opened, and we both rode in that; and that, I suppose, was the flip side of the egalitarianism they were known to practice.

Coming to the prison part, I arranged for a visit to the open-air prison we had at Moula Ali, making the drawing of comparisons difficult. For details of the Chinese legal system and glimpses of social life in China as seen by us, instead of going purely by memory, I would rather refer to my article 'Law and Justice in China', published in the *Journal of the Bar Council of India*, Vol. 9(3), 1982, excerpts of which were also published in *The Hindu* in October 1982. After that visit to China, when I returned to Hyderabad, my friend R. Tagore of Tagore and Co., my auditors from inception, invited me to give a talk at a breakfast meeting of the Hyderabad chapter of the Institute of Chartered Accountants. After I narrated what I had observed, there was a barrage of questions from the audience, wanting to know more about life, development and society in China. It was perhaps understandable, since we in India hardly knew much about what was happening in our neighbouring country.

Amongst the many trips abroad to attend lawyers' conferences, the one I enjoyed most was my trip to Buenos Aires, Argentina, to attend the twenty-second biennial conference of the International Bar Association (IBA), considered the foremost organisation for international legal practitioners and bar associations. Though IBA has many sectional conferences, their biennial conferences attract a few thousand delegates globally. For some years BCI had been boycotting the IBA conferences since IBA had recognised the Bar Association of India as the premier body to represent the Indian Bar. In 1988, when I was chairman of BCI, senior advocate R. K. P. Shankar Das (Kumar) had been elected president of IBA; and so I thought that it was time—particularly when one from our own Bar was heading the organisation—to attend the conference, making our position clear, that while BCI was the statutorily recognised apex body of the legal profession in India, BAI was a premiere voluntary organisation, with many doyens of the Indian Bar closely associated with it.

Soon after I moved to Delhi, I became a member of BAI, of which Fali Nariman was the president, and I was made member, executive, and later a vice-president. Attending meetings presided over by the legendary leader of the bar, Fali Nariman, with many legal luminaries present, was always an intellectually stimulating experience. It is gratifying to learn that the then honorary secretary, Lalit Bhasin—whom Fali characterises as a 'Master-Organiser', while acknowledging his unstinted support, help and initiative—is presently the President of BAI. I must add here that I felt deeply grateful to BAI for inviting me to Delhi—almost a decade after I quit practice and left Delhi—and felicitating me on 3 December 2019, presenting me with a plaque of honour and distinction, 'For Outstanding Contribution to the Development of the Legal Profession in India and Highest Standards at the Bar'. What a magnificent gesture which, in effect, invalidates the age-old adage, 'Out of sight, out of mind'.

While in Buenos Aires, I felt very much at home, with Kumar heading the IBA as chairman, making the visiting Indian delegation immensely proud. Kumar, I think, was equally happy that I, a friend for whom he had high regard, was heading the delegation from India. I also had the good fortune of running into an Argentinian friend, whom I had known almost a quarter century earlier when he was also doing his postgraduate law course in London, and we got acquainted on the tennis courts. I lost contact with him and so I was wondering if I could get to meet him. In fact, I barely remembered his name—it was something like Alfredo, Roberto, first and middle names, with the surname Uriburu, as that of a past president of Argentina. After arrival and registration, the first evening was a welcome party for the leaders of developing bar associations attending a seminar preceding the main conference, hosted by the Argentinian Bar Federation. As I walked in, I saw a person with a familiar face receiving the guests; he was apparently an office-bearer of their Bar Federation. When I walked up to him and asked if he could remember someone from his student days in London, he immediately recognised me as his tennis companion and started pulling my leg, telling all his friends that I was looking for ball pickers on the tennis courts in London. I enjoyed his hospitality, visiting high-end restaurants on the waterfront.

I also got to have an Indian meal of sorts at the home of an Indian lady who had married an Argentinian. She was related to neighbours of my niece Padma in Chennai, and Padma got me her phone number and wanted me to call her up for her neighbour's sake, which I did, and she was very pleased to receive my call and insisted on my visiting her to meet her friends at dinner. She and those other ladies were apparently devotees of Satya Sai Baba and had made a few visits to his ashram at Puttaparthi. Another spiritual connect with India I encountered was at Santiago airport in Chile, where I had to transit on my way to Rio de Janeiro, Brazil. In the coach at the terminal was this young Caucasian in saffron robes, and I greeted him, addressing him as "Swamiji". He belonged to the Hare Krishna movement and was mighty pleased to have someone greet him reverentially. He then told me that his brahmachary group was running a vegetarian diner in Santiago by the name 'Govinda', and said that should I happen to visit Santiago, I should go there. I was, of course, thrilled to hear that, though I had no occasion to have a vegetarian meal at Govinda.

After the conference concluded, Anil and I flew to Rio de Janeiro, the first leg of our planned travel to few places, before heading back to India. Some other delegates from India also visited Rio after the conference. Rio was a vibrant and populous city, whose people seemed oblivious to the dismal state of economy of their country, with the inflation soaring by the day and hour. This came as a revelation to us when we noticed people thronging in large numbers at the banks late in the evening every day. The reason, as we learnt, was that no one wanted to keep Brazilian money with them or in their bank account overnight since the next day the value would be much less against hard currencies like the American Dollar. So they used to convert their currency into US Dollars on a day-to-day basis. When asked how he managed his professional fees, a Brazilian lawyer explained that his fees were in terms of American Dollars, and so when a client engaged him, all he needed to do was to check out the exchange rate for the day from the newspaper and collect the amount in local currency. None of this had noticeably affected the spirit of the Brazilians, who seemed to live for the sheer joy of watching football, besides planning for and participating in the yearly carnival.

We then flew to Manaus, capital of the Brazilian state of Amazonas, in the midst of the rainforest from where the river Amazon originates at the confluence of two rivers, Solimos and Negro. The waters from these two sources run side by side for more than a mile without mixing—a fascinating phenomenon which is clearly visible from the banks as well as from the boat you are sailing in since there is a slight colour difference between the two streams. From there the tour operator was to take us to the treetop lodge deep in the rainforest for a two-night stay. As we landed in Manaus, we had transport, with an English-speaking chauffeur-cum-guide to take us to the downtown hotel. On the way we noticed huge billboards with pictures of two individuals prominently displayed all the way into town. It was evident that there was some election in the offing. Our chauffeur said it was the impending municipal election with the incumbent, a corrupt politician seeking re-election as mayor, and his opponent, a lady candidate, seriously campaigning against him. On inquiry, he said that the incumbent was likely to be re-elected. When asked, "How come, if he is known to be so corrupt?", he responded by saying, "That is a good question. It is because our people think that an old mouse is better than the young ones". A purely pragmatic approach—given the rampant corruption, and no one believed to be above it, better to settle for the old who might, after all the opportunities he or she had, be a little less greedy.

I remember quoting this much later while meeting with some foreign journalists in Delhi. At the time, the Jain *hawala* diaries cases were being dealt with by the Supreme Court, with all the attendant media coverage. There was this delegation of European journalists visiting Delhi who came to interact with lawyers in the Supreme Court as part of their schedule. The Bar Association had invited a few senior advocates, including myself, to meet with the delegation. There was this discussion, naturally veering to the ongoing hawala litigation in the Supreme Court, and when they started quizzing us on the issue of corruption, most of us became defensive, admitting the despicable levels of corruption in public life, as if ours was the only country afflicted by the malady. After a while, I intervened, quoting what the chauffeur had said in Brazil, to make my point that corruption is not uncommon in developing countries, and that we at least had this hope of our body politic being cleansed of it, with our institutions like the judiciary firmly in place. Of course, I didn't go to the extent of saying that corruption can also have the positive effect of accelerating economic growth, as propounded by a lawyer-politician at a seminar. My own view was that being overly obsessed with the issue of corruption might be counterproductive, and instead the focus should be on possible systemic changes to minimise the scope for corrupt practices. Some state governments have addressed the issue, coming forward with citizens charters and putting to optimum use information technology. We see the same implemented by the Central government, having a salutary effect in departments such as income tax. If there is political will and increased awareness amongst the public, I have no doubt that there will be significant diminution of corruption, even if it is not totally eradicated.

Manaus, being in a rainforest area without easy access, was sparsely developed. The government therefore had allowed duty-free shopping for Brazilians up to a limit of 800 USD or so to promote tourism, and so the Main Street was full of huge shops with electronic goods and top-end luxury products of renowned international brands. Most of those shops, interestingly, were owned by persons of Indian origin and a five-star hotel that was coming up was said to be owned by an Indian entrepreneur. When we went to Lima, Peru, on our way to Machu Picchu—the one-time seat of the Inca civilisation— we also noticed this phenomenon of admirable entrepreneurship of the Indian diaspora, which naturally made us proud. When I was getting organised for this trip and applying for visas, my colleague in the Bar Council representing Rajasthan, N. K. Jain (NK)—who later became a judge and served as the Chief Justice of the High Courts of Madras and Karnataka for about five years—got wind of it, insisted on informing his relatives in Lima, and was keen that I should contact them. When I got there, NK being a close friend, I gave them a call as he had advised, and this young man, brother of NK's brother-in-law, came to see us at the hotel and take us around a bit. His family was into the jewellery business, and there were billboards widely advertising their shops and products—if I can recall correctly, it was the Jhaveri Brothers. The interesting part is that they were not selling jewellery made in India; they were actually making Peruvian jewellery, in Peru, for the local market. When this young man got to know that we were flying to Cuzco, to visit Machu Picchu, he insisted that his manager there would meet with us. Well, the manager came and took us to a movie theatre owned by his employer, where they were showing a Hindi Bollywood movie, with Spanish subtitles. The entrepreneurship of our diaspora was truly amazing. Our spiritual thought and religiosity is the other thing that had noticeably spread even to those parts of the world.

The next IBA conference I attended was the one in Cannes, France, particularly famous as the venue for international film festivals. This time round, Radha accompanied me. We stayed in Nice and took a coach to Cannes for the conference. The big social events were the beach parties on the French Riviera, with laser shows and good wine, a delightful experience. The conference as such was of course the usual, with large number of delegates from Europe and the Americas busily networking, and everyone had a great time.

After the conference, we planned to meet up with my brother-in-law, NRC, and Prabha in Paris, and to drive to Vienna for a couple of days. Actually, they wanted us to visit them in the UK, and I persuaded them to agree to make this trip to Vienna, which I was keen to visit. I suggested that we hire a car in Paris for the trip to Vienna and back, and fly back from Paris to our respective places. Not being enthusiastic about driving, NRC cut a deal with Prabha that only we both, that is, she and myself, would drive. In Paris, we met at the airport and hired a car. There, when asked to produce her licence while hiring a car, Prabha rummaged in her bag and put up a blank face, saying that she seemed to have forgotten to bring it with her. And so I was to be the only official chauffer, with NRC available to relieve me if needed. We got back to the hotel. Since the night was young, that, too, on a Saturday, we decided to drive to downtown Paris to see some action. NRC was at the wheel when we had this accident—at a junction, a vehicle coming from the lower road ran into us at the merging point. The ease with which you can handle such situations there is something astounding. The police officer who came made both vehicles move to a side road, whereupon the driver of the other vehicle, a commercial vehicle, called his office and started kicking up a shindig. We called the car hirer and, when we gave the particulars from the insurance documents, we were asked to leave the car and find our way home and, believe me, we could carry on as if nothing had happened. Nevertheless, since it was a bit of a jolt, we wanted to drop the road trip to Vienna. But then when we contacted Siri, my nephew, in the UK—who was our man to go to, particularly since he had lived in Paris for more than a year while doing his MBA at Insead—he gave particulars of the hirer who would be open on Sunday and wanted us to pick up a car the very next day and go ahead with the planned trip. Which we did, and thanks to Siri, we had this memorable experience of visiting the famous concert halls and attending concerts of some renowned orchestras. That delightful experience made us forget all our travails, including anxious moments of driving around aimlessly to find accommodation for a comfortable stay since most of the hotel rooms were sold out.

There are a couple of other trips Radha and I made to attend conferences, one of which was to Manila, for the Law Asia Conference where CJI Justice Verma addressed the plenary, and the other was the South Asian Association for Regional Cooperation (SAARC) Law Conference, closer home in Kathmandu. At a buffet dinner there in Kathmandu, I heard someone calling me from behind, saying, "Reddy *garu*". I wondered who it could be, since the only other Telugu-speaking delegate there was P. P. Rao, who would not address me so formally. I turned around and found that it was a delegate from Pakistan. Though I cannot now recall his name properly, I have a vivid memory of his background. He was a judge in Pakistan who resigned when president Ayub Khan imposed martial law, and he had been practicing in Lahore High Court ever since. He told me that his parents hailed from the Godavari district of AP and that his father, being a government officer, was transferred to Karimnagar in present Telangana state, where he spent his childhood before Partition, when the family migrated to Pakistan. He was ever so proud that P. V. Narasimha Rao, then PM of India, was from his district, Karimnagar. More interestingly, he told me that his grandmother always used a Telugu adage or phrase to drive home something important. It was so inspiring and poignant to see him fondly remember his childhood and the language he was familiar with then. Though I was keen to have him invited by the government to one of the World Telugu Conferences, I couldn't figure out his name from the list of delegates. Typical indeed that sloppiness and lethargy put paid to realising good intentions.

21 Introspection

Within the country, there used to be visits to many places to attend conferences, seminars and events organised by BCI and various State Councils. Something I can never forget is the invitation to be a guest speaker at successive State Lawyers Conferences, a yearly event organised by the Karnataka State Bar Council and other lawyer bodies there, reflecting the close bond I had developed with the legal fraternity there. Besides those, as managing trustee of the BCI Trust, I had to attend events organised by the Trust, more significantly, those which related to the continuing legal education (CLE) programme. There were few more such workshops; at least two I can recall were in Nainital and Trivandrum. I am not sure if the BCI or the State Councils are still conducting such workshops. I remember meeting the lady who was director of the CLE programmes during the IBA conference, and could appreciate the kind of importance attached to them in developed countries.

Though there were many pleasant and gratifying experiences worth reminiscing, with the satisfaction of rendering real-time service to the fraternity, stressful moments arising out of rancour caused by the individual political mindset of some colleagues became far too frequent. There were things which some of us used to find unpleasant. For instance, BCI's financial position was far from healthy, with most of the State Councils not remitting their share of the enrolment fee collected—the prime source of revenue for the BCI. Some members would repeatedly seek time for their State Councils to remit the amount to BCI. In fact, when I pleaded with the Law Ministry for some amendments to the Advocates Act, the foremost needed for the BCI's very survival was to ensure that its share of enrolment fee was remitted directly into BCI's account by the candidates. My successors may have had the benefit of it since the amendment came into force after my term.

While the financial position was utterly grim, members were not willing to show restraint in curbing travel expenses. In my initial year the practice was to have a retired judge or an eminent lawyer as a co-opted member of BCI's Disciplinary Committees. It was indeed a wholesome practice which would enhance the prestige of the Committee, against the orders of which an appeal lay only to the Supreme Court. On my committee there used to be Justice Talukdar, and after his term we had co-opted Justice M. Krishna Rao, who had retired as a judge of AP High Court. On the insistence of some members this practice was departed from, and co-opting a member of the State Bar Council became the new norm, with the object of pleasing members of the State Bar Council. As such opportunities to co-opt State Bar Council members were limited, a member from Uttar Pradesh evolved this ingenuous plan of obtaining the co-opted member's resignation after a few months and co-opting another in his place, so that by rotation more had the opportunity to be co-opted. Merely being a co-opted member might not be of much use in the absence of opportunities to travel to various places—Mumbai being the most preferred destination—and this would necessarily lead to pressure on the staff to post cases somehow or the other and assign them to the Disciplinary Committee regardless of the financial crunch faced by BCI.

While we were with difficulty carrying on, it became necessary for us to vacate the premises occupied by our office. Our office was located in one of the AB type bungalows in front of the Supreme Court, and it was required by the authorities to build the proposed Lawyers' Chambers. We were allotted a plot of land in Rouse Avenue and asked to build our own office there. With increasing pressure to vacate, we decided to construct our own office. An architect known to the secretary was engaged and plans were got ready. It was quite a grandiose plan, with a medium-sized auditorium and guest rooms, besides the regular office space and library. I think V. C. Mishra (VC) was the chairman then. When the architect started pushing for floating tenders, I made my position clear—that the work should be entrusted only to a public sector undertaking (PSU), and also had a resolution adopted to that effect by the BCI. Even so, when I was in Hyderabad, there was this call from the office saying that the tenders were being finalised for execution of the work by private builders. I shot out a telegram, insisting that any deviation from the BCI's resolution cannot be sustained. VC then called to say that no PSU was prepared to take up the work, and asked me to find one. I went to Delhi, met with the managing director of National Buildings Construction Corporation (NBCC), who, though not inclined to take up such a small work, on my insistence relented. The building came up while I was in Delhi—though I was not associated with BCI then—and I attended the inaugural function.

Another embarrassing situation was during the silver jubilee celebrations of BCI. VC was the chairman and, with a view to make it a grand national event, invited Rajiv Gandhi, the then PM, who was kind enough to agree to be the chief guest. It was a very well-attended meeting, with many lawyers from UP and other neighbouring areas present. VC, in his welcome address, with a sense of bravado, said something to the effect that, "Mr PM, as chairman of BCI, I was not able to secure an appointment from your office to see you. If this is the situation for chairman BCI, one can imagine the plight of a common man." It was indeed shocking that he should say such a thing to the chief guest in a celebratory function. But then he received a proper slap when Rajiv Gandhi in his address said that, after hearing the BCI chairman, he could understand why an appointment as sought for may not have been forthcoming from his office. The entire audience applauded the PM when he said that, compounding our embarrassment. I remember going to the office of the *Hindustan Times*, where my friend Kishan Mahajan was the legal correspondent, to issue a statement, and Kishan said that instead of a statement I should write a letter to the editor, which he would publish in toto. I did that, and also wrote to the PM, clarifying that what the chairman said did not represent the views of the Council. How embarrassing! A greater embarrassment was the event leading to litigation, culminating in the adoption of a motion of no-confidence against VC, then BCI chairman, under the aegis of the Supreme Court.

The purpose of recalling some of these unpleasant experiences is only to lay bare the lacunae in the system and to highlight the need to address these. That said, I must say that the sense of fulfilment derived from contributing to various initiatives which produced positive results far outweighs the unpleasantness of some of the developments in the functioning of a body comprising members from diverse backgrounds and different regions of the country. Bearing relevance to this are some of my suggestions in the presentation I made at the BAI conference in Goa, and the amendments to the Advocates Act that I pleaded for, some of which were mercifully given effect through the amendment bill introduced by the government.

On my return from South America, after attending the IBA conference in Buenos Aires, during my talk on my experiences to the members of the High Court Advocates Association in Hyderabad, I remember highlighting the cheerful disposition of the Brazilians despite the financial crisis faced by them, with their currency changing its colour and name ever so often on account of its devaluation. What was 'Cruzeiro' would become 'Cruzado' or something else. Another thing I mentioned was my meeting with a functionary of the Brazilian Bar Federation at the IBA conference. This person, who introduced himself as a secretary of the Federation, tried to impress me by saying that there were some 70,000-odd lawyers in Brazil, and that it was the largest bar in the region. I in turn introduced myself as chairman of the BCI and said that we were some 4,00,000-plus when I left. Though I enjoyed seeing his face going pale, numbers were always a serious issue for the legal fraternity, with all the concomitant problems. I did try to limit the burgeoning strength of the new entrants churned out by the mushrooming private colleges, since overcrowding would lead inevitably to a fall in income below sustenance level and encourage unethical practices. There was this practice of the BCI sending an inspection team of two or three of its members on receipt of application for recognition of a private law college even before the concerned university conferred affiliation. Considering all factors, including the financial crunch faced by BCI, as chairman, I gave strict instructions that unless an application was accompanied by a certificate of affiliation from the concerned university, it need not be considered, leave alone proceeding with inspection, and also decided to collect a specified amount as inspection fee from the applicant promoter. There were a few applications from Hyderabad pending for long, and while sending a team I remember giving them a hint that they should look into the need factor besides fulfilment of other conditions, and accordingly, they cleared just two. After my term there were, I think, about twenty-two colleges which secured recognition, leading to the AP High Court taking up the matter as public interest litigation (PIL). Besides such issues of in-house management, there were undoubtedly some major issues that leaders of the fraternity were often called upon to address.

There was this unfortunate episode of a confrontation between the bar and the law enforcement agencies in Delhi, which dragged on for weeks and months. This may be, for brevity, referred to as the Kiran Bedi episode. What was perceived as unacceptable aggression and assault by the law enforcement agencies led to the bar bodies in Delhi boycotting the courts and resorting to agitations, backed by resolutions adopted by their respective Bar Associations. Even the Supreme Court Bar was under tremendous stress, and I recall the then president Murali Bhandari seeking my intervention as BCI chairman. The Supreme Court Bar then constituted an action committee, headed by noted activist and senior advocate Gobind Mukhoti, who formally requested BCI to intervene. In that scenario, some of my activist colleagues wanted BCI to give a call for a nationwide boycott of courts by lawyers. Few of my friends and I were firmly of the view that, BCI being the highest statutorily recognised disciplinary authority of the Indian Bar, calling for such boycott would be inappropriate. I had nevertheless expressed my solidarity and offered my support to the leaders of the Supreme Court Bar in upholding the prestige of the profession by means other than BCI calling for a boycott. This brings to mind my appearance before a Supreme Court Bench dealing with the legality of strike/boycott by lawyers, where I strongly pleaded that there cannot be any absolute bar against recourse to such means by advocates, as pleaded by the petitioner in the PIL.

Another issue which often arises is taking recourse to boycott of courts in order to protest against a particular judge or judges, and Bar Associations adopting resolutions against members of the judiciary. I always firmly believed that it is a part of the professional duty of members of the fraternity to protect the prestige and image of the judiciary, the credibility of which is the bedrock for the edifice of the judiciary and rule of law. As BCI chairman, a few instances of lawyers denigrating some members of the judiciary, making wild allegations and ignoring avenues for remedial measures, came to my notice. I took the initiative to constitute a judicial committee of three retired Supreme Court judges to whom we could refer any transgression of probity by a judiciary member, particularly of the higher courts, and seek advice. On such a reference, the committee could make its own discreet enquiries and advise us on prima facie substance in the allegations or otherwise. In the press release handed out at the press meet, attended by many legal correspondents, direct reference to such enquiries into allegations against judges was discreetly avoided, though it was very much on our minds to utilise the services of the proposed committee. Due publicity was given to this decision of the BCI and on our request, the three eminent retired SC judges, namely Justices A. N. Sen, O. Chinnappa Reddy, and V. D. Tulzapurkar, were kind enough to agree to serve on the committee. It is a different matter that shortly thereafter, I ceased to be associated with the BCI, and, apparently, my successors chose not to take benefit of such course of action. Even individually, I used to take strong exception to allegations of misconduct by judges being given publicity without any competent authority probing to see prima facie substance in such allegations. I recall my article 'Judges and Medals', published in *The Indian Advocate* (The Journal of Bar Association of India; see Appendix 5), when serious allegations of misconduct involving three judges of the Karnataka High Court were made, and also my letter to the editor of *Frontline* on the opinionated piece published against Chief Justice A. S. Anand.

When my second term as member BCI was coming to an end, I made up my mind not to seek re-election, though with some remainder of my term as chairman still left, getting elected to the State Council, and from there to BCI, would not have been a problem. I did not reveal my mind, lest there be pressure from friends and well-wishers to continue. In fact, my calling it a day came to be known to all only when my nomination in the State Council elections was not received. I have no regrets really. I had served the organised Bar with a sense of commitment and thought it was time to give others an opportunity.

A discerning reader would no doubt notice my focus on serving the organised Bar and my sense of pride in being part of the legal fraternity. Well, from the time I joined the profession, I never considered it to be a springboard for the goal of judgeship, which is generally perceived as the culmination of a successful legal practice. I was, in a way, an oddball character in the legal profession who firmly believed these two things to be essentially two different paths, albeit interchangeable. This, I believe, is precisely the thought process that led me to decline the offer of judgeship.

It was in the year 1988 when Justice Yogeshwar Dayal, judge of Delhi High Court, took over as chief justice of the AP High Court. In or around August that year, I was making plans for my trip to Argentina to attend the Biennial Conference of the IBA in Buenos Aires. Justice M. Jagannadha Rao, then a judge in the AP High Court, sitting on the Bench with the Chief Justice, called me to say that Chief Justice Dayal wanted to see me. When I called on the CJ at his residence that evening, Justice Dayal told me that he wanted to send my name for judgeship and sought my consent. Since it came as a surprise, I naturally requested him for some time to apply my mind and revert to him. Being one who had come from Delhi, he could make out that it might not be a positive response from me. And so he sought to ensure that I would not be bogged down by any doubts of his proposal getting stuck at some level by saying that he had ascertained the views of the functionaries who had a role to play, and that they were all positive to the proposal. Nevertheless, I insisted that I may be given at least a day to consult my family, which he reluctantly agreed to, saying that he would expect to see me the next day and that he would not accept a "no". Well, it was obviously persuasion, and not so much a pressure tactic. I did give serious thought to it, being one who never doubted the importance of the role of judges in the administration of justice. I could not, however, convince myself that I had the aptitude for judgeship. I went the next day to convey with trepidation my decision to decline the offer. Siddharth, who drove me to the CJ's residence, had apparently guessed that I was going to decline. Justice Dayal was, no doubt, disappointed but took it in his stride by saying that he could understand my reluctance. It was, indeed, gratifying to know sometime later from the horse's mouth, as it were, that the then CM, N. T. Rama Rao, was also keen to propose my name for judgeship. The only person in the family who was disappointed with my decision was my father, who couldn't possibly figure out any valid reason for my decision.

22 Back to Business—Advocate General of Andhra Pradesh

Thereafter focus shifted to professional work, which may have suffered to some extent during the period of my active involvement with BCI. My constant availability in Hyderabad made it easier to handle work in the office and courts. I occasionally used to make trips to Delhi to argue cases of my clients in the Supreme Court, using the skeletal office created there with P. S. Narasimha (PSN) attending to my work along with his own practice, sitting in the front room of the government bungalow on Purana Quila Road allotted to Surender Reddy, who was then member of Parliament.

Then came the change in the political dispensation in Andhra Pradesh with Nedurumalli Janardhan Reddy (NJR) taking over as CM, succeeding Dr M. Channa Reddy. R. Venugopal Reddy, the incumbent Advocate General, tendered his resignation and it became known that NJR might want someone else for the post. Though I had no acquaintance with NJR, my name came into currency as a strong candidate under consideration. Enquiries in political circles revealed that the CM was very much inclined in my favour, except for the lurking doubt in his mind of a possible negative reaction from the backward class (BC) leaders in Telangana. There was then a very strong lobby of BC leaders and legislators in Telangana area, and the CM's anxiety to avoid any possible adverse reaction from that lobby was quite understandable. I did not try to contact any of the BC leaders, though most of them, particularly G. Rajaram, C. Jagannatha Rao, Manik Rao and others were closely known to me from the time when Nukala was a senior minister. I did not want to embarrass them by contacting them. My junior Mr Devaraj, who was an astute thinker particularly in matters involving politicians, came up with this idea of contacting G. Venkataswamy, undoubtedly the tallest of Scheduled Caste leaders of his time in Hyderabad. He used to take such keen interest in the welfare of slum-dwellers in and around

Hyderabad that he came to be fondly known as 'Gudisela (hutments) Venkataswamy'. He was later a member of Parliament for long and also a Central minister in Delhi when I had moved to Delhi. He had deep affection and regard for me and my family. He would accept our invitation for any important get-together hosted by us while in Delhi and, despite his busy schedule, used to be one of the first to arrive. Pursuant to Devaraj's advice, I remember calling on Venkataswamy at his residence. When I explained to him the CM's dilemma, his immediate reaction was, "How can there be any criticism if someone like you were to be appointed as Advocate General?" He then said that he would speak to the CM to allay his fears.

My appointment as Advocate General came through and I took charge in January 1991. The Andhra Pradesh government wanted a new team of law officers and government pleaders, and left the selection entirely to me. The then law secretary Sanjeeva Reddy, a district judge on deputation, used to be in touch with me. Before the appointment of the new team of government pleaders, the incumbent GPs were carrying on, and there was no decision as such not to reappoint any of them, which was only proper. But I was averse to have any from the outgoing team, though some like L. Ravi Kumar, Vineeta Reddy were deserving of being seriously considered for continuance. There was, however, this unpleasant development I had to face during that interregnum. One of the GPs from the outgoing team was representing the government in a writ petition by a civil contractor, raising issues of alleged breach of terms by the government. The petitioner's strategy was to have the disputes referred to arbitration. The government pleader concerned mindlessly gave consent and also agreed to the appointment of the one suggested by the petitioner as arbitrator. A writ appeal was filed and before the matter came up for hearing, the whole process of arbitration was completed with an award granting substantial sums of money to the contractor. I had to argue the matter and since the stakes involved were pretty high, the petitioner-contractor had engaged Soli Sorabjee, senior advocate at Delhi, to argue and sustain the order in the writ petition. The writ appeal came up before a Bench presided over by Justice A. Lakshmana Rao, who was highly regarded by all without exception. I had this unpleasant task of having to denigrate the mindless manner in which the GP conducted the matter, with the concerned gentleman sitting next to me. Needless to say that the government was averse to reappoint him after that, and so I remember making him a standing counsel for some corporation.

Thereafter, the task of selecting candidates for appointment was completed pretty smoothly. I counted on my juniors, particularly Nagarjun, Devaraj and Niroop, to help me since I was not familiar with many from the younger section of the bar. Surprisingly there was no pressure on me from any quarters, barring a couple of well-meaning suggestions or requests. Devaraj wanted Anand Reddy, an elderly lawyer, to be accommodated, which I gladly did. Whether one likes it or not, the process was akin to cabinet formation in many ways, with regional, caste and other interests having to be balanced. Since I had no special interests the selection was as objective as it could be, given the overwhelming number of aspirants. From my office, D. Sudarshan Reddy, who had varied experience, was made a government pleader and a few years later he came to be appointed as advocate general, and T. Durga Reddy was appointed assistant GP and has now been continued as GP in recognition of his integrity and hard work. While scouting for a suitable candidate for a particular slot, I thought of C. V. N. Shastry who, after many years of practice in the districts, had shifted to Hyderabad a few years earlier. I had seen him arguing on a few occasions and found him conducting himself with dignity. When I floated his name, there were some doubts raised by my advisers if he could cope with writ work which would be the major chunk. I didn't take it seriously and thought he would be best suited for cases of revenue department where his past experience could stand him in good stead. Shastry did so well that his name was proposed for judgeship and he served the office of High Court Judge with distinction and retired a few years ago.

Another such instance was my choice of Krishna Kaundinya as one of the GPs in the Advocate General's office to assist me. I had seen him arguing some income tax matters as a junior of Suryanarayana, the standing counsel for the Income Tax department. His senior, whose term as standing counsel had just then expired, came to me to recommend Krishna for being accommodated in a suitable slot. I readily took him in as GP, along with Subramaniyam and Ravinder

Back to Business—Advocate General of Andhra Pradesh

Rao as special GPs, to assist me. Sadly, Subramaniyam, who was shaping up well, passed away prematurely, while Krishna Kaundinya and Ravinder Rao have done well, availing the opportunity provided by the assignment and are now designated senior advocates handling considerable government litigation. Chandraiah, who was also a GP in the team, retired recently as judge of the Andhra Pradesh High Court and keeps himself busy with voluntary social work, and has recently been made Chairman of the State Human Rights Commission, while Eshwaraiah, also part of the team, was elevated to the Bench and after retirement held the post of Chairman, Backward Class Commission at the national level. Vijayalakshmi, who was also attached to my office as assistant GP, is another who used to be a great help and she is presently Judge, High Court of Andhra Pradesh.

Motilal Nayak, one of the GPs, was later judge of the High Court of Andhra Pradesh and after retirement he was appointed chairman, Debt Recovery Appellate Tribunal at Delhi. I remember the GP's office finding it difficult to cope with his short temper. Many years after I moved to Delhi, my office had accepted a matter for appearance before that tribunal and the briefing counsel came the previous evening for a conference. Not having appeared before that tribunal earlier, I was surprised that the brief was accepted. On questioning Kannan, my secretary, it came to light that he mistook it for a matter before the Company Law Appellate Tribunal, before whom I had appeared earlier. I then enquired who the chairman of the tribunal was and was told by the briefing counsel and his clients that it was Justice Motilal Nayak, a retired judge of High Court of Andhra Pradesh. I then wanted them to find someone else to appear for them, since having known Nayak, it would not be right for me to appear before him. As the client and his advocate were apparently not used to such niceties, there was no way I could return the brief, particularly at the last minute. So the next day, I went to appear in the matter. As Motilal Nayak walked in, he saw me and, taking his seat, said, "Oh! I am seeing Mr V. R. Reddy after a long time." How smart! He openly made it known to all that he knew me so that there could be no whispering later. Anyhow, there was an interim application that day, after which, the brief was promptly returned. It was a pleasant surprise to see Nayak conducting himself with the calmness and composure befitting the office he held.

It is a matter of immense gratification that most of the GPs I had in my team had done exceedingly well, fulfilling my expectations of their potential when I chose them for appointment. While on this subject I must also mention the one that got away. Soon after I started the exercise, I pitched upon Vilas Afzalpurkar for appointment as special GP in the Advocate General's office since I knew that he would be able to take some load off my shoulders. So, I called him over and invited him to join. But then Vilas had a problem leaving his senior M. L. Ganu's office and could not accept my offer. Vilas was later elevated to the Bench and served as a judge of the High Court of Andhra Pradesh with distinction.

Once my team of government pleaders was in place, I had to start the process of selecting standing counsels for various statutory bodies and corporations. Here again, I kept my own counsel in the selection of candidates, and couldn't believe that there were no pressures, as was widely considered unavoidable. I cannot claim that subjectivity and a personal element have absolutely no place in such matters of selection for assignments. A personal element—as long as it does not reek of rank nepotism or favouritism—may not always be an unwelcome factor. As an illustration, I can mention the case of the appointment of the late Ram Mohan Raj, an advocate who hailed from Cuddapah district. He had apparently worked as secretary of a market committee and at a later stage came to Hyderabad to practice in the Andhra Pradesh High Court. He was obviously comfortable with the few criminal cases he used to get. He was a very pleasant, elderly man who often used to chat with me, and I had developed a liking for him and thought he deserved some help. Knowing of his exposure to the working of market committees, I suggested his name as standing counsel for market committees. I could help him without compromising the quality of legal services required for the department. Then there was B. S. A. Swamy, who had political inclinations and was known for passionately espousing the cause of the backward classes. I wanted him to involve himself more with court work. One day he walked up to me in the corridor of the court to say that someone from Andhra Pradesh State Financial Corporation had called him to say that they want him as their legal advisor; he then added that he figured that I must be responsible for it. Yes, I had recommended

Plate 61 VRR's felicitation on assumption of office as Advocate General of AP; (L to R) VRR, Katikaneni Jagannadha Rao, President Bar Association, CM N. Janardhan Reddy, Justice M. Jagannadha Rao.

Plate 62 CM at the venue; (L to R) VRR, Niroop Reddy, D. Sudarshan Reddy, CM, E. Ayyapa Reddy.

Plate 63 CM greeting attendees; (L to R) K. Raja Reddy, CM, C. V. Nagarjun Reddy and others.

Plate 64 At the function; (R to L) P. Babul Reddy, Justice A. Seetaram Reddy and others.

Plate 65 VRR with Nori Rajeswhar Rao and Justice K. Ramaswamy.

Plate 66 (L to R) K. Raja Reddy, VRR, R. Venugopal Reddy, former AG, Ram Mohan Raj.

Plate 67 With the CM and K. Madhava Rao, PS to CM.

Plate 68 VRR with 'Senior' P. Ramchandra Reddy and colleagues Venkatram Reddy and Nagaseshiah.

Plate 69 VRR, chief guest at conference of Indian Lawyers Association; (L to R) Jwala, C. Padmanabha Reddy (President IAL).

Plate 70 VRR with Surya Rao (3rd from left), K. Raja Reddy, N. R. Devaraj and others at the conference.

PLATE 71 VRR with friends, Justice Parvatha Rao and P. Ramachandra Reddy (ex-speaker Legislative Assembly and minister).

PLATE 72 VRR speaking at the IAL Zonal conference in Vijayawada; on the dais, Karavadi Venkateswarlu (Ongole) and others.

Plate 73 CJ Obul Reddi Memorial Lecture delivered by Justice A. M. Ahmadi; (L to R) Prof. Ranbir Singh (Director NALSAR), VRR, Justice Jayachandra Reddy, Justice Devinder Gupta CJ AP, Justice A. M. Ahmadi (ex-CJI), P. Shivshankar (partly seen).

Plate 74 Pandit Govind Ballabh Pant Birth Centenary Seminar; on the dais (L to R) advocate K. J. Sethna, CJI R. S. Pathak, ex-President Shankar Dayal Sharma, VRR, former Union law minister V. Shankaranand.

Plate 75 VRR and members of BCI with guests of honour.

Plate 76 Jawaharlal Nehru birth centenary seminar at Jaipur; (L to R) N. K. Jain, CJI J. S. Verma, Justice E. S. Venkatramaiah, VRR, R. N. Bishnoi.

PLATE 77 VRR speaking at Commemorative Conference on 40 Years of The Advocates Act, 1961, organised by BAI at Goa in 2001.

PLATE 78 VRR, with Justice Lahoti lighting a lamp to inaugurate the All India Moot Court Competition held by University College of Law, Karnataka University, Dharwar, in 2001.

Plate 79 BCI Trust workshop on constitutional litigation at Shimla; (L to R) VRR, N. R. Madhava Menon, K. D. Sood, P. P. Rao and others.

Plate 80 VRR with Madhava Menon, Ramakrishna Hegde, Justice R. S. Pathak, at workshop organised by NLSIU and BCIT in Bangalore.

Plate 81 VRR receiving Justice Hidayatullah, Vice President of India, Ashoknath Banerjee, Governor of Karnataka and others at NLSIU's inaugural function.

Plate 82 At the inauguration of NLSIU on 25 February 1984, Justice Hidayatullah, CJI Y. V. Chandrachud, CJI Ramakrishna Hegde, Karnataka CM, CJ Malimath, Governor Banerjee, Ranjit Mahanti, BCI Chairman Ram Jethmalani, VRR and others.

PLATE 83 Justice Chandrachud and wife with Justice Malimath, Shetty, Upendra Baxi, Ranjit Mahanti, Rangaraj, Tippana, VRR and others.

PLATE 84 Justice Y. V. Chandrachud unveiling the foundation plaque.

Plate 85 Ram Jethmalani.

Plate 86 Justice Bharucha with CJI A. S. Anand and VRR.

PLATE 87 VRR and other members of the executive committee at the 2000 convocation.

PLATE 88 VRR at inaugural of Centre for Education and Training in Human Rights, with Justice Krishna Iyer, Michael Kirby (Australian judge), Puvaiyya, Prof. Madhava Menon and others.

Plate 89 VRR with law officer colleagues at the Supreme Court; standing (L to R) Ashok Desai AG, VRR, Andhyarujina SG; sitting (L to R) K. N. Bhatt, Usgaonkar, Altaf Ahmad.

Plate 90 Government staff of VRR when he was an ASG during Siddharth's wedding. Pandyan (attender), Vijay Kumar (PA), Khanna (PS), junior advocates Pragasam and Nageswar Reddy.

PLATE 91 With former president, S. D. Sharma.

his name, not that he asked for it, nor did I tell him. Many are such instances which, at the end of the day, give me a sense of fulfilment for having done my duty to the best of my ability without in any manner compromising integrity.

Work in the court was pretty much the usual. During the morning I had to be in the first court for admission work, writ appeals and bench writ petitions. Barring my occasional appearance in some important cases, I had made Ravinder Rao totally in charge of the 'Habeas Corpus' writ petitions. As I found from experience, delegation is normally the key for successful discharge of heavy responsibilities. Choose the right person and make him feel responsible for carrying out the work assigned to him.

When I took over office, there was this major litigation with significant political implications. Elections for managing committees of cooperative societies were not held for long after they became due, and in writ petitions filed concerning the matter, a Division Bench of Shivaraman Nair and M. N. Rao JJ. came down heavily against the government and directed that elections be held within the period fixed by them. Since the party in power was totally unprepared to face the cooperative society elections, not having done their homework at the grass-root level of enrolling members, the government wanted the judgement to be challenged and so the matter was carried to the Supreme Court, and on my advice, senior advocate K. Parasaran was engaged to represent the government. We managed to secure an extension of time for holding the elections more than once, and finally the Supreme Court fixed time peremptorily, and in view of the mandatory direction there was a danger of the government facing contempt action for noncompliance. But every time I went to the CM's office for a meeting, his ministers, including my lawyer friend D. K. Samarasimha Reddy, would strongly plead that more time be secured for holding the elections, as otherwise their party was likely to lose hold over many cooperative societies. In that situation, when I made it known that there was no room for any further extension, a meeting of all concerned was convened at the home office of the CM, and I was to attend the same.

The meeting was attended by the chief secretary, the secretaries of cooperative societies, law, the registrar of cooperative societies, besides some ministers. When the CM, NJR came in, I explained the seriousness of the situation. The CM said, with a sense of bravado, something to the effect: "What will happen if we cannot hold the elections within the time fixed—contempt action against the officers concerned. Why against them? It should be against me." Then, with all present pleading for restraint, he cooled down and after pondering briefly, came up with the proposal that the Cooperative Societies Act be amended by ordinance to provide for inclusion by nomination of two women members in the managing committee of every society. All present were taken by surprise by this brilliant though radical proposal and there was silence. The law secretary didn't react except to say that it would surely be challenged in court; the chief secretary said that if the advocate general thinks it can be legally sustained, it would be an eminently suitable solution for the problem. I then expressed my view that we may have an arguable case for defending the same on the ground of encouraging participation of more women members in the management. The meeting concluded; and the Act was amended through the proposed ordinance, which, as expected, was strongly challenged by the opposition parties who cried foul. Before the Bench, the petitioners strongly urged that if encouraging women members was the true object, it could be ensured by reservation of seats and not by nomination, which was patently opposed to the norms of democracy. A very valid argument indeed, which I successfully countered saying that given the social scene at the grass-root level, many women might be wary of going through the electoral process, and reservation cannot as such serve the purpose fully. So the government took the considered view to promote their participation through nomination, which seemed an appropriate process at least to start with. It clicked, and the petitions were dismissed.

Special leave petitions (SLPs) were filed in the Supreme Court, and when the matter came up before the Bench of Justice Khare, I was there on caveat, and the Bench ordered notice declining the stay pleaded for by the petitioners, making it clear that the notice was being issued only to decide the legal validity of the nomination process. Thus, the CM's brainwave saved the day for his party and government. It is a pity that a leader known for his administrative ability and sharp mind should lose office on account of adverse remarks by a Bench of the High Court of Andhra Pradesh while dealing with matters concerning grant of permission for establishment of private medical colleges in the state. By then I had demitted office as Advocate General and had moved to Delhi as ASG. It may be apt to record my experiences, belying the general perception of governmental pressures and interference. Well, I would imagine that such instances depend on the perception of the pliability of the law officer concerned.

23   Additional Solicitor General of India

Within a few months of my taking over as Advocate General, there were general elections to the Lok Sabha, during the course of which the tragic incident of Rajiv Gandhi's assassination occurred. The Congress Party romped home, their electoral prospects boosted immensely by the sympathy factor after the tragedy. P. V. Narasimha Rao, who was minister for external affairs in Rajiv Gandhi's cabinet, became prime minister and, in a surprise move, he made K. Vijayabhaskar Reddy (VBR) the minister for law and justice, assigning some other portfolio to H. R. Bharadwaj, who was earlier the minister for law. When VBR came to Hyderabad after he was sworn in, I called on him to greet and congratulate him. He made me stay on and, when I was alone with him, he told me that the PM and he had decided to appoint me Solicitor General (SG) of India. I was quite surprised and while expressing my gratitude for their kindness, made known my unease for leaving the post of Advocate General, which might not be to the liking of the CM here. He then said all that will be taken care of and that I should await formal intimation. VBR visited Hyderabad a couple of weeks later, when I was sent for and informed that some hitch had developed. He was obviously not happy with that development and so took pains to explain that earlier it was decided to have someone in place of G. Ramaswamy (GR), who was then the Attorney General for India, and myself as SG, and that later the PM told him they were to continue with GR for the remainder of his term as Attorney General. In view of that change in decision, the PM apparently expressed reservations about having me as SG as it might seem that both top law officers of the country were from the south. I suppose such thinking was bound to arise in the PM's mind since he was the first PM from the southern states, and much was being made of that in the media. Honestly speaking, this, in a way, came as a relief to me, and I told VBR that I was happy here in Hyderabad as Advocate General, and so he need not feel bad about the development.

Sometime later, when VBR came to Hyderabad, he came up with the idea of making me First Additional Solicitor General (ASG) of India. There was such a ranking at that time, with statutory recognition for it as well. Fali Nariman was the first one to be appointed ASG of India. When yet another had to be appointed ASG of India, Nariman came to be designated First ASG. Thus started the ranking of ASGs, and the Advocates Act also provided for the First ASG as an ex-officio member of the Bar Council of Delhi. In fact, I continued as ex-officio member of the Bar Council of Delhi even after the ranking system came to be dispensed with. I was in a quandary when this offer was made, and I had this occasion to visit Delhi and I called on senior advocate Santosh Hegde, a close friend and former ASG, to seek his advice. Santosh was pretty clear in his mind and he strongly advised me to take up the assignment if I had no issues in shifting to Delhi. I then gave my consent and I was appointed First ASG of India. I took charge on 18 August 1991 after resigning as Advocate General of Andhra Pradesh.

I went alone, since allotment of the official bungalow and staff would take time. When my appointment as First ASG became known, before I left for Delhi to take charge, I was overwhelmed by a call from Soli Sorabjee, by then amongst the top doyens of the bar, inviting me to join him at dinner on reaching Delhi, and I couldn't but admire Soli's warmth of heart. In fact, on account of my long stint with the BCI, many senior advocates and some judges in the Supreme Court had personally become known to me. While in Hyderabad, I had the honour of some chief justices of India visiting my home and accepting my hospitality while in office. I gratefully acknowledge the affection of the Hon'ble Justices E. S. Venkataramiah, Ranganatha Mishra, Ahmadi, and A. S. Anand who visited Hyderabad during his term as chairman of the National Human Rights Commission.

Appointment as ASG and the consequential shift to relocate ourselves in Delhi was fraught with some issues regarding management of our establishment in Hyderabad. Ever since the passing away of Nukala, Mother-in-law was living with us, and she moved with us to Somajiguda from the Hyderguda house. She preferred staying in Hyderabad, presumably to be with my son Siddharth, who had to continue in Hyderabad, being in the middle of his engineering course.

In Delhi, I chose the chambers for myself in the main building of the Supreme Court, two or three rooms away from the Attorney General's chambers. From the bungalows on offer for my residence, I chose AB15 on Mathura Road. AB14 was occupied by Altaf Ahmed, and K. T. S. Tulsi (KTS), who was also an ASG along with me, was in a bungalow on Purana Quila Road. Bungalow AB15—being in front of Pragati Maidan, and five minutes' walk to the Supreme Court—was very convenient for me. It took a couple of months for the premises to be refurbished, and by the year-end, Radha also moved there and we had settled down. We had taken Venkati, our junior cook from Hyderabad, and for the office I had two attendants, besides a PS and a PA assigned by the government; Mr Khanna, who had earlier worked with Parasaran, joined as PS, and Vijay Kumar was the PA.

The Central Agency, the nodal office for handling the administrative work of litigation involving the Government of India, had an excellent team of lawyer-officers, then headed by Subhashini, with Parameshwaran, Anil Katiyar and a few juniors like Prasad joining later. They kept track of the cases and had them allotted to the different law officers for appearance in court, and to the advocates in the panel to brief and assist. KTS and Altaf from the previous team were continuing, as was GR, the Attorney General. Though for the briefs from the Central Agency there was a briefing counsel from the panel, I had my own juniors as well to assist me. Narasimha continued to work with me and V. G. Pragasam, an advocate who had moved to Delhi after practicing for few years in Pondicherry, joined me as junior. While they were the mainstay, a couple of other young lawyers also used to work in my chambers.

Though initially the workload may have seemed heavy, particularly on the miscellaneous days i.e., Mondays and Fridays earmarked exclusively for miscellaneous work, in a couple of months the whole process got systematised. In the absence of a Solicitor General—which post remained unfilled for almost six months after I took over—I had to take on a considerable workload and deputise for the Attorney General in his absence, even on formal occasions like full court references. Besides the Central Agency briefs, counsel of state governments, public sector undertakings and corporations also used to engage us in important cases and, if I may say so, a substantial amount of our income would come from those engagements since we could charge them like private counsel for those briefs, while fees for the Central Agency briefs were pretty low. Unlike in the case of an advocate general in a high court, who couldn't accept a brief only if it was against the government, the rule for law officers of the Supreme Court was more stringent, in the sense that they were not permitted to accept any brief except those of the Central and state governments, or public sector undertakings and corporations. Only with special permission could one appear for anyone else. I had sought for such permission in only one case, which I was handling and was mid-way through.

Apart from the briefs for appearance in Supreme Court, we had engagements in various high courts as well. I used to have many such out-of-station briefs to represent various state electricity boards, coal corporations, etc. besides state governments, and would quite enjoy appearing in different high courts, particularly since the judges there would be most accommodating. I had appeared for the Central Bureau of Investigation (CBI) a few times in Patna High Court in the fodder scam cases involving Lalu Prasad Yadav. I clearly recall appearing before the Bench of former chief justice Markandey Katju while he was in the High Court in Chennai. His light-hearted comment, heard by my assisting counsel N.C. Ramesh, when I took out my pocket diary for suggesting the next date of hearing, was none too complimentary for the senior advocates practicing in Delhi. But then Justice Katju was known for speaking his mind. When I was trying to sustain a challenge to the high tariffs allegedly affecting the industrial sector, he sermonised, saying no one will respect your country unless you are economically strong and that the industrial sector should be allowed to flourish. I was one of those who appreciated his forthrightness while dealing with matters before him as a judge even while in the Supreme Court. Going back to his comment about senior advocates from Delhi having to check their diaries before suggesting the next date of hearing, Ramesh, being one who personifies the *satvik* nature, did not repeat the comment to me till we had left the court to avoid any possible retort from me—that was his nature.

Ramesh also engaged me and briefed me in a few matters, including a heavy international arbitration relating to disputes arising out of a power purchase agreement that his client Tamil Nadu State Electricity Board had entered into with Videocon for power from the proposed project close to Chennai. Justice Mohan, retired judge of the Supreme Court, and Justice Pendse, retired CJ of Karnataka High Court were nominees of the Board and Videocon respectively, while Mr Veeder QC from UK was the presiding arbitrator. Senior advocate P. Chidambaram was representing Videocon as senior counsel and the venue for arbitration was Singapore, though we had a couple of sittings in Hong Kong as well. Must say, I thoroughly enjoyed delving deep into technical aspects during the many conferences with Ramesh and the concerned functionaries of his client, particularly to prepare ourselves for examination and cross-examination of witnesses. This included the time spent in conferences at my holiday home in Coonoor during summer vacation. A long association with Ramesh, entailed by the two of us working closely together on several other cases, led to a lasting friendship, and I always look forward to spending time with him when I visit Chennai.

Besides the court work, we had to deal with piles of briefs referred for opinion. While some were issues referred for opinion as guidance to the decision makers, a major chunk used to be from the Central Agency for opinion about the fitness for filing SLPs in the Supreme Court against judgements of high courts and tribunals. One had to go through the judgement sought to be impugned and the comments thereon of the department, and tender an opinion regarding fitness of the case for seeking special leave to appeal in the Supreme Court. I used to be quite conservative and, unless it was a strong case with significant adverse impact, would never suggest carrying the matter further to the Supreme Court. There were cases where the time for approaching the Supreme Court had long passed and nevertheless the department sought filing of SLP with petition for condonation of delay. There were also cases with delay of years, and when we said it would be pointless to file SLP, the department would come back often highlighting the adverse impact of the impugned judgement and wanting the ASG to reconsider his opinion. Worse still were instances where the department would have the temerity to suggest that some senior advocate, considered effective by them, be engaged to argue the petition for condonation of delay. GR once mentioned to me this ridiculous trend, and I agreed with him and also conveyed to the concerned in the Law Ministry that seeking to engage private counsel, barring in exceptional cases, outside their panel of law officers, including the Attorney General, reflects a lack of confidence in the ability of their own law officers.

On the practice of obtaining a law officer's opinion for filing SLP in SC, I am reminded of the practice in the US, as narrated in the book, *The Tenth Justice*. The title reflects the status of the Solicitor General there, whose opinion not to carry a matter to the Supreme Court gives finality to the judgement under consideration, and in that sense the Solicitor General's opinion is considered akin to a Supreme Court judgement, and hence the title 'Tenth Justice'—as one in addition to the nine judges of the apex court. Alas, back home, the tendency of the concerned in the government to keep litigating till their view is accepted perhaps contributes significantly to the heavy filing of SLPs in the Supreme Court. The fact that almost 90 per cent of SLPs get dismissed at the threshold does not deter this mindless pursuit. To an extent, a trust deficit may also be an issue, for government functionaries are often wary of accepting an adverse decision until it ends with a seal of finality from the Supreme Court.

After some months of my appointment, the post of SG was filled with the appointment of Dipankar Prasad Gupta, senior advocate, and former Advocate General of West Bengal when Siddhartha Shankar Ray was the CM. It came as a great relief to me, the major takeaway being more free time during SC vacations, enabling me to spend time in Hyderabad. Dipankar, who sadly passed away recently, was eminently suited for the post with his experience and dignified persona. He and his wife Anjana Gupta, a very pleasant lady, were our family friends. A couple of months before his demise, his son, Jaydeep Gupta, who has done exceedingly well and made for himself a name at a young age as a competent Senior Advocate in the Supreme Court, brought his parents over to Hyderabad, and we were happy to spend time with them when they visited us. Dipankar was under medical care for heart ailment for some time, which in no way diminished his warmth. He passed away a couple of months later, yet another autumn leaf falling, saddening my heart.

Things got smoothened and I started enjoying the work, particularly the tight schedule—besides the stress on miscellaneous days—and it was like living the dream. Though to say that there used to be fifteen to twenty SLPs to be handled on a Monday or Friday might make it seem highly burdensome, but once you develop a system and procedure, it isn't a burden at all and instead becomes an exciting experience. Running from court to court used to be quite like a fielder running to save a boundary on the cricket field. Prioritising cases depending on their importance was also a factor. For billing, presence in court when the case is being disposed of was crucial, regardless of your contribution, though "Deemed Appearance" was a concept the ever witty GR had innovated. There was one Sunday when I was flying back to Delhi from Bangalore and I was informed by my office that next day my list was pretty long, with twenty-two SLPs to be handled. I instructed the office to request Narasimha to come to the airport with the list and, believe me, most of the briefing was over before we reached home, in the car. That is because a good many of them would normally be cases which had been dealt with earlier. Even otherwise, Pragasam used to note the core issue and pages to be referred to on the first page. That brings to mind the comment of Venkati, our cook. One day when a pile of briefs were delivered from the Central Agency late in the evening, and Radha was apparently annoyed, Venkati's smart comment was, "Ayya does not read the whole file. He only sees what Pragasam sir underlines", in effect saying, don't think that your dear husband does a great lot! Well, it might be something for a psychologist to unravel.

Social life made our stay in Delhi quite pleasant and enjoyable. Altaf and his devoted wife Nighat, our next-door neighbours, were like family and we often used to enjoy the delectable Kashmiri *wazwan* at their place. KTS would not miss out any special occasion to have friends over at his place, and he and his wife Suman were known for their superb hospitality. There used to be dinner meets often organised by senior advocate friends, notable amongst them being Fali Nariman, Soli Sorabjee, Tehmtan Andhyarujina, Anil Divan, Ashok Desai, P. P. Rao, K. K. Venugopal, M. L. Varma, G. L. Sanghi, Abhishek Singhvi, Joseph (Mohan) Vellapalli, and others. The list is too long to include all here. Radha used to have close relations with the ladies, which helped to keep contacts alive even after we left Delhi.

Besides friends from the legal fraternity, we had cousin Venu (Dr Y. V. Reddy), holding a key assignment in the Ministry of Finance, and his wife, Geetha, living there, and also some senior officers including those from the AP State cadre. They were: K. Padmanabhaiah, home secretary, P. Abraham, power secretary, Jayabharath Reddy,

G. P. Rao, M. Gopalakrishna, chairman REC (formerly Rural Electrification Corporation) Ltd., R. Rajamani, environment secretary, B. N. Ugandhar, PMO secretary, Dr Chakravarthi, K. Kosallram, Sujatha Rao et al. In the political circle, we had friends hailing from AP. R. Surender Reddy was there, who used to visit Delhi as MP and stayed close by on Purana Quila Road in our initial period of stay in Delhi. Then there was T. Subbirami Reddy, MP, who also had his bungalow close by. Subbirami was known to me for long and he would often insist that I was his lawyer. I represented him or his brother, the late T. Rajagopal Reddy when there was a commission of enquiry probing into issues relating to the 'Perubhatla Palem Deep Cut' contract in Hyderabad. Subbirami and his loving wife Indira were our family friends from the late sixties. Subbirami could wear many hats with ease and élan. He has been a promoter of art and culture for many years in Hyderabad. He is well known for his spiritual bent of mind. He is also a successful entrepreneur as civil contractor, hotelier, promoter of power projects, etc. Despite the incredible diversity of his activities and accomplishments, one common thread that is noticeable is his warm-hearted, cheerful and friendly disposition.

The other and most highly-regarded political leader we had for a friend was Jaipal Reddy, a cabinet minister held in high esteem. Jaipal, Mrs Reddy and his family were close to us. Before I completed penning this memoir, on 8 August 2019, to our utter shock we got the news of our dear friend Jaipal passing away. He was a great political leader who fought his way with commitment and courage of conviction and rose to great heights at the national level, defying his physical disability. He could garner admiration for his intellect from the intelligentsia and adulation from his constituents for his warmth of heart and egalitarian mindset. Fortunately, I could lay my hands on a copy of the letter I had addressed to him, when an article by Sachidananda Murthy rightly characterising him as 'The Gentleman Politician' was published in *The Week* in 2009, and I include below an extract from it, as my tribute to the leader.

> Dear Jaipal,
> I read an article with delightfully analytical arithmetic of the composition of the central cabinet, by Mr. Sachidananda Murthy in *'The Week'* dated June 14, 2009 under the caption:

"The gentleman politician". This at once brought to my mind the joke often repeated by lawyer baiters, of whom there has never been any dearth, which goes like this. This young man who was visiting his friend in the countryside, while strolling in the cemetery area, noticed what was engraved on a tombstone and asked his friend, "How come your people bury two in one grave while there is so much space available?" The local friend, who was baffled by the remark, went close to the tomb-stone and found the inscription: "Here lies the gentleman lawyer...".

Though belonging to that profession, I have no hesitation in yielding this reputation to politicians who seem to deserve it more. But then, after all, it takes an exception to prove the rule. Thank you for doing old-timer friends like me, who continue to value decency in public life, proud.

Yours sincerely
V. R. Reddy

In my very first year in Delhi as ASG, N. V. L. Nagaraju, secretary of the Delhi Telugu Academy, approached me to be president of the Academy. My friend G. V. G. Krishna Murthy had held that office previously and, after his term, presumably on his advice, I was approached. I was hesitant, saying I may not be able to spare time, but then they promised to hold the executive meetings at my place itself, if it made things easier for me. Naturally, I couldn't disappoint them. My association with the Academy was, however, short-lived; after just one executive meeting and annual function, I realised I may not be able to contribute much, and so I politely parted company. But I was quite impressed by Nagaraju's enthusiasm, and I think he has now made Hyderabad the base for the Telugu Academy's activities.

Overall, with such a pleasant life and tight work schedule, time passed briskly and smoothly, and my initial office term of three years was to end in August 1994. On the eve of that there was this unpleasant episode relating to the renewal of my term. On 14 August, Mr Agarwal, a senior officer in the Law Ministry who had taken over as head of the Central Agency, came to my chambers during lunch recess to inform me that he had instructions from his Ministry that, since my term as ASG was to end by 18 August, briefs were not to be marked to me from the 17th. He sounded terribly embarrassed to convey the same to me. I put him at ease saying that he should not feel bad about it since my juniors had private briefs ready for my appearance from the 18th. Then, H. R. Bharadwaj, one of the guests at dinner at our place that evening, mentioned while leaving that the file for my fresh term was with the PM's Office. The next day was Independence Day, and as was the practice, we had an invitation for the 'At Home' at Rashtrapati Bhavan, which Radha and I attended. Owing to unexpected showers, the venue was shifted from the lawns to the entrance hall indoors. Former president N. Sanjeeva Reddy, then visiting Delhi, was a special guest on the occasion. The President and the Prime Minister were seated in the lounge on the upper floor. We were keen to greet them and also meet Sanjeeva Reddy, so Radha and I went up to the upper floor and there we saw the President, PM Narasimha Rao and Sanjeeva Reddy seated together. We duly paid our respects to all three of them. The PM then asked me how my work was progressing. I responded saying it was going well and that my term was about to end. When he looked at me quizzically, I told him that according to my information, the file for my fresh term was pending in his office. He immediately called his PA Krishnamurthy, who was amongst the invitees, and told him to put up the file to him immediately and to "rush it". On 17 August, Mr Agarwal came to my chambers to sheepishly inform me that the notification for my renewed term was on its way. What I got to know later was that the proposal for my renewed term got linked up with the proposal for creating an additional post of ASG, and so it was stuck in the PM's Office. Needless to delve into whether it was an inadvertent occurrence or a deliberate attempt to delay orders for my fresh term. What was conveyed to me by Bharadwaj was without doubt suggestive of the latter.

Actually, I never considered my moving to Delhi as permanent. I retained my moorings firmly in Hyderabad, though profession-wise, Delhi became the base. While I was ASG, I never missed an opportunity to leave Delhi and spend time in Hyderabad, availing every vacation of the Supreme Court, and always intimating the Ministry well in advance that I would not be available in Delhi. I used to often combine Dussehra and Diwali vacations, bunking court for that week in the middle. Holi and other vacations were also made good use of. In Hyderabad, I used to spend time with old friends. Among the senior group, Panda Punnaiah, chairman of Navbharat

Ferro Alloys, and former judges like Justice O. Chinnappa Reddy and Justice Ramachandra Rao were close to me. They, together with Seetaramaiah (of Brahmaiah and Co.), Swaminatha Reddy, Surender Reddy and a few other senior citizens, used to have frequent dinner meets. Though the minimum age of the members of that group was seventy, and I had quite a few years still to get there, I had the privilege of being invited to join in. Even while I was in Delhi, Punnaiah, one of the most amiable and affectionate people I have known, used to check with me if I was going to be in Hyderabad on the day they were planning to have a get-together. The fact that I was counsel for the AP State Electricity Board—against whom Ferro Alloys had a major litigation regarding the power tariff—and my strongly fighting for the Board's cause did not sour our relationship even a wee bit. Those were the values the old-timers adhered to. In fact, it used to be fascinating for me to hear their experiences of earlier times in the erstwhile Madras State. One evening I was hosting the get-together at my place in Somajiguda for the group, and Punnaiah remembered that G. Ramaswamy, his close friend and former AG, was reaching Hyderabad that evening on a visit. I then asked Punnaiah to invite him over on my behalf, and the sight of the former Attorney General for India walking into my house is something etched in my memory. He was casually attired in a t-shirt and trousers, with chains dangling around his neck, but then that was GR for you.

Another close friend, who would always insist on taking me out for lunch during my visits to Hyderabad, is Vinod Poddar. Vinod, who never failed to see me whenever he visited Delhi during my stay there, is an affectionate friend with whom I spend quality time even now and have the most interesting conversations. Vinod, who hails from a reputed business family in Calcutta, is a keen follower of political developments in the country, particularly at the state level. This trait is perhaps traceable to the legacy of his illustrious father B. P. Poddar, who was a minister in the cabinet headed by Dr B. C. Roy in West Bengal. Though Vinod claims to have wound up all his business interests, having closed down operations of his factory in Hyderabad, he is incredibly busy travelling, and the manner in which he can reel off his itinerary, particularly upcoming trips to various places, is impressive. He is an interesting conversationalist and has a range of travel experiences to recount, including to Tibet and Lake Mansarovar in the north, and places down south right upto Kanya Kumari. I am fascinated by his keen interest in and his ideas for development of agriculture, organic farming and power sector.

That apart, I even continued to file my income tax returns in Hyderabad. Suryanarayana, finance manager in the office of the Bar Council of AP, used to attend to my accounts and filing of returns from the inception and he used to visit Delhi to finalise my accounts while I was there. It is amazing how impactful and lasting certain associations prove to be. Suryanarayana, in the years before his demise, involved his son Machi Raju in the bookkeeping exercise for me and my family, and Mr Raju, who passed the preliminary chartered accountancy exams and completed his law, continues to be associated with me even after my retirement. One significant takeaway from maintaining Hyderabad as my base was that I was the recipient of the Income Tax Department's 'Samman' for the financial year 1998–99, as the highest taxpayer in the segment, which may not have been possible if I were based in Delhi. Radha and I were visiting US that summer, and Raju called to say that the auditor would like me to be in Hyderabad to receive the Samman. I can recall my jocular response to Raju, saying that I don't want to show myself as the fool who paid such taxes. Anyhow, I left it to my auditor to receive it on my behalf.

Another relationship that extended beyond a generation is that of Shiva (Sambashivaiah), chauffeur-cum-personal attendant, who is counted on to handle diverse household chores, and is the third generation staff of a family that I have personally known. Shiva's father, Raghuramaiah (Raghu), who was my father's driver, now takes care of my interests in my ancestral village. I have elsewhere referred to Shiva joining our service as an attender in my Delhi office. Our chef Govind, from Nepal, started as a watchman looking after our Defence Colony property while it was being readied after we bought it, and later moved with us to Hyderabad. Yet another karmic relationship of sorts is with Manemma, whom Radha engaged as an ayah to look after Siddharth as a toddler. Manemma stayed on even after Siddharth grew up, and moved with us to Delhi. There she had a serious spinal problem, which persisted despite all the medical care provided; and so we shifted her to our Somajiguda house, making provision for her needs, and later admitted her into a private old-age home, where she has been for more than a decade now. Radha and Deepa get calls even if there is a problem with her personal TV. Well, one should consider oneself blessed to have these lasting relationships, and I believe it takes more of EQ than IQ to sustain them, which the mother and daughter Radha and Deepa seem to be endowed with in good measure.

During this period, Milon Banerji, who was appointed Attorney General after GR's term ended, was continuing in office, and one couldn't but admire his beautifully-crafted opinions and references in court. After his term, Ashok Desai took over as Attorney General for India and was continuing when Deve Gowda was sworn in the PM. It was indeed a great pleasure to have him as leader of our team. Ashok and his loving wife Suvarna have been our close family friends over the years. I remember sending my letter of resignation as ASG when there was a change in the political dispensation. Ashok had then called me over and expressed his keenness to have me continue as ASG, saying that the government was not averse to having some of the incumbent law officers continue. Tehmtan Andhyarujina was appointed the SG. Though I had no issue with that, I recall Ashok explaining to me that, Andhyarujina being senior to me in all respects, I should have no reservations on that score. Andhyarujina, who was based in Mumbai, was known for his expertise in constitutional law, especially with the kind of exposure he had working with H. M. Seervai, veteran jurist, former Advocate General of Maharashtra and author of the magnum opus *Constitutional Law of India*. Besides, Tehmtan was a great human being, down-to-earth, and a highly disciplined professional. We were good friends and held each other in high esteem.

When the Bharatiya Janata Party (BJP) came to power, with the universally respected statesman-politician A. B. Vajpayee as prime minister, I once again tendered my resignation and insisted on the same being accepted. Not that I had anything against the new dispensation; I thought it was only proper that having been appointed and worked for long when the Congress—in many ways the polar opposite of the BJP—was in office, I should quit and leave the new government to have its own team.

24 Independent Practice and Retirement

Thus started the new phase of my career as senior advocate, practicing in the Supreme Court. Logistically, the first step for transition was to acquire suitable premises for residence since the government bungalow had to be vacated. I had, in fact, started scouting for such property for some time even before my resignation, and with the help of P. S. Narasimha who, as family, had a good understanding of our needs and tastes, we pitched upon the property D-223 in Defence Colony, which was in the final stages of construction. Radha and I sought a few changes and had the interior and furnishings done with the help of Rajiv and Meena Mehta, a friendly couple running a firm for architecture and interior designing. My basic requirement, of having my office attached to the residence—with the lower ground floor made into an office area with enough room for my study, conference room, and workstations for juniors—was deftly met with and executed by them. A set of *All England Reports* from inception and *Halsbury's Laws of England* were procured and, to make room, *All India Reporter* reports of high court cases were weeded out and sent to Hyderabad. C. Kannan, referred by someone I cannot remember, came to see me to offer his services as secretary. I do, however, recall him pompously saying that he hailed from Kanjeevaram, the native place of C. N. Annadurai, first Chief Minister of Tamil Nadu, and I engaged him as my secretary. It didn't take him long to learn his ropes and become manager of my office. He rendered excellent service, with integrity and commitment for almost fifteen years, till I quit practice and moved back to Hyderabad. He is now an advocate practicing in Delhi, and the bond developed continues. V. G. Pragasam continued working with me, while Narasimha used to have his desk in my office to meet his clients and take care of his work. When needed, he would also lend me his assistance, but Narasimha was more like family with whom I could open up my heart and seek advice.

Sunil Murarka, who was a junior along with V. Kameshwar Rao under Justice Arjan Kumar Sikri before he was elevated to the Bench, joined me as junior, and so did Sakya Singha Chowdhary (SSC). Sakya used to assist me in electricity-related work besides some arbitrations. Since by then the New Electricity Act had come into force, he used to assist me during my appearances before the Central Tribunal also. It is heartening to see Sakya attain recognition as an expert counsel for power-related litigation. Another lawyer who worked with me as junior for a short period and made significant progress in his career is Vikramjit Banerji, a sharp and ebullient lawyer who, after a brief stint in my office, moved on to practice in Calcutta and was appointed advocate general of one of the North-East States. He later shifted back to Delhi to practice in the Supreme Court and is presently Additional Solicitor General, Supreme Court—yet another junior of mine to hold the post of ASG, which I once had the honour of holding, doing me immensely proud.

I also had three lady juniors: Sara Khan from Karnataka; Shruthi Devi, daughter of V. Kishore Chandra Deo, MP from AP; and Altaf Fatima, a graduate from the National Academy of Legal Studies and Research (NALSAR) in Hyderabad, who continued in Delhi even after I moved back to Hyderabad, working with Bharati Reddy, standing counsel in SC for AP, and her husband Ramakrishna Reddy. Bharati practiced in the AP High Court and moved to Delhi to practice in the Supreme Court, where she did well to be recognised for her competence. Fatima now practices in Hyderabad along with her lawyer husband Mr Bose, commanding substantial corporate litigation work. Menaka Guruswamy, daughter of Mohan and Meera, first cousin of Radha, used to breeze in and out of my office as a busy junior of Ashok Desai, with her own clientele and work even in the early years of her practice. Menaka had graduated from NLSIU, Bangalore, and kept her word to me that she will get the medal for best student advocate—an award I had instituted. As a Rhodes Scholar at Oxford University, she was awarded D. Phil. and won a Gammon Fellowship for Masters in Law at Harvard Law School. A professor of constitutional law at Columbia University, US, and visiting faculty at Yale Law School, Menaka had the distinction of being designated a senior advocate by the Supreme Court at a young age, making an exception to the norm of forty-five as the minimum age. Menaka has played a pivotal role in several landmark cases, and was on the April 2019 list of *Time* magazine's '100 Most Influential People'. I would say she is a work in progress, with many more academic and professional laurels expected in times to come.

Speaking of moot court competitions—success in which leads to award of the best student advocate medal—I am reminded of the first all-India moot court competition, conducted by the BCI Trust while I was its managing trustee, in Hyderabad, in which second-year students of NLS had participated. I was overjoyed when M. G. Poojitha and D. Sundari from NLS won, and I had occasion to meet Poojitha and Nandan Nelvigi during my visit to the US. Nandan, who was with White & Case, New York, set up a meeting with the chairman of the firm, who was keen to understand prospects of American law firms being able to operate in India. I had the pleasure of making the acquaintance of young students of the initial batches of NLS, including Dayan Krishan, Nikhil Nayyar, Sajjan Poovayya, and closer home, D. Sundari and Bindu Mohana.

About that time, two young lawyers from AP evinced interest in joining my office as juniors. They had put in a few years in Delhi, and I thought it best that they carry on and build up their practice and so advised them accordingly. One of them, G. Nageshwar Reddy (GNR), nevertheless used to often spend time in my office and discuss his cases with me, and I in turn used to follow his progress in the profession with keen interest. GNR did well for himself, working with commitment and competence, and was appointed standing counsel for AP and some state corporations sometime after I left Delhi. Mercifully he has developed an Eklavya sentiment towards me, which I heartily reciprocate. The other young man, Palvai Venkat Reddy, who took to the parallel course of attracting private clientele, has also done well for himself and we continue to be in close touch.

A couple of years after I started practice as private counsel, I received a letter from Krishnayan Sen, who had graduated from National University of Juridical Sciences (NUJS), Calcutta, introducing himself and enclosing some of his articles published in law journals of repute. He expressed his keenness to join my office as a junior. His parents, Udayan Sen and Nandita Sen as lawyers ran a reputed law firm in Calcutta. Frankly, even now I remain fuzzy about how and why Krishnayan decided to work with me. He had not interned with me nor were there any significant dealings of his family firm with me. Whatever it may be, our association developed into a '*guru–shishya*' relationship of the '*gurukula*' tradition. His devotion and hard work were highly impressive and over a period I started counting on him to assist me on heavy briefs and major arbitrations. One day, I noticed the attender carrying tea to the office much before the normal office time of 8.30 a.m. I was told that it was for Krishnayan, and when I wondered why he came in so early, I was told that he hadn't gone home the whole night. It is his persistent efforts that have resulted in my penning this memoir, as acknowledged in the Preface.

While remembering the juniors who have worked with me, it may be apt to also remember the one that got away—Rajshekhar Rao, a product of NLS, whom I was keen to have in my office, but by the time I made my intention known, he had already committed to and joined some other senior.

Besides the juniors, I have fond memories of some budding lawyers who interned in my office for brief periods as students of law schools. While I was ASG, I had two such young men from NLS Bangalore who were sent by the university to my office as interns. It is indeed gratifying to see that both have done exceedingly well in their careers. One of them, Sashikiran Shetty, was designated senior advocate in the High Court of Karnataka at a relatively young age. The other, Mr Srikar, on completing his law course in NLSIU, was selected for the IAS with a high rank and assigned to his home state of Karnataka, where he is now a highly-regarded senior officer.

Notable amongst the others was Shubhankar Dam, a student of NUJS Calcutta. In the few days that he was with me, his remarkable research skills did not go unnoticed. When there was a ruckus in Parliament on Sonia Gandhi supposedly chewing gum in the House, I wanted him to dig out some material on chewing gum and norms of chewing habits while attending Parliament. He produced relevant material, based on which I wrote an article, 'Chewing Gum and Spewing Venom', which was published in *The Hindu* on 14 May 2002. Shubhankar was a soft-spoken and quiet sort of guy, and having noticed his passion for research and his analytical mind, I sent a letter of commendation to the director of his law school when he completed his internship with me. Shubhankar went on to become an accomplished academic, taught constitutional law at universities in Singapore, Hong Kong and USA, and is now a professor of public law and governance at the University of Portsmouth, UK, along with stints as a visiting professor in prestigious universities in the US. He has authored a book titled *Presidential Legislation in India: The Law and Practice of Ordinances*, and regularly writes on issues pertaining to law and governance in India in leading English dailies and magazines. Association with such bright young persons while in practice as senior advocate is indeed intellectually stimulating.

I may have appeared in cases covering diverse fields including service jurisprudence, capitation fee, the Terrorist and Disruptive Activities (Prevention) Act (TADA), human rights, besides many relating to the power sector. The cases I used to passionately involve myself in were PILs concerning vehicular pollution, environmental degradation, the Bhopal Gas tragedy, and the Drugs and Cosmetics Act. Appearing in these matters was indeed an enlightening experience. On vehicular pollution, the technological difference between single-stroke engines and others; the reduction in environmental pollution by switching to compressed natural gas (CNG) fuel; the logistical issues of making CNG available on the highways and the feasibility of switching to propane gas; the adherence by vehicle manufacturers to the permissible levels of emission; best practices to be followed by oil refineries, etc.—all these were matters in which, once assigned to me, I had to ensure my presence whenever they came up, week after week, often giving up appearances in highly lucrative briefs of corporations and states.

Justice J. S. Verma, as presiding judge of the Bench, used to bestow serious thought and attention in dealing with environment-related matters such as deforestation, ecological and vehicular pollution. I can recall the overbearing activism of the Bench presided over by Justice Kuldeep Singh while dealing with oil refineries. In these matters, to ensure proper assistance to the court in the unlikely event of my absence, I used to insist upon having senior advocate Dinesh Kumar Goswami—a fine person who, along with his wife, practiced after retiring as a judge of the Delhi High Court.

In matters relating to relief for victims of the Bhopal Gas tragedy, I have represented the Union of India as well as the concerned officers of the Madhya Pradesh government. Wasim Quadri, a hardworking panel counsel, used to assist me in all those matters. There was this interesting episode of the former Solicitor General of UK claiming to be a trustee of the trust created by Union Carbide under court orders. Sir Ian Percival took the trouble to visit me in my chambers to explain his stand, which made no difference to my view that, though the creation of a trust for the specified purposes was ordered by the court, the appointment of trustees to manage its affairs was entirely within the province of the Union of India. Not pleased by my firm stand, he had supposedly complained about my opposition to his claim of being a validly-appointed trustee.

One of my reasons for calling it a day in Delhi and moving back to Hyderabad was the sought-after prospect of being able to spend time with the two grandchildren, Shloka and Abhinav. But then, by the time we came here, they were almost in their teens, with busy schedules of their own. Besides school, Shloka used to practice dance and Abhinav was busy with his tennis, and the two together would attend classical music classes a few evenings of the week. I often used to taunt them, telling people that we need to take an appointment to spend time with them. Time has passed so fast that they are now poised to complete their schooling and join college. Radha and I are happy about our decision to move back to Hyderabad, quitting my practice as senior advocate. Learning about former colleagues going strong as practitioners might engender mild disappointment. Yes, initially it is something to be expected, particularly in the mornings when you no longer need to hurriedly get ready and plan the work schedule for the day. I may have suffered the least on that score since I started planning my retirement from 2007 itself, though I gave effect to the decision only in 2010. While spending time during Christmas and New Year with Siddharth's family in Hong Kong, I had this inspiration to put down my decision poetically in Telugu on the morning of 1 January 2007:

సంవత్సరాల పరుగులో సంబరాల మెరుగులో
మనోతృవికమను సురతములు మూటకట్టి
మానవ కళ్యాణమునకు నడుము కట్టి
ఈ ఆశయం ఇది నూతన సంవత్సరాయానమా?
వేచి చూడండి వేసవివరకు.

Roughly translated, it means: "As the years race along, with celebrations glittering, it is time now to wind up the legal legacy of Manu, and contribute to people's welfare. Is it a New Year resolution? Wait and see till summer". Having thus made a commitment to myself, packing up from Delhi was just a matter of time.

As I was mulling this thought of quitting practice, there was this incident of my office getting inundated with storm water. That was the time when preparations were being made to develop infrastructure for the Commonwealth Games. Leaving aside the allegations of scam in the media, I was a victim of mindless planning. To create parking space for vehicles, the major sewage-pipe or *nala* behind my house in Defence Colony was blocked, and one day when there was a heavy downpour, the storm water couldn't get drained through the sewage-pipe, resulting in water flowing into my office, ruining furniture and, more importantly, hundreds of books on the shelves. We had to engage electric pumps to bail out water from the premises and it took weeks to retrieve at least part of the library, drying the volumes in the sunlight on the terrace. Narasimha was incharge of the operations, along with other juniors and staff in the office.

My decision to quit was made irreversible by my progressive impairment of vision. Since there was a family history of glaucoma known to Dr Gangadhar Reddy (who had treated my mother), he advised a proper check-up, which I got done by ophthalmologists in Delhi, and was using medicated eye drops. Meanwhile, cataract had developed in both eyes and I decided to have it attended to while in Hyderabad on vacation. I had the surgery done on one eye in October 2008, which unfortunately got botched, leading to loss of vision. I then went to L. V. Prasad Eye Institute (LVPEI), the globally reputed eye care institute in Hyderabad, and though specialists are normally wary of taking up cases which have been messed up elsewhere, they were kind enough to help me. Dr Raja Narayanan, consultant ophthalmologist, trained in Harvard and Yale (a qualification which would amaze anyone, and more so, a lawyer), conducted a corrective procedure, which helped to some extent. Responding to my son Siddharth's anxious enquiry, he said: "Your father has central vision of 80 per cent, but in the end percentages have no meaning. What is more important is that your father has to get back on track to lead a normal life, which we have more or less achieved now." What a morale booster! Since then, I have been under the constant care of Dr G. Chandrasekhar, Vice Chair, Consultant, VST Centre for Glaucoma Care at LVPEI, and visiting professor of various reputed universities in the US. Though my other eye needed cataract surgery, he said, "What is the urgency while you are able to carry on?" One day, after a regular examination, I tried witty banter to make him depart from the overly cautious approach, saying, "Doc, whatever may be the issues affecting my vision, my golf seems to have improved". He naturally asked, "How so?" I cheekily told him that every ball I hit was going out of sight. Sharp as always, he promptly replied, "Oh! That's good! What really matters is that you are able to connect the ball". What a profound statement, with philosophical underpinnings! I had no choice then but to give up and carry on with my hazy vision.

Hazy or otherwise, I had vision, for which I am beholden to the doctors of LVPEI, who treated me with deep concern and care. If I were to confer an award, it would be the *Drishti Data* Award. That said, I will be failing in my duty if I do not acknowledge with gratitude the stupendous initiative of Dr Gullapalli V. Rao, Founder Chair, in creating an institute of high global standards for eye care and providing a magnificent platform for renowned experts in the field to render service and conduct research. Yet another institute in the field of specialised medical care that brought fame to Hyderabad is the Asian Institute of Gastroenterology (AIG) Hospital, India's foremost gastroenterology hospital, established by Dr D. Nageshwar Reddy, Chairman and MD. I had known Dr Nageshwar for some years. While practicing in Delhi, I consulted him on my visits to Hyderabad for gastric problems like acidity, flatulence, etc. I would have an appointment to see him at his clinic but more often than not, it would be in the late evening; sometimes it would materialise close to midnight. Even at that late hour, after a whole day's hectic schedule, I would be amazed to find him most equanimous and pleasant, as if I were his first patient of the day. No wonder he was able create an institution like AIG Hospitals. Radha and I always enjoyed friendly relations with Nageshwar, his accomplished wife Dr Carol Ann Reddy, and other family members. I had, in fact, known his father Dr Bhaskar Reddy, and am immensely happy and proud of Nageshwar's stupendous contribution and success.

While at it, I am reminded of another renowned expert in a related area of medical science. Dr K. Rajender Reddy is Director, Hepatology, at the Penn Medicine, University of Pennsylvania, Ruimy

Family President's Distinguished Professor of Medicine, author of many treatises and reference books on the subject, and the recipient of several awards. I had the pleasure of spending time with him during my visit to the US in September 2019, and found him to be a down-to-earth, warm-hearted Indian who loves his country and its legacy immensely. I was fascinated to learn that during his brief visits to India, he tries to visit as many ancient monuments in the country as possible. For someone like Rajender, it is the due recognition of his accomplishments in his own country that would please more than all the awards and honours earned elsewhere, and hopefully, it might not be long before that happens.

The inevitable problem faced in carrying on with hazy vision was compounded by the hearing impairment I developed. Though not severe, it caused difficulty in court halls and while in a group. On the advice of my long-time friend and ENT consultant Dr T. V. Krishna Rao, I had tests done by a reputed audiologist, Rajinder Tickoo, in Hyderabad, who advised using a hearing aid. I was wary of doing so, especially as I had noticed that a lot of people develop this problem in their late fifties but ignore it, following their own ways to carry on, like lip-reading or simply asking people to repeat what was said. When I visited the main dealer of the imported brand of hearing aid then popular in India, what I saw made me change my mind. There, on their pinboard, I saw a copy of a picture of the then PM and defence minister, both using hearing aids. Though these devices cannot give back our God-given hearing ability, they can certainly make life more comfortable.

While I would joke with friends that there is a glitch with my *son et lumiere* (sound and light) system, the impairment of two vital faculties, however, made me serious about quitting practice. I, therefore, put forth my keenness to swiftly implement my decision to Narasimha, who forthrightly said: "Yes Sir, I agree with you, since I wouldn't like anyone to point fingers at us." Thus, I was indeed fortunate to have had a junior who was a true well-wisher, who was with me when I forayed into practice in the Supreme Court, arguing my briefs myself, and who was also with me to bid an affectionate farewell for a happy retirement when I was to leave Delhi for Hyderabad. It was always a matter of immense gratification for me to see Narasimha rise in the profession and come to occupy the position of Additional Solicitor General of India with distinction and dignity. Not to say that I am unduly enamoured of high and coveted positions as much as the value I attach to the respect one commands amongst one's peers. I was disappointed when Narasimha was disinclined to consider the offer of judgeship to High Court, for which I thought he was temperamentally well-suited.

When we moved back to Hyderabad, Radha thought that it would be better for us to stay in the Stone Valley Apartments than in our marital home in Somajiguda, and so we plonked ourselves here in Stone Valley Apartments, a well-maintained gated community, leasing out our Somajiguda house. Living in the Banjara Hills area makes it convenient for us to visit Deepa and Shyam's place in Jubilee Hills, and equally for them to see us every now and then. It didn't take too long for life to fit into the new routine, with considerable time spent at the desk, reading newspapers, journals and fiction as substitutes for briefs, and a spot of TV-watching for sports and news channels after lunch and dinner. Thus, life was good, generally speaking. And then came this activity of doing up the villa we bought in a vast gated community known as 'Banyan Tree Retreat' (BTR) developed by MAK Projects. Though it was more a tax-planning measure, it turned out to be an excellent decision. It is a beautiful and quiet place, with a few retiree friends living nearby. More importantly, it has a small nine-hole golf course, a mini-course really, enough to provide sufficient exercise and engrossing sporting activity for me, while Radha keeps herself busy with gardening, which she normally enjoys most while in Coonoor.

Speaking about Coonoor, sometimes taking snap decisions without too much mulling over prove to be most positive and beneficial. For some years from the mid-seventies onwards, we used to spend some time during summer in Ootacamund (Ooty), in the Nilgiris. Our stay mostly used to be at a club there or at Surender's house in Ooty. During one such visit, Narasanna, Nukala Narasimha Reddy, Radha's relative, took me along with Surender to show some lands he had bought to develop into plots, and one such was the land in Pemberley Estate, close to Wellington, almost a part of it, in Coonoor. One look at the captivating greenery of the valley and beyond, and I instantly decided to buy a plot there; and Surender, not being disinclined to buy the neighbouring plot for himself, made me firm up my decision; thus I became owner of a plot for housing.

Without losing much time, I proceeded to build a house, with Vikram Devraj as the architect and Kaiwan Patel, a reputed developer in that area, undertaking the construction work alongside many other such constructions his company was carrying out in the area. The house got ready in a year, and we had the gruhapravesam puja in 2001.

We used to fly to Coimbatore from Delhi and drive up to our house to spend time for a few weeks about twice a year—once during the summer months, and once during what is known as the second season in August–September, before the North-East Monsoon sets in. The location of our house being practically in Wellington, the area is maintained with the typical precision of army establishments. Really speaking, more than the salubrious weather and scenic beauty, it is the opportunity to spend time with new friends and acquaintances which makes short stays either in Coonoor or in our villa at BTR refreshing. In Coonoor, we have our dear friends the Sebastins and the Sreedharans. We always spend a few evenings together with General Sebastin and his gracious wife, Thamkam Sebastin. Radha and I once visited them at their estate in Kottayam district of Kerala. They have a beautiful house there and the estate is a plantation of rubber, pepper and other commercial crops. Apparently, some of the trees were planted during the General's grandfather's time, and General Sebastin, who has a fascination for agriculture and particularly floriculture, had developed the estate with great interest.

The family closest to us in Coonoor, from the time that we bought land there, is that of Sreekumar. Sreekumar's father, Mr Sreedharan, is a noted criminal lawyer in the Nilgiris. Sreekumar and his wife Nandita are also lawyers, and it is an acknowledged fact that practically every major real estate transaction in the area goes through their office, with one of the parties to the transaction seeking their advice. My acquaintance with them goes back to the time when I had just acquired a plot of land and was seeking to start construction of a holiday home, while practicing as a senior advocate in Delhi. There was this young man, Anup Nair, who joined my office as a junior in Delhi. Anup's parents, P. S. Nair and Indira Nair, were advocates practicing in Jabalpur. P. S. Nair, who handled substantial litigations for various coal corporations, used to engage me as senior counsel for his cases in Supreme Court and also for some of his matters in Jabalpur. When Anup got enrolled, Nair made him join my office as a junior. Anup, who learnt that I was planning to build a vacation home in Coonoor, told me that his cousin Nandita, a lawyer herself, was married into a lawyer family in Coonoor and wanted me to contact her husband Srikumar. I thus got acquainted with Srikumar, and our connection bloomed into a close friendship of families. Srikumar is the one we go to for any help while we are in Coonoor.

There are, of course, some cousins and close friends from Hyderabad who also have their vacation homes in Coonoor, like Jagdish, Santosh, Ram, Ramana et al. in Tiger Hills and Woodsborough. Special mention has to be made of my hostel-mate while in Loyola College, Madras, Homi Dhunjibhoy, whom I got to meet after five decades during one of my initial visits to Coonoor. Homi was with the Tea Plantations after college and, after retirement, he settled in Coonoor, living in Tiger Hills Cottages along with his wife Khorshid, who hails from Hyderabad. Must say, Homi has successfully retained his sense of humour all these years, and we have a fun time together during our stay in Coonoor. The real icing on the cake is Surender being my immediate neighbour, and if he is there during our stay, not a day passes without us spending time together. The other neighbour is B. S. Reddy (BS), father of Dr Rajnesh, a reputed gastro surgeon in Apollo Hospital, Hyderabad; while in Coonoor, BS has an open house for friends like me who are interested in a game of cards in the evening. A short walk from home, we have the Ayurveda Retreat run by Kantilal Chordia and his wife. Thus, life at the 'Pine Cliff', our house in Coonoor, is pleasant and refreshing, particularly with a short round of golf in the mornings at the Wellington Club thrown in. Lately we also have senior advocate Mohan Vellapally spending time in his house in Coonoor, shuttling between Cochin, Bangalore and Coonoor.

Another instance of old acquaintance almost faded in memory blooming into close friendship is Sobha Koshy. Sobha and Ashok Koshy were our guests once at a dinner along with the Sebastins and few other friends; when I introduced myself, Sobha smilingly said, "Sir, I had visited your office and had meetings with you while you were ASG in Delhi." Sobha was Secretary, Health Ministry, and had briefed me in some matters of her Ministry that I was handling. She and Ashok, also a senior IAS officer, have retired and now live in their bungalow in Coonoor. A wonderful couple that we love to spend time with.

Besides enjoying good times with friends residing in Coonoor, Ooty and Coonoor being popular hill stations, especially during summer, we often have friends dropping by to spend time with us. One such notable visit was by Rammohan Rao, former governor of Tamil Nadu. I had known Rao while he was a highly-regarded senior police officer in AP and in the Intelligence Bureau at Delhi. While he was on a summer sojourn at Ooty in the Raj Bhavan as governor, I invited him over to visit us sometime. Known for his amiable and down-to-earth disposition regardless of the office he held, Rao made time to visit us with his wife and son, and have tea with us. Needless to say that such a gesture would undoubtedly make the bond of friendship stronger. Similar was a visit by Justice Satish Agnihotri, with his wife, while he was the acting chief justice of the High Court of Tamil Nadu. Amongst senior advocate friends, P. P. Rao, who used to spend summer vacations in Ooty, would without fail accept our invitation to join us for lunch or dinner. My ebullient friend senior advocate Anup Chowdhary would drop in, along with Vikramjit Sen and Mukul Mudgal, after a game of golf at the Wellington Club. Senior advocate Gopakumar Nair, my friend from the time of his association with the Kerala State Bar Council, has also visited me and we have fondly reminisced about the old times. It is quality time that we spend with friends when we get to meet in such a relaxed holiday atmosphere. All my juniors have standing invitations to join us for a holiday in the cool climes of Coonoor during their court vacation, and some of them have.

At our villa in BTR, which is like a country home, I have a good physical fitness schedule, with Bhupal (Bhupal Reddy) ensuring that I don't miss out on my morning walk, and friends, Jagan (Dr Jaganmohan Reddy), Damodhar (Damodhar Reddy), playing golf with me, a short round really, enough to qualify us for sipping some fancied beverage together on some evenings. Most of the villa owners at BTR spend time there infrequently, using their villas as vacation or weekend homes like us. We are however fortunate in having, on our three sides, Bhupal, Vijayabhaskar, who has retired from Agricultural University and Osmania University, and Mahender Reddy, Senior

Police Officer who retired as IG Prisons, who reside there on a regular basis. I also get to spend quality time with Innayat, though he lives a little further away from us, sharing our liberal views based on our varied experiences in life.

I visit Rajampet and our village Seetharamapuram on and off, though such visits have become infrequent when compared to what they used to be while we were in Delhi. It is always a happy feeling to meet people whom I had known from my younger days.

In the village I have made my two-storied ancestral home available for running the government school. There was this close friend of mine from my college days, a lawyer, K. Rama Raju who was the president of Rajampet Mandal Parishad. He was known for his sincerity in public life. His being at the helm of affairs was an inducement for me to let the school function in my building. I had noticed that in the absence of a proper school in the village, children were being sent to private schools in Rajampet, hiring auto rickshaws. Besides the cost involved for the parents, it was a great strain for the children. When the school was not getting many admissions, on one of my visits, I promised the teachers—who were most enthusiastic—every assistance from my side to help them attract the villagers to admit their children in the school. They wanted a computer, which I immediately arranged. Such encouragement made the headmaster and teachers issue a pamphlet advertising the facilities available in the government school, and even meet the parents to explain to them the benefits of utilising the school in the village instead of sending their children to the town at great cost. The school is functioning, though the strength has not improved over the years. Recently I organised some proper benches and desks for the students. Inspired by my initiative, some enthusiastic young men of the village organised uniforms and photo identity cards for the children, and evinced interest in taking steps to make the school popular in the villages around. One thing still lacking is a trained teacher for spoken English, and I have noticed it is this facility which makes the private schools charging high fees attract students. I haven't given up on all this since I strongly believe that the focus should be on primary education, and a well-run government school will provide an immeasurable impetus to poor villagers to educate their children. There are many ways of encouraging public participation in this endeavour, which hopefully governments in the states and at the Centre will focus on and formulate schemes.

After the *Badi* (school), the other area that I wish to make a contribution to in terms of time and effort is the *Gudi* (shrine). While in Delhi, I had a temple in Hatyarala renovated. Hatyarala is a place few kilometres away from Rajampet, on the road to Penagaluru, on the banks of Cheyyeru river. There is a Shiva temple, and a *tiranala* (fair) is held there for three days during Maha Shivaratri. There is also an ancient temple of Parasurama, which the Archaeological Survey of India had renovated recently. In that cluster, there is a temple of Gadadhara Swamy (Vishnu), with which our family ancestors have been associated. The temple needed extensive repairs, and Father would often think of getting it done, but sadly he passed away before he could do so. So I had the temple renovated and had the *punah prathishta* (reinstallation) of the deity on 10–13 February 2005 with all the requisite pujas. It is learnt that there is a temple of that deity in Gaya, Bihar, where devotees go to perform obsequies for their ancestors. Since in the south this was the only such temple, the place was apparently referred to as 'Dakshina Gaya' (Gaya of the South). In the recent past, however, the temple seems to have lost its special significance for want of publicity. I am now in the process of organising a temple to Lord Shri Ram near my house in the village which, though bearing the name Seetharamapuram, has no temple dedicated to Sita and Ram. The small one we had next to our house had become dysfunctional over the years.

So presently I visit the village to oversee the Badi and Gudi, besides the small mango garden I maintain for old times' sake. I suppose that is enough activity to keep me occupied during my short trips to Rajampet, essentially to keep in touch with the villagers and friends in the town. This brings to mind the thought that philanthropy is the age-old tradition of our society, more particularly if it is directed to one's own native place. The problem is one of credibility. One doesn't know whom to trust to utilise the money donated for the chosen cause. If only governments could evolve schemes to invite contributions for promoting education and health in rural areas, providing a sense of involvement to the donor, a flood of donations can be expected to flow in from NRIs, besides those in the country.

I seem to have painted a rather rosy picture of post-retirement life. But then, it is a factual account, which will, I hope, infuse confidence in the minds of lawyers and judges that when, after long years of practice, they do finally choose to retire, life can be most pleasant and enjoyable—*if* one has the appropriate mindset for it. It is said that if you do not seek power, fame or notoriety, the allure of peaceful retirement is irresistible. I am tempted to add lucre as well to the list. I believe that after decades of active, successful practice, when you do decide to hang up your robes, a sense of fulfilment helps you enjoy your retirement peacefully, shorn of all the stress and anxiety associated with professional responsibilities.

Many might find it difficult to cross that line, unmindful of the fact that lawyers also have a 'Best Before' date. Fortunate are those who are unaffected by aging, which in most cases is known to cause at least impairment of vision or hearing, if not any other serious disability. For most, the desire to stay active and relevant to society seems to outweigh the allure of peaceful retirement. It is really a matter of individual choice. Here, I am primarily addressing only those who are deeply apprehensive of the very prospect of retirement from practice as a lawyer.

There are books authored by specialists offering tips for a happy retirement. When I started toying with the idea of quitting work, I too had in fact bought one, by an American author, which wasn't much use since, with the typical American mindset of a retiree, he had focused more on financial security. One important piece of advice I can, however, recall is that for planning retirement, one should not try to arrive at the amount of money to be saved as retirement funds to meet one's requirements as a retiree, since that figure will progressively increase with the passage of time, a concomitant upward movement of lifestyle, and inflation. Instead, he suggests that endeavour should be to figure out how little one can make do with—excellent advice indeed. What is needed, really, is the mindset to make saving a habit to create at least a modest retirement fund, and the determination to do so. These days there are many schemes on offer to help one in this regard. It is heartening to see some state governments also taking initiatives in this regard. More has to be done by governments, both at the state and Centre levels. Bar Councils and Bar Associations, too, should seriously explore the possibility of group insurance and pension schemes.

The other important consideration that troubles decision-making relating to retirement is one's ability to overcome the apprehended boredom. Here again, the sooner one starts preparing for it the better. This is, if at all, something faced by persons regardless of the profession or career pursued. The clamour among government officers to push back the retirement date as much as possible and the attendant controversies relating to date of birth are too well known. So is the clamour for post-retirement assignments noticeable even among members of the judiciary. It is really a matter of developing an appropriate mindset and preparing oneself to make the best of the inevitable—retirement. The much-touted advice, to develop a hobby, may not be feasible for all. Reading books beyond the field of law is intellectually invigorating for a lawyer, besides being an absorbing activity. Enjoying music is also something I would strongly recommend. I have known several retirees and others spending time attending cultural events with great interest. Notable amongst them are Umapathy Rao and Anjaneya Reddy who retired as senior officers in the IAS and IPS respectively. Umapathy, who sadly passed away recently, used to attend without fail all Deepanjali events—particularly Deepika's performances. Anjaneya, as a person with flair for Telugu literature and the performing arts, is often seen at related cultural events. Dr Chakravarthy, IAS (retired), is of course one who renders yeoman service in promoting music and dance, and our cultural legacy as head of the South Indian Cultural Association (SICA).

In my school days, I used to see elderly gentlemen in Chennai on their way to office silently singing *keerthana*s during the bus ride and tapping their thigh for beat, and the sublime joy on their face as they did that. It was a fascinating sight. Those were the days one could hear only classical Carnatic music the whole day on radio, which led to my developing a liking for Carnatic music. Classical Hindustani took me a while longer to familiarise myself with, and to acquire a taste for. Initially, if I attended a Hindustani vocal concert, I would wait for the artiste to finish the *raga* and move on to the *thumri*. But then, over a period, I started enjoying it from start to finish. You need not be an aficionado to be able to enjoy music, of any kind, just be totally absorbed and derive joy out of it. My dear friend senior advocate Murali Bhandari and his wife Justice Sunanda Bhandari used to host classical vocal concerts of noted artistes visiting Delhi from Maharashtra and across the country at their house, and they would invite a few of their friends—nothing but sheer love for music and the spirit of sharing its exquisite joys with kindred spirits. I must admit, though shamefully, that as far as I can remember, I first mindfully heard and enjoyed Pandit Jasraj's recital only when the most revered Sadguru Jaggi Vasudev, head of Isha Ashram in Coimbatore, had the maestro perform during the Shivaratri celebrations at his ashram a few years ago. The Shivaratri programme at the Isha Ashram, presided over by a legendary spiritual leader of our time, is something I rarely miss watching live on TV year after year. It is remarkable how the Sadguru makes music and dance inspire spiritual thought and a sublime, absolute *ananda* amongst the thousands of devotees who flock to be in his divine presence at the ashram that night, and the tens of thousands others watching the programme live.

Sometime back, while surfing channels on TV, I came across a *qawwali* concert of the legendary and iconic Sabri Brothers from Karachi, performing at the Kamani Auditorium in Delhi. I was so captivated by the sheer vibrancy and soulfulness of their rendition that I post-haste called a couple of friends to tell them to tune in to the channel. How I wish I could understand the lyrics; but then, observing their gesticulations and superb voice modulation, I could discern that these accomplished Sufi artistes were reaching out to the Supreme One with the intense love and devotion conveyed through their sublimely beautiful music. When the music is so pure, so divine, the mind is of itself elevated to heights of spirituality.

My gravitating to spiritual thought as I became a septuagenarian is something I did not fail to notice. It is a different matter that Krishnayan, in one of his mails the context of which I cannot now recall, had asserted that he always found religiosity to be a central trait in me. It may well be so. I cannot in any case dispute Krishnayan's view, based as it is on keen observation of his mentor.

Well, nowadays, religiosity and faith in the divine seem to permeate amongst all age groups, not just the elderly. During my school and college days, however, visiting temples and places of worship was certainly not so common amongst young people. The transformation

Independent Practice and Retirement 185

that has taken place over the years makes the religiosity of the younger generation much more manifest today. We witness gestures of gratitude to the divine on the cricket ground when a batsman makes a century or a bowler captures a prize wicket, regardless of the faith the concerned player belongs to. While appreciating the strong minds of non-believer friends, I hold on to my belief that faith inspires hope in all people at all times and, equally, it imbues humility, a sense of gratitude and cherished humane virtues in life.

I have been a regular visitor to the famous temple at Tirupati from a young age. Entry into the temple and *darshan* used to be relatively easy then, unlike the present times, and I used to make a quick visit whenever possible, particularly on my trips to Rajampet. In fact, while I was practicing in Delhi, I had the good fortune of appearing for the TTD in their numerous cases in the Supreme Court, arising out of their action to clear encroachments in the Mada Streets in Tirumala, and for using land near a tank for TTD staff housing. Narasinga Rao, the then joint executive officer of TTD, and one deeply committed to the cause of the temple, used to visit Delhi to brief me. On one such visit, he brought for me the temple *prasadam*, an unusually large *laddu* as big as a melon, which he gave me before leaving in the evening. I called my juniors into my room to share it with me, and noticing the astonishment on their faces at the enormous size of the laddu, I asked them if they could guess how much it cost. When they expressed their bafflement, I told them that it cost thirty thousand rupees, or the amount that would be normally charged for court appearance in such a matter, since I was not charging any fees for representing the TTD in Supreme Court, as my humble offering by way of service to the Deity.

While such was my deep devotion to Lord Venkateshwara, I somehow missed the opportunity of visiting the popular temple at Srisailam despite living in Hyderabad. This was mercifully remedied a few years back after my friend Meher Jha, Judge, Patna, who used to assist me in matters before the Patna and Ranchi High Courts, visited me in Hyderabad. Having just completed a visit to Srisailam, Meher enthusiastically described how beautiful the ambience was and how much he enjoyed being there. After hearing him, I had to sheepishly admit that I hadn't been to Srisailam, which, of course, surprised him. I then lost no time in requesting Mohan Sharma, alias Bhaskar Panthulu Mohan, who used to then practice in the High Court and was known to visit Srisailam often, to arrange for my visit to the temple, which he did, and I enjoyed the visit and the darshan at Srisailam in his company. Mohan, presently Judicial Member, National Company Law Tribunal, Amaravati, had visited Rajampet on my invitation. From Rajampet, he took me to Tirupati to meet with Bondu Chandrasekharam, Associate Professor, Rashtriya Samscrutha Vidyapeeth at Tirupati, whom he respectfully refers to as his 'Guru'. This Guruji is a young unassuming person who radiates equanimity and compassion. In the evenings, after returning to his modest ashram home near Tirupati, he sits in the tin-roofed shed and shares his profound knowledge of Hindu scriptures and mythology with ordinary folks, who join him on their way home from work. It was his simple unassuming nature and his spiritual knowledge that impressed me most. The presence of some gifted individuals like Professor Chandrasekharam permeates sublime peace, and that I believe is the essence of what we call *satsang*.

The narrative willy-nilly seems to have become much longer than anticipated. So it may be apt to conclude here, expressing my deep gratitude to my family for making my life's journey smooth and serene, and to all my juniors, colleagues, friends and well-wishers, for making my career as a member of this noble profession fulfilling.

That said, I shall sign off, recalling the beautiful words I had seen on a placard held by a fan in the stands of Providence Stadium in far-off Guyana—when the Indian women's cricket team beat the much-fancied Australian team in the last match of the league stage—which read: "LOVE MY INDIA, PROUD TO BE INDIAN". Nothing can be more gratifying than spending my sunset years with that profound and overpowering thought.

GOD BLESS.
VRR

Appendix 1

'Justice Delivery System'
Speech delivered by V. R. Reddy, as Chairman, Bar Council of India, at the National Convention of Lawyers on 22 August 1989, New Delhi.

THE efficacy of the 'justice delivery system' as it exists today is engaging the minds of all thinking people in our country. The Hon'ble Prime Minister in his Independence Day address referred to the weaknesses in the judicial system, especially the cost and the time involved, that are causing hardship to the common man. Law's delays have become proverbial, what, with cases pending for over twenty years in the highest court of the land. The total number of cases pending in different courts of course runs into astronomical figures.

This depressing scenario found poetic expression at the hands of Shiv K. Kumar, a recent winner of the Sahitya Academy Award for English poetry, who, referring to the plight of litigants perched on the benches of the Tis Hazari Courts, says,

> On the rickety wooden benches
> the waiting pilgrims have left
> their bones for their progeny to collect.

While delay is only one of the 'ugly features' of today's justice delivery system, equally serious is the cost factor. In spite of the demoralising prolixity, and oppressive cost which have become inseparable parts of the litigation scene in India, it is heartening to observe that people have not lost faith and confidence in the system of justice. One wonders whether this dogged faith in the justice delivery system is on account of the Indian society's ancient belief that justice springs from a divine source. Apart from the generally positive attitude of the public to the judicial system, it is significant that the youth of today with a modern outlook also repose considerable faith in our courts and judiciary. A recent study by an American professor amongst the law students of Delhi University revealed an "extraordinarily high level of support" that legal institutions enjoy among the student population and that courts were perceived as a "moral institution enjoying a deep reservoir of general approval". Such faith notwithstanding, the stark reality today is that the system of justice is under severe strain and one cannot expect it to sustain its efficacy and relevance unless some far-reaching reforms are ushered in, without any loss of time.

With the advent of the many social welfare legislations and increased awareness of rights amongst even the poor and downtrodden, the judicial system has a far greater and a more positive role to play, if it is to fulfil the rising social aspirations and Constitutional goals. In this context there is urgent need for ensuring that courts are made more accessible to the members of the lower economic and social strata of society. Extending the system of justice to the grass-root level by ensuring devolution of judicial powers to Panchayat institutions is but a necessary corollary to the momentous initiative taken by the Hon'ble Prime Minister, for achieving democratic decentralisation by strengthening the Panchayat administration and the Urban Local Bodies, through the recent amendments to the Constitution. The concept of 'Nyaya Panchayats' recommended by the Law Commission of India under its 114th report therefore deserves serious consideration.

Apart from accessibility, there is need for evolving less complex procedures. It is time to consider the desirability of continued dependence on the adversary style of adjudication, particularly in the matter of resolution of disputes involving the rural masses and the working classes. A pragmatic approach of retaining the essence of the adversary system, with the necessary operational changes and innovative newer methods to suit our ethos and social needs, is necessary. Further, focus of attention may have to be shifted more to the conciliatory processes. The emphasis in a sound judicial system ought not to be on encouraging litigation, but on ensuring its reduction. The Constitution of Mediation Committees in every neighbourhood to resolve all minor disputes by arbitral process, as is the practice in some countries like the Peoples' Republic of China, merits consideration. Pre-trial conciliatory proceedings, as tried out by the Himachal Pradesh High Court, is also a measure which deserves wider application.

A major part of today's litigation, particularly in the higher courts, involves governments and public authorities. The judicial system, which is already burdened with mounting arrears of cases, can ill afford the manifold increase of cases assailing administrative action. Methods may therefore have to be devised by which there is objective determination of the challenge to governmental action, in the first instance by the administrative machinery itself.

One of the major contributing factors for the deficiencies in the legal system and the delay it entails is the use of archaic methods and procedures. It is indeed paradoxical that in this modem age of advanced science, computer technology and innovative managerial methods have remained alien to the justice system of our country. An eminent English judge speaking about the legal methods in his country remarked: "If our business methods were as antiquated as our legal methods, we should be a bankrupt country". Needless to say that this observation is as valid or perhaps more valid in the context of the situation obtaining in our country.

Other than judges, the major component of the Justice Delivery System is the legal profession. The role of the legal profession in strengthening administration of justice in the country is a matter engaging the attention of the profession as well as others. It is significant that the Law Commission in its recent report rejected the oft-repeated suggestion that lawyers must be excluded from appearing before certain tribunals and courts and in certain types of cases. It further observed that the legal profession provides a healthy check on the angular behaviour of the presiding judges and that experience of excluding members of the legal profession from appearing in certain cases has neither contributed to the expeditious disposal of the cases, nor to a more satisfactory resolution of disputes. This should dispel misgivings, if any, regarding the appearance of lawyers before all tribunals and courts as envisaged under the Advocates Act. The legal profession is very hopeful that the much belated notification, bringing into force Section 30 of the Advocates Act, will be issued by the Government without any further loss of time.

To the legal world it was most gratifying to hear the Hon'ble Prime Minister's words, on Independence Day, reflecting the firm resolve of his government to improve the judicial system, even if it involves making changes in the existing framework. This important declaration, coming in the wake of democratic decentralisation through the Constitutional Amendments, augurs indeed well for the attainment of the Constitutional goal of an egalitarian society where justice, social, economic and political shall inform all institutions of national life.

Appendix 2

'**Practice of Law in the Multimedia Era: An Indian Perspective**'
Paper presented by V. R. Reddy at the Regional Conference of the International Bar Association on 5 November 1999, New Delhi.

It was not long ago that communication, particularly for professionals such as lawyers, was confined to the written word and telephonic talk. In the recent past technology has developed the world over so rapidly in the fields of communications and servicing of information that its influence is felt by every profession. There is a convergence of telephone, television, computer and the Internet. Users of computer networks and the Internet may not only have instant access to each other but also to a vast sea of information at their fingertips. Transmission of messages on e-mail, the delivery time of which is measured not in days or hours but in minutes, is a widely used practice even in the developing countries. It is predicted that if the Internet keeps growing at its present pace, practically every person on the planet will have a net address in ten years. The online data banks available are helping enormously seekers of information from every profession and from every walk of life.

It is axiomatic that the legal profession is generally slow in adapting itself to changes, more particularly if it means a near transformation of its very style of functioning. It might surprise one to know that in one of our high courts in India, namely, the Calcutta High Court, court orders even now provide for payment of costs in guineas—a measure of money used in UK traditionally—more than fifty years after British rule ended. It also seems to take lawyers longer to exploit the potential of technology fully in its use in their offices and in courts. In India, where precedent is a source of law, an average lawyer even today is more comfortable poring over the case law digests and commentaries to find authorities, than have recourse to data banks through computers or the Internet. It may partly be on account of the absence of an efficient on-line computer network. A few years ago, the idea that a person could be a better lawyer by using a computer would have been greeted with incredulity in most legal circles. There is however a slow but definite change in attitude today, and those who earlier grudgingly acknowledged the value of technology are gradually becoming committed users of the same.

Instead of scheduling conference calls, as is commonly the practice in the technologically advanced countries, video conferences are bound to become the popular medium for interaction shortly. Paper, which had served humanity for centuries as a medium for recording, communicating and disseminating thoughts and information, might cease to play a vital role and it may not be long before paperless law offices become a reality. Hypertext briefs are expected to replace their bulky paper counterparts. There is already serious debate on the utility and efficacy of such briefs, with the proponents highlighting the advantages which such a system would bring in its wake, while others apprehend that the high cost of producing these could tip scales in favour of parties who can afford to present them. Sourcing information with regard to law from one's own jurisdiction or from other jurisdictions has become so much easier with tremendous saving of time and energy. While these are some of the changes in the functioning of law offices and lawyers, courtroom procedures can also be expected to undergo drastic changes with the use of modern technology. The Internet, besides being a tool for the practitioners of law to access information or to interact with clients, is increasingly becoming the medium for dispute resolution through courts.

Litigation hitherto has been confined to courtrooms, where the examination of witnesses, recording of evidence and presentation of arguments took place. Litigants of the future might be able to resolve many disputes from their homes over the Internet rather than going to court. A consultation paper of Lord Chancellor's Department in UK contains proposals envisaging a "virtual court hearing" in which people can communicate with the judges and lawyers over the Internet via their television sets. With such a procedure, many of the traditional trappings of courts including legal documents, books, papers and formal court hearings are likely to disappear or will be limited only to particular circumstances and defined cases.

The prospect of litigation outside a courtroom, dispensing with live witnesses, judges and lawyers in appropriate attire and other paraphernalia that is so familiar, might horrify many, particularly the older members of the judiciary and legal profession. Referring to the experience of the High Court of Australia, Justice Michael Kirby observed that the use of video links has not led to any diminution in the effective use of judicial and lawyer time and that, on the contrary, hearings by video-link tend to be shorter, since "the living presence of human beings somehow breathes into all concerned, prolixity and oratorical flourishes that disembodied impersonal electronic form appears to control and minimise."

While the legal profession and courts in some countries are rapidly moving into the electronic age, the effect of technological advances in the field of law is not quite as rapid in the developing countries. The degree of change would necessarily depend upon many factors such as the size and structure of legal profession, the nature of the judicial process and court practices followed, access to technology and suitability of the modern techniques to serve the needs of the end users of legal services. It might be apt in this context to refer to our experience in India, in putting to use these technological aides in the area of legal services and administration of justice.

Speaking about India, I should say that popular use of information technology and computer network is at its infancy in India. It might seem paradoxical that the progress in this area is not anywhere near what is obtaining in the developed countries despite the fact that Indians today constitute the largest group of expatriates in the United States of America, that is most successful in the field of software technology. Slow progress in this area is on account of inadequacy of efficient infrastructural services such as telecommunications and also partly on account of the slow growth of awareness of the potential of information technology, particularly in rural India.

India has the second largest legal profession in the world with more than 5,00,000 lawyers. There are, besides the Supreme Court of India, 18 High Courts, 430 District Courts and a few thousand county courts. Legal practice in the country is by and large litigation-oriented in the sense that about 80% of the professional time of lawyers is devoted to litigation in courts. Most of the lawyers are solo practitioners, with 'law firms' being essentially an urban concept. There are law firms mainly in the metropolitan cities such as Delhi, Bombay, Calcutta, and in some of the cities where the High Courts are situated. The size of the law firms that we have is also not large and only a few law firms engage more than 100 lawyers and have offices in more than one city. The role of lawyers, and the manner in which the profession is structured, may be responsible for the modest use of computer and Internet technologies by the legal community.

As of today the Supreme Court has become successfully 'computerised' in many applications, such as, registration of cases, management of offices and providing information on status of pending cases. This information has been made available to over 700 terminal points all over the country. In the High Courts, too, similar infrastructural sprucing up has taken place. The idea for computerising the 430 District Courts has also been mooted and as of today, the process is complete in 382 courts. Computer data banks are being provided by some of the publishers of law journals and others, of the decisions of the Supreme Court. Over 3,000 subscribers access the more popular of these providers.

Computerisation has helped the Supreme Court of India, which is perhaps the most overburdened highest court of a country in the world, immensely in reducing the tremendous backlog of cases that had accumulated. In 1990, 1,60,000 cases were pending before it and computerisation has helped in categorisation of cases, which had in turn accelerated disposal of cases, bringing the backlog down to 20,000 in 1999. It might be of interest for lawyers of other jurisdictions to know that on a Monday of every week there are as many as about 500 petitions seeking special leave to appeal, which are taken up for consideration by the Supreme Court of India. This is in striking contrast to the number of cases taken up by the Supreme Court of the United States. Information regarding the progress of a case and the status thereof can now be had by the litigant public from any part of the country, thanks to an information bank known as 'Court NIC' organised by the National Informatic Centre, a Government of India undertaking. Each day over 200 litigants and advocates access this information bank. Besides computer facilities, a similar system is available over the telephone known as IVR (interactive voice response system).

If one considers the increasing use of multimedia technology it cannot be long before we can hope to see optimum utilisation of technology in the field of law. There has been increasing awareness of the need to train lawyers of the future in diverse computer applications. Many law schools in the country are providing training in the use of computer technology. For those who are already in the profession, Bar Associations are taking initiative to provide facilities for accessing data bases and Internet services.

With the fascinating possibilities of using information technology, one can expect to see a radical change in the practice of law and the administration of justice. We are in the transitional phase or at the threshold of the move from the 'industrial print-based society' into what is called as information technology-based society.

Prof. Richard Susskind in his work, *The Future of Law*, envisages that in the world to come much of the lawyer's work will shift from being advisorial in nature to becoming, in large part, a form of information service, a kind of legal service which might meet most of the needs of individual citizens and businesses, yet differ markedly from the traditional means of working of a lawyer. Legal service in the form of information-service would help immensely in providing the necessary legal input required in domestic and business life, which hitherto may have been inaccessible, conventional legal service being too expensive or impractical in the circumstances. Information technology is expected to help bring legal guidance to this 'latent legal market'. Unlike in the traditional model, where a lawyer provides the client on a one-to-one basis an advisory-based service for an agreed fee, in the emerging system, legal service becomes information service and a new setup of relationships is established. "Those who are guided become users, the lawyers who analyse and organise the material become the legal information engineers and the organisations who develop and market the legal information products and services become the providers". Looking at the positive dimension of this transformation, it can be said that with a demystification of the law and its far wider availability will come the perception that the law helps rather than hinders. Instead of regarding law as restrictive, users of legal information service will gradually appreciate that the law can be a source of empowerment and a powerful weapon, which can be marshalled in support of the exploitation of opportunities and the attainment of all manner of objectives.

In developing countries such as India, where society is based on rule of law with the basic human rights assured to people, it is often said that all these freedoms and other fundamental rights guaranteed would remain merely on paper unless awareness is created among people of the rights so guaranteed. In this context some NGOs, law schools and others have hitherto been organising legal literacy programmes. On account of the complexity of laws and prolixity of litigation, some suffer in silence what they perceive as deprivation of their rights, while many are totally unaware of their rights under the law and protection envisaged under law against exploitation. Transformation of legal service into information service and easy access thereto on the information highway would help enormously in promoting legal literacy and ensure recognition of the role of law as one that is supportive and not obstructive. While this could be a significant contribution of the legal profession to society, any apprehension of the diminishing importance of the legal profession may not be wholly justified. The liberation and emergence of the hitherto 'latent legal market' will create a range of opportunities for lawyers to package and sell their expertise in innovative ways. This apart, the traditional advisory role of the legal profession will still be called for, since information services available might not suffice to meet the requirement of every situation. The upshot of it all is that while lawyers have no choice except to move with 'electronic times', the influence of technology of the multimedia era can be expected to contribute towards raising the quality of professional skills, while making the profession more 'user-friendly'.

Appendix 3

'The Role of Bar and Bench in Administration of Justice'
Address by V. R. Reddy as guest speaker at the Golden Jubilee celebrations of the Rajasthan High Court on 4 September 1999, Jodhpur.

I deem it an honour to be invited to associate myself with the Golden Jubilee Celebrations of the High Court of Rajasthan. Though fifty years may not be considered such a long period in the history of a judicial institution, any high court born after Independence which could fulfil in a fair manner the rising aspirations of a democratic society governed by the rule of law can justifiably feel gratified.

The people of Rajasthan represent a rare mix of vibrancy and colour on the one hand, and sobriety on the other. In that sense this State can be said to be an oasis if one takes into account its general neighbourhood. The High Court, which is the apex judicial institution of the State, has over the years displayed in great measure sobriety which lends lustre to any judicial institution. I have great pleasure in extending hearty felicitations to everyone who has been associated with this prestigious institution on this occasion of its Golden Jubilee.

These celebrations, apart from promoting bonhomie among those associated with administration of justice, provide an occasion for one to recall the achievements of the past and reflect upon what remains to be achieved.

It is no exaggeration to say that the Judiciary is perceived by the people of the country as the best performer out of all the constitutional organs of the State. We can take legitimate pride in the fact that the Judiciary, led by the Supreme Court of India, has acquitted itself admirably over the years. The innovative and path-breaking initiatives of the Supreme Court, particularly in the areas of judicial interpretation of the Constitution, Statutes and public interest litigation, have helped in improving the quality of life of the people and toning up the administrative machinery. Without going into the specifics, suffice it to refer to the contribution of the Court in the field of protection of ecology and environment, the norms laid for curtailing vehicular pollution, garbage disposal, protection of monuments, and preservation of forests. In the area of social upliftment we have any number of instances of judicial action for eradication of bonded labour, child labour, protection of women and generally speaking the poor, weak and under-privileged. Jurists from advanced countries have paid encomiums to our judiciary, admiring the innovative jurisprudence that our courts have evolved.

It is also a well-known fact that courts have become the last resort when it comes to a question of solving some of the intractable problems encountered. This is because of the credibility that judicial institutions enjoy, particularly when there has been a steep decline in the credibility enjoyed by the other organs of the State. While these are matters of immense gratification, it is necessary and also appropriate that the Bar and the Bench should introspect on occasions like this and address the deficiencies.

While dealing with the problems that the 'administration of justice' is beset with in the country, the first and foremost question to be addressed is whether the system is capable of providing speedy and cost-effective justice. Law's delays have become proverbial. It is a depressing scenario, if one takes into account the situation with cases pending for more than twenty years and the pendency in different courts in terms of numbers running into astronomical figures. Cost of litigation would inevitably become prohibitive on account of sheer delay even if one were to ignore other contributory factors. Inspite of the demoralising prolixity and oppressive cost, which have become inseparable part of the litigation scene in India, if people have not lost faith in courts all together, it can only be either because of our society's ancient belief that justice springs from a divine source, or on account of the sheer lack of alternatives. Perhaps we do not know of many who need to have justice done shying away from courts. We might also not know the capacity of the disappointed to raise their voice of protest. This indeed is what makes it necessary for us to take serious note of this and try and find solutions without waiting for someone to shake us out of our apathy and inertia.

Besides the issues of cost and delay, there are certain other major issues such as systematic deficiencies to be considered. As an example we can consider what is happening on the crime scene in the country today. The two major issues people have never been tired of talking about in the last few years are 'rampant corruption' and the 'criminalisation of politics'. Laws relating to prevention of corruption have undergone changes from time to time and these changes were intended to make the prosecution of the offenders more effective and speedy. We had these offences of one time under IPC 161 to 165 and later we had the Prevention of Corruption Act 1947 and the present Act of 1988. In the year 1962, the Government of India constituted the Santhanam Committee "to suggest changes in law which would ensure speedy trial of cases of bribery, corruption and criminal misconduct and make law otherwise more effective." The Committee, after collecting a lot of material from the public relating to the nature of corruption in the administration, had this to say: "We heard from all sides that corruption has in recent years spread even to those levels of administration from which it was conspicuously absent in the past." It is a different matter that the Santhanam Committee's recommendations had led to the amendment in 1964. The law now provides for appointment of Special Judges for disposal of these cases and the courts have upheld the constitution of such special courts for dealing with cases involving persons holding high public or political offices. Justice Krishna Iyer had in his inimitable style said: "No party to a criminal trial has a vested right in slow motion justice since the soul of social justice in this area of law is prompt trial followed by verdict of innocence or sentence." Despite all these, what we see today is that investigations do not touch even the periphery when it comes to corruption in high places, and where prosecution is launched, there is interminable delay in the proceedings. As to how many political functionaries have so far been convicted in our country, there is difference of opinion; while some say none, others refer to one instance in Uttar Pradesh which had supposedly occurred years ago. I refer to cases of corruption in high places since it has an utterly demoralising affect upon the society.

With respect to the normal run of criminal cases, the Supreme Court has time and again had occasion to deal with the right to speedy trial in cases like Sheela Barse, Antulay and more recently, in the Public Interest Litigation initiated by Common Cause, the court has had to go to the extent of directing grant of bail or discharge in cases where the trials have been pending for long before courts, depending upon the nature of offence for which the accused is charged. Despite all this, it is common knowledge that hundreds and thousands of persons accused of crimes are languishing in jails without judicial determination of their cases. Another aspect which one might like to gloss over is the fact that an impression is created in the minds of the people that those with resources can escape the clutches of law. It might seem to be so since what normally happens in most such cases is that the loopholes of law are exploited to the maximum. Our criminal jurisprudence, not being based on something like the inquisitorial system prevailing in some countries, makes it immensely difficult for even a well-meaning investigating agency to be effective in the absence of co-operation from the public.

There is another related problem, namely, the criminalisation of politics. As we all know, power has become the political goal or end in itself, and one's journey to it has to start with elections. It is therefore not surprising that criminality should manifest itself more in the electoral process. The Election Commission has been doing its utmost to curb this; the Law Commission of India has been seriously considering this issue and their report is to be made public shortly. Here again though, the preventive measures are strictly speaking not in the realm of judicial administration; when it comes to any possible deterrence by way of speedy and effective action, there are interminable delays that seem to affect the whole process. With the amendment of the R.P. Act, 1966, election petitions are now shifted from the jurisdiction of the Tribunals to the High Court. There is a time frame of six months fixed, with 45 days for the presentation of the petition, it works out to $7\frac{1}{2}$ months from the date of election. One really wonders as to how many petitions are being disposed off within the time frame. The Law Minister of India, sometime back in June 1998, said that there were 372 petitions pending in the High Courts and 41 in the Supreme Court, and that many were 5 to 8 years old. The sting of the laws, however severe they may be, is lost if there cannot be immediate enforcement thereof.

If this is the fate of criminal prosecution, [it is] needless to speak of litigation between private individuals and litigation between individuals and government organisations. The party against whom relief is sought, and particularly the party in whose favour there is an interim order or an order under appeal, would seek to have the case delayed or for the litigation to be unduly protracted. This has given rise to serious disenchantment with the judicial system in the minds of many, with the result that even persons with genuine claims hesitate to approach courts of law. It might be seen that this is one way of limiting litigation, but then if the justice delivery system is unavailable for genuine and worthy causes, its very existence becomes purposeless.

In this kind of a situation one is seeking a solution to the problem through the method of Alternate Dispute Resolution, and we now have the Arbitration and Conciliation Act, 1996. This alternate dispute resolution, some prefer to call it Appropriate Dispute Resolution or Additional Dispute Resolution. Whatever be the name, the object essentially is to ensure dispute resolution with speed, informality, flexibility, and limiting cost without sacrificing fairness. Some jurists expressed the view that the primary responsibility is of the government to provide a civil justice system, which maintains and advances the rule of law and furnishes the means to secure legal rights and enforce legal duties. If so, why not incorporate the essence of the Alternate Dispute Resolution mechanism into the main system itself and thereby, without undue emphasis on legalism, make it user-friendly and cost-effective.

Though, I am digressing from the topic of discussion, namely, the 'Role of the Bar and Bench in Administration of Justice'. If I were to adopt a nuts and bolts approach, I would have been content with suggesting changes in methods of disposal, cutting down on call work time, adjournments, brevity in judgements, etc. But then the problems that the administration of justice is beset with today are far more serious, warranting comprehensive systemic changes or reform. For this the initiative in my opinion should come from mainly the Bar and the Bench. Today fortunately the judiciary in the country enjoys the kind of independence which one can scarcely find in any developing country in the world. The executive, it must be said, is not in a position to resist any initiatives from the judiciary. It is therefore for us to take time out from our routine rush of work and address these issues.

Yet another aspect I would like to touch upon is one concerning legal services that the profession is in a position to offer today. It is a matter of deep concern that there is a steep decline in standards. If there is a decline in the standards of the profession, it will necessarily reflect upon the standards of the judiciary as the judges are after all one-time members of the bar. One of the factors for the fall in standards is of course the lack of proper legal education.

Some years ago there was no realisation that imparting legal education is a serious business. There was considerable amount of casualness with which they viewed legal education. This was the position when there were very few law colleges in the country. The Law Commission of India headed by the late Shri Setalvad had in its 14th Report lamented the poor standards of legal education.

There has since been a mushroom growth of law colleges. Without going into the history of it all, I can say that today it is most heartening to know that there is general acceptance of the 5-year degree course as the best way to impart legal education. The experiment of the National Law School of India University at Bangalore has been such a tremendous success that practically every state in the country is today trying to establish one. I cannot forget the time when there was tremendous and bitter opposition to both these proposals, from within BCI and outside. The issue was even sought to be politicised. There was a State Bar Council which elected its representative to the Bar Council of India on a definite commitment of opposing these measures. Change is generally resisted, and I suppose it is bound to be more so with lawyers, who one can say are traditionalists. As I said, we are happy that today there is far greater realisation of the need to improve the standards of legal education. And even the toppers are today choosing law as a career. There is great dearth of junior lawyers with proper educational background and they are in tremendous demand from law firms and corporate houses. This is indeed a very important development particularly in the context of the imminent opening up of legal services, if not immediately, maybe after a decade or so. The World Trade Organisation in its next round of negotiations will be dealing with the 'Service Sector', and the Government seems to be having consultations with the different sections as to what our stand can be (GATS). It is time that the profession starts gearing itself up, though whatever be the outcome, it might in the initial period affect only a minuscule section of the Bar.

Apart from the qualifying course for the new entrants it is time that the other members of the Bar, who have many more years of career ahead of them, acquaint themselves and not feel left out in the technological revolution that is taking place today. In many countries, and particularly in America and Australia, one is not looking to computers and internet merely as tools that help a counsel. Even the court proceedings are expected to make the best of the advanced technology available today [says] Michael Kirby.

These have to be on an organised basis taken up under the CLE programmes for lawyers and also for judicial officers. Judicial academies are coming up in every state to take care of this need. In so far as lawyers are concerned, our problem basically is one of numbers. Whatever be the problems encountered, the profession has no choice if the administration of justice is to fulfil the rising aspirations and the societal needs.

Appendix 4

'Reminiscences and Random Thoughts'
V. R. Reddy's article, penned on '40 Years of The Advocates Act, 1961', published in a commemorative volume on the occasion of the Bar Association of India Conference, 30 September–1 October 2001, Goa.

WE had witnessed a lively debate when the Government decided to set up the Constitution Review Committee, with the object of reviewing the working of the Constitution and to recommend changes appropriate to meet the emerging demands of good governance and democratic polity in the country. Some jurists and public figures expressed doubts with respect to the purpose and usefulness of such an exercise. Be that as it may, any attempt at reviewing the working of the Advocates Act 1961 is not likely to meet with any informed criticism, since the need for such an exercise is generally accepted by the Bar and the Bench, besides others concerned with the administration of justice. Today, 40 years after the Advocates Act came into force, need is felt to bring about the necessary changes in the statute for facilitating reforms in professional legal education and training, and to make the legal profession more responsive to the emerging needs of the public and particularly those arising out of liberalisation and globalisation. It is but appropriate that the legal profession itself should address these issues in the first instance with candour and objectivity and try to evolve a consensus with respect to the comprehensive changes required. The Bar Association of India (BAI), as a noted professional body at the national level, consistent with various initiatives it has been taking in the field of law and legal profession, is setting the process in motion with this commemorative conference, and for this the BAI and, more particularly, its President, Mr Fali Nariman and the Secretary Mr Lalit Bhasin deserve to be complimented.

The Advocates Act, while seeking to maintain the autonomy of the legal profession, seeks to govern practically every aspect such as—legal education, enrolment, disciplinary jurisdiction, promotion of legal aid, lawyers' welfare, law reform and a host of related matters. The conference has as many as seven working sessions, each focusing upon a specific topic, besides the inaugural session in which the dynamic Union Law Minister Sri. Arun Jaitley, the President of BAI Sri. Nariman and the Chairman of Bar Council of India (BCI) Sri. D. V. Subba Rao and others are expected to deliver their addresses. Though undoubtedly this is the maximum one perhaps could hope to achieve in a two-day conference, there may be some other related issues, which I am sure the participants will be touching upon during the course of the deliberations.

My experiences during my long association in the past with the BCI and my continued association with the National Law School of India University (NLSIU), Bangalore, inspires me to recall to memory some of the developments in the context of the working of the Advocates Act, and to express some random thoughts.

Legal Education and Law Universities

It is not surprising that the working sessions of the conference are to commence with "Quality of Legal Education". It is axiomatic that the quality of professional service lawyers and standards in administration of justice would necessarily depend upon the quality of legal education. Legal education had never enjoyed any particular importance or primacy in the academic world. The 14th Report of the Law Commission headed by Sri. M. C. Setalvad, Attorney General for India, referring to standards in law colleges, bemoaned that in the chaotic state of affairs prevailing in a number of these institutions, there is hardly a pretence at teaching. The Commission went on further to comment, "It is true that our country has produced eminent practitioners in law and learned judges. Their achievements probably arise from their own intellectual brilliance and capacity rather than from the education received by them at the universities". Dealing with the steady deterioration in standards, the Commission highlighted lack of motivation amongst the students and lack of earnestness in teaching as factors leading to the dismal state of legal education. How true it is. Students of the early days of Madras Law College remember the opening lecture of one of the popular professors, in which he was known to remind them that "they were there since they could not be elsewhere". There was this vice-chancellor of an university, who had earlier occupied a high position in the Judiciary, who recalled to memory his days as a student of law addressing the law faculty, and stated matter of factly that law courses were never serious educational exercises.

There was always this belief that professional knowledge and skills are to be gained by a lawyer more during his initial association with a senior or in courts, than through a study of law. Whatever may have been the reasons for the poor state of legal education in the early period, there was further deterioration with the mushroom growth of law colleges with an unmanageable number of students, compounded by the dearth of competent law teachers and commercialisation of legal education.

In this scenario of a dismal state of legal education, it must be said to the credit of the BCI that it took the necessary initiative as a body charged with the responsibility of laying down and ensuring compliance with standards of legal education under the statute. The legal education committee of the Bar Council headed by Justice Hidayatullah, after wide-ranging consultations with the universities, the UGC and others concerned, came out with a proposal for restructuring legal education, by introducing a five-year course from the 10 + 2 stage. More or less simultaneously, the BCI decided to establish an autonomous institution dedicated solely to law, namely the 'National Law School of India'. This unique national level institution was intended to act as a "pace setter and a testing ground for bold experiments in legal education." The simultaneous ushering in of these two schemes had led one to believe that one depended on the other. Despite wide-ranging consultations over a long period of time by the Legal Education Committee, presided over by Justice Hidayatullah, who was not only gracious enough but enthusiastic to continue his association with the committee even after assuming the august office of the Vice-President of India, the decision regarding the five-year course evoked strong opposition. Many of us have fond memories of the hospitality of the Vice-President's house and the dignity and stature enjoyed by the committee, which had as its members stalwarts like Messrs. Ram Jethmalani, Rajendra Singh, Ranjit Mohanty from the legal profession besides those from the academic world, prominent of whom being Prof. Upendra Baxi. It is a different matter that the decision to switch over to a five-year course with a cut-off date could not be implemented owing to vociferous objections, particularly from the lobby of the private law colleges and a section of law teachers. There was also a genuinely felt apprehension regarding the desirability of making a student decide upon law as a course of study soon after completing 10 + 2. There was yet another misgiving that such a switchover to a five year full term course would disable those who wish to pursue law as a part-time course with a view to improve their prospects in the employment held by them or to facilitate meeting of expenses from the earnings from such employment. So intense and acrimonious was the debate that some started characterising the five-year degree programme as anti-poor.

The problems with regard to the National Law School were far more formidable. The BCI, with its changing composition, did not continue to subscribe to the idea with conviction and commitment. Many State Bar Councils had serious reservations. Amongst members of the BCI, the vocal proponents were very few, with the others either strongly opposing the project or being indifferent to the proposal. In such a scenario it is not perhaps surprising that, a newly elected member of the BCI, when approached for support for my candidature for chairmanship of the council, said with candour and aplomb that I can expect his support only if I was prepared to join the opposition to the five-year course and the National Law School, since such was the commitment made by him to his colleagues in his state Bar Council when he was elected as member of the BCI. Needless to say that I neither could secure his support nor succeed in the election on that occasion.

To compound the problems was this reluctance of the University Grants Commission (UGC) to confer deemed university status upon the institution. This could be eventually overcome by the unique piece of legislation of the Legislature of Karnataka, viz. the National Law School of India Act, 1986 (Karnataka Act 22 of 1986), by which the National Law School of India University came to be formally established on 29.8.87. At its infancy the institution had to face multifold problems, without any infrastructure and financial resources. The apathy and indifference with which our approaches for financial support were met with are still etched in my memory. Thanks to the innovative methods that Dr Madhava Menon, the first Director of the School, and his team of committed academics could evolve, which enabled the school to overcome the severe financial crunch felt in the initial years. It is a different matter that once the institution gained recognition, one had to become selective in accepting offers of support.

This ambitious project, which is and will remain "a national showpiece of the legal community", is a major and significant contribution of the organised Bar in the country for improving standards of legal education. The standard of professional legal education imparted in the National Law School and more importantly the quality of product, namely the students of the school had in fact become the talk of the town from the very inception of the school. The student community of the school came to be recognised as comparable to those of the most prestigious law schools in the world. The manner in which they performed in

'Moot Court' competitions, including those at the international level, the scholarships and fellowships including 'Rhodes' are some of their significant achievements. It is therefore no surprise really, that the graduates passing out of the school are in such tremendous demand from law firms, lawyers and the corporate world.

To my mind the most beneficial impact of the NLSIU has been the greater awareness it created of the importance of and imperative need for quality legal education in the country. Secondly, the experimentation in NLSIU has demonstrated the merit and efficacy of an integrated five-year course as the most desirable programme of professional legal education. The Committee of Judges, consisting of Mr Justice A. M. Ahmadi as its Chairman and Mr Justice M. Jagannadha Rao and Mr Justice B. N. Kirpal as its members constituted by the Chief-Justices Conference in the year 1993, strongly approved the five-year programme and recommended establishment of National Law School type of institutions in each state. Such of us who felt that the vociferous objections from some members of the Bar, law lecturers and political functionaries, highly irrational and most disheartening, are today willing to view such expression of opposition as an opportunity to dear the cobwebs in one's mindset. It is most gratifying that there is all round acknowledgement of the fact that the introduction of the five-year course and establishment of a model institution such as the NLSIU are the best things that could happen for retrieving and reforming legal education from the dismal state that it had assumed.

It is all well that we have today, besides NLSIU, four other similar institutions and the general mood is also such that the five-year law programme to the total exclusion of the three-year course had found acceptability. Though this development augurs well, the magnitude of the problem being what it is, the effect of it can be felt only in a very small measure and that too after a very long period. There are over 400 recognised law colleges in the country. Ensuring that each one of these institutions imparts quality legal education is going to be a stupendous task. Merely providing an agenda or a road map prepared by the NLSIU and other law universities would not suffice. The major problem of acute shortage of competent law teachers has to be addressed immediately. The NLSIU has launched a new scheme in this direction, which is needed to be strengthened and the other law universities also should undertake such a task. Law teaching must be made attractive in terms of remuneration, prestige and avenues of mobility for the academics, be it into legal practice, judicial and governmental assignments on a tenure basis, should be seriously explored. Each one of the law universities should take steps for developing requisite infrastructure for adopting the law colleges of the other universities on a limited basis for a specified period and thereby upgrade the standards of academic culture of such colleges. There should be a co-ordinated synergy in the approach and promotional activity of the law universities in the matter of facilitating upgradation of teaching standards of the various law colleges affiliated to the other universities. For achieving these objectives by co-ordinated effort the law universities, i.e. the universities dedicated solely to the study and research of law, should have a co-ordinating body. Adequate resources should be made available to such body by the Government of India and to the extent possible by the state governments.

While pursuing such an effort through law universities, the BCI, which is charged with the responsibility of legal education and the function of recognising and supervising the law colleges in the country, should also evolve suitable strategies. Originally the Act envisaged inspections by the BCI, while by the 1993 Amendment provision is made for involving the State Bar Councils for the purposes of visit and inspection. While pleading for the said amendment, which was eventually introduced in 1993, I distinctly recall the unsuccessful effort made by us for amending the Act so as to enable the BCI to deal with and de-recognise an individual law college. Now if there is a college, which is conducting its affairs in breach of the norms, action by the Council can only be either through the University, failing which action is to be taken for de-recognising the degree of the University as a whole, which in many instances might prove to be far too drastic a measure. We were however not successful in persuading the concerned with regard to the change in this respect. The responsibility of overseeing the functioning of so many colleges cast upon the Bar Councils with their limited number of members is far too heavy, and the Bar Councils may therefore have to evolve suitable strategy for effective discharge of this function. To sum-up, the organised Bar, the Bench and the law academies should continue to be focused on overhauling the system to ensure improved standards.

Pre-entry Training and Test

Most legal practice in India being oriented towards litigation, the fact that entrants into the profession are neither properly equipped in law nor exposed to the culture and etiquette of courts becomes far too obvious when a newly enrolled advocate appears in court. This has led to the belief that the remedy lies in reverting back to the old practice of apprenticeship, pre-entry test before enrolment. These requirements which a candidate had to fulfill before enrolment were deliberately dispensed with after the introduction of three-year law course in the place of the two-year course then existing. The endeavour was to build into the curriculum of the three-year course practical training by way of moot courts, visits to courts and study of the procedural laws. If this programme was earnestly carried out by all the law colleges in India, there perhaps may not have been an occasion to consider re-introduction of apprenticeship and pre-enrolment tests. In the case of those passing out of National Law School of India and few other law colleges which provide practical training by way of placement of students in law offices, mandatory visits to courts, teaching of procedural laws and practices and participation in moot courts, I do not think that one would feel the need for any further time being spent on training by way of apprenticeship or in qualifying in the pre-enrolment test. It is therefore a matter to ponder as to whether, at a stage when we are about to switch over to a five-year course ensuring reasonable standards, it will still be necessary to compel candidates to spend one additional year for apprenticeship and to again qualify in a test conducted by the Bar Council.

Further, experience shows that there will normally be neither adequate motivation amongst the candidates nor earnestness amongst those enforcing such rule. An apprentice in the early times when such practice was in vogue was, more often than not, unwelcome appendage in an office, with hardly any senior evincing interest in training the apprentice. In most of the cases apprentices were hardly spending their time in court and the maintenance of diaries was reduced a shallow formality. Though some Councils used to arrange for lectures and were serious about the conduct of tests, in many others, the impression was that the candidates ran the risk of failing in the test only if the invigilator did not know the correct answer. While such was the position earlier, I do not think that there was any noticeable change when recently the BCI sought to re-introduce the system by framing Bar Council of India Training Rules, 1995. During the period 1997-98 as Chairman of the Committee appointed in the place of Delhi Council, I had the opportunity along with my esteemed colleagues who were members of the committee, to interview candidates and particularly with reference to the period of apprenticeship that they had spent and the diaries maintained by them. Though few of the candidates had made good use of their association with a senior, most of the others were evidently biding their time, making superficial entries in the diary of the proceedings in courts supposedly followed by them. The view that apprenticeship earmarking of the period of one year for training under a senior would have major beneficial effect may not be wholly correct. The question therefore would be whether it is desirable to make a candidate spend a one-year period when the benefit from training can only be marginal in most of the cases.

As far as the pre-enrolment test is concerned, here again no particular purpose would be served if it is to be yet another examination. If the training and the tests are to be meaningful and beneficial to the candidates, they should be structured in such a way to create sufficient impetus and motivation for the candidate concerned to seriously apply himself to the said task. The entrance examination may have to be structured in a way that a candidate has a choice of subjects or combination of them qualifying in which, in the long run could help him to claim specialisation in such subjects. This has to be backed by a programme for capsule courses by way of week-long lectures and distance education. This exercise, run simultaneously along with the apprenticeship under a senior, to my mind might produce better results if recourse to apprenticeship and pre-enrolment test is found unavoidable.

Continuing Legal Education (CLE)

'Once a mortgage is always a mortgage' goes the adage. Lawyers are prone to believe that once you qualify and are enrolled, your right to practice as a lawyer should remain unaffected for all time to come except in cases of disciplinary action. There is equally no particular enthusiasm to keep oneself upbreast, nor are there opportunities for such exercises. This lead to the BCI Trust, of which I had the honour of being the Managing Trustee, launching the CLE Programme in the year 1980 with the first CLE workshop on Criminal Law held at Hyderabad. There was then the first workshop on Administrative Law at Bhubaneswar. These were followed by many on diverse subjects such as labour laws, arbitration, company law, etc. Many of the legal luminaries of the country participated with enthusiasm as members of the faculty. The organisational ability of Prof. N. R. Madhava Menon, who was during the said period the Secretary of the Trust, coupled with enthusiastic participation of the faculty and participants made the programmes a resounding success. This lead of the BCI was followed by some of the State Bar Councils, which had successfully conducted some CLE programmes.

What has been achieved in regard to CLE is wholly inadequate. To have a continuing legal education programme on a regular basis, making participation therein convenient for advocates from different parts of the country, an institutional mechanism has to be evolved. Such a project may not be possible for the Bar Councils to undertake given the limited resources available to them. The International Bar Association (IBA) has created a chair for CLE in the National Law School of India, thanks to the efforts of Shri R. K. P. Shankardass. Network of institutes for CLE will be necessary if such a programme is to be available to advocates in different parts of the country. Besides helping an advocate in updating his knowledge, properly structured CLE programmes with due certification procedure can help members of the Bar seeking to specialise in specific areas of law and legal practice. Move seems to be afoot too for introducing renewal (re-registration) of enrolment as a requirement for continuing eligibility to practice law. If such procedure for renewal of enrolment is to be enforced it can be linked to participation of an advocate in courses under CLE programmes. Whatever may be the merits of introducing such statutory requirement for re-registration of an advocate, institutionalising the CLE programme, providing impetus and easy access to such programmes to members of the Bar in all parts of the country desirous of availing the same is undoubtedly essential if standards are to be ensured in the legal services.

Ethics of the Profession—Advertisement and Contingency Fees

Consistent with autonomy, an essential attribute of the profession of law, the Advocates Act confers upon the BCI the power to prescribe by rules, standards of professional conduct and etiquette. The disciplinary jurisdiction is also specifically vested in the Bar Councils, and their respective disciplinary committees. The BCI has framed rules prescribing standards of professional conduct and etiquette, the preamble of which states that "an Advocate shall, at all times, comport himself in a manner befitting his status as an officer of the Court, a privileged member of the community, and a gentleman, bearing in mind that what may be lawful and moral for a person who is not a member of the Bar or for a member of the Bar in his non-professional capacity may still be improper for an Advocate." The Preamble, really speaking, sets the tone and the rules containing canons of conduct and etiquette are said to be "general guides" which are in no manner to detract from the generality of the obligation set out therein. Like in all walks of life though the core ethical values remain static, approaches may vary with the passage of time. A review of the rules, framed by the BCI in such spirit, I think is essential at least with respect to two of the canons.

Rule 36 of the rules provides that an Advocate shall not solicit work or advertise either, directly or indirectly whether by circulars, advertisement, touts, personal communications, interviews not warranted by personal relations, furnishing or inspiring newspaper comments or producing his photograph to be published in connection with cases in which he has been engaged or concerned. This part of the rule in a comprehensive manner covers "soliciting work or advertising" by means set out therein. The rule to the extent relevant for the present discussion provides further that the signboard, nameplate or stationery should not indicate his specialisation in any particular type of work. The essence of the rule, which is found in Section IV, dealing with "duty to colleagues" seeks to forbid soliciting work or advertising, obviously with the intention of preventing competition of the market place amongst advocates. It is indeed a very wholesome principle viewed from the point of view of an advocate's duty to his colleagues. There is however another aspect which requires consideration in this regard, namely, providing necessary information to a person seeking to engage the services of an advocate in a way that he can make an informed decision. It is said that an important function of the legal profession is to educate laymen to recognise their problems to facilitate the process of intelligent selection of lawyers, and to assist in making legal services fully available. In the days when the legal community was small and the reputation of the local lawyers for competency and integrity were widely known, a potential client could make an informed choice. Even if one had no personal knowledge one could rely upon the advice and recommendation of third parties, be it relatives, friends or acquaintances. It must be recognised that there was unavoidably a great deal of touting either direct or indirect on behalf of some of the advocates, particularly in the seats of District Courts and High Courts, since a prospective client's information and knowledge did not extend to such areas. One other traditional mode used was to rely upon the advice of the counsel whom the client had known at the local level. The effectiveness of such a selection process, apart from ethical considerations, is by no means sufficient to enable a potential client to make an informed choice. With the number of lawyers increasing multifold and special tribunals and commissions being constituted in increasing numbers, the problems of a prospective client in selecting a suitable counsel have become more acute. It is therefore necessary that the professional bodies should themselves evolve a suitable method for dissemination of information and/or should in a restricted manner permit notifying through any recognised listing agency the essential particulars of the services offered by an advocate. It is in this context that one has to consider listing in yellow pages or other dedicated directories or maintaining a website on the Internet. Whatever be the mode, it appears imperative that the total ban be removed and instead a restricted process be permitted.

The related issue is whether apart from permitting an advocate to notify particulars, such as educational qualifications, the place of practice, experience and the courts in which he practices, one should be permitted to claim specialisation in any particular area or branch of work. No doubt, "competitive advertising would encourage extravagant, artful, self-laudatory brashness in seeking business, and this could mislead the layman". This however may have to be balanced with the need to enable a layman to choose an advocate best suited for his particular requirement. Specialisation in some branches of law is accepted today and we are bound to see more of it in the years to come, which to my mind is by no means an unwelcome development. All the same, it cannot be left to the individual lawyer to claim specialisation by himself. Hence, the need to evolve norms for recognition of specialisation-claims. In this context factors such as specialised courses of study during the pre-entry training period, as already referred to, and certification obtained for the CLE programmes participated in, besides basic education and the practical experience may be taken into consideration. To assist the Bar Councils in the matter of acceptance for one's claim for specialisation, special committees for accreditation may have to be constituted. Whatever be the methodology, there ought to be dissemination of information for the benefit of persons requiring legal services to enable them to make an informed selection of the counsel suited for their requirement.

Yet another aspect while dealing with rules of professional ethics which may require review is Rule 20, which provides that an advocate shall not stipulate a fee contingent on the results of litigation or agree to share the proceeds thereof. While contingency fees is traditionally an anathema, in many jurisdictions there has been a departure from the norm. Though, there perhaps cannot be two views with respect to laudable purpose of the rule, at the same time we may have to consider whether exception ought not be carved out in respect of cases such as land acquisition compensation and motor vehicle accident claims. If one takes into account majority of the cases of land acquisition, such as acquisition made for the purpose of irrigation projects, laying of roads, housing schemes, etc. claimants are poor land owners who cannot be expected to commit themselves to pay fees with reference to the quantum claimed, not being sure of success. Similarly, it is hardly logical to expect victim of a motor vehicle accident or members of his family to commit to pay a fee chargeable based on the claim or such fees that an experienced lawyer might charge, without knowing whether their claim would meet with at least partial success. Because of the impracticability implicit in the said norm, it is common knowledge that it is observed more in breach. I think it is time to accept this ground reality. The relevant rules of ethics give rise to many clandestine transactions, leading to, in some cases, denial of most of the compensation to the client when the case of the claimant meets with success. Courts have, with a view to avert such unethical practices, directed payments to be made only into the accounts of the client by way of cheque so as to protect the clients from becoming victims of the avarice of his lawyer. Therefore, it is necessary to evolve a suitable procedure permitting transparent arrangement for receipt of contingency fee in specified cases, fixing ceiling thereto so that the interest of the litigant public can be better protected, while avoiding room for doubting bonafides of the advocates concerned.

Disciplinary Jurisdiction

The Advocates Act, 1961, confers jurisdiction upon the disciplinary committees of the State Bar Councils and BCI. Prior to the Act, High Court alone could award punishment for professional misconduct. The change brought about by the Advocates Act reflects due recognition of one of the essential attributes of the profession, namely autonomy. Greater responsibility therefore rests upon the shoulders of the elected statutory bodies of the profession to ensure accountability of the profession and penal action against the erring members of the fraternity.

Reservations may be expressed in certain quarters regarding the efficacy and effectiveness of the exercise of disciplinary jurisdiction by members of one's own fraternity. Sometime ago it was commented, after a review of the working of disciplinary committees, that the disciplinary committees of the BCI seemed more lenient than those of the State Councils. Such an opinion drawn on the basis of scrutiny of the some of the decisions may not reflect any liberal approach having been deliberately assumed. While our concern is not so much with respect to justification for the opinion expressed, the fact remains that the exercise of the disciplinary jurisdiction by one's own peers should withstand critical scrutiny. Section 9 of the Act provides that a disciplinary committee shall consist of 3 persons, of whom 2 shall be persons elected by the Council from amongst its members and the other shall be a person co-opted from advocates who had put in 10 years or more of practice. Till a few years ago, it was the practice to co-opt a retired judge of a High Court or other senior members of the Bar to the disciplinary committees of the BCI; that no longer appears to be the practice followed. Without dwelling into the matter, the suggestion for consideration is that due care be taken to co-opt as far as possible seniors, whose presence can enhance the stature and credibility of the committees. It is also, I think, equally important that the practice of inducting members of State Bar Councils as co-opted members of the disciplinary committees of the BCI should be avoided. Section 9, which provides that the seniormost advocate amongst members of the committee shall be the chairman thereof, also seems to pose certain practical difficulties since the said provision might give rise to the tendency to co-opt someone who will not become the chairman by virtue of his seniority. Suitable amendment providing for a senior amongst the two members elected from the Bar Council concerned shall be the chairman of the committee might be a practical solution, justification for the same being that logistically it might be more convenient for members of the Bar Council to guide matters relating to meetings of the committee and posting of cases.

Yet another aspect that requires to be addressed is the period of one year specified under Section 36(B) of the Act, pendency beyond which results in automatic transfer of a case from the disciplinary committee of a State Council to a disciplinary committee of the BCI. One year being too short a period, practical experience shows that a number of cases stand transferred to the BCI, leading to a backlog of cases before its committees. I recall pleading with the concerned to bring about an amendment in this regard prior to the 1993 Amendment of the Act. This was not acceded to on the grounds that increasing the period would make it appear that the sense of urgency is deliberately being diluted. The fact however remains that very often automatic transfer of cases to the committees of the BCI, instead of serving the purpose of expeditious disposal, leads to further delay of the process.

General Functions—Review

Any review of the working of the Advocates Act would be incomplete if one does not take into account the functions of the Bar Councils as set out under the Act. The functions of a State Bar Council include organising legal aid to the poor. Similarly under Section 7, functions of BCI include organising legal aid. This organising legal aid is one of the functions of the Bar Councils specifically provided under the Act. The councils are conferred with the power to constitute legal aid committees. Despite emphasis laid on legal aid as one of the functions of the Bar Councils, there may not have been any significant contribution in this area by the Bar Councils. While dealing with the Legal Services Authorities Act, 1987, in the Chairman's page of the *Indian Bar Review*, I had, while acknowledging that it was a significant step in the pursuit of one of the Constitutional goals, commented that, "what however stands out from the provisions of the Act is the fact that the organised Bar in the Country is not assigned any significant role under the Act". I had to no doubt further add that, "it is perhaps the failure on the part of the organised Bar in taking the initiative in legal aid that has lead to its relegation to the background". This to my mind continues to be the position. The BCI at one point of time had decided to set up a Legal Aid Cell to assist victims of the Bhopal Gas Tragedy, which did not really materialise owing to the financial crunch that the Council was beset with at that time. Even now, with the Legal Services Authorities Act and other legal aid programmes the Bar Councils can still make a significant contribution in promoting legal aid. For a start, every State Bar Council should run a legal aid window in its office, which invariably will be located in the seat of the High Court. Considerable assistance can be lent by engaging the services of a handful of junior advocates by paying them a stipend to man the cell or the window on all working days. While assisting the litigant public in providing them information and guidance, they can arrange for the services of a counsel from the panel of advocates who volunteer to serve the cause, maintained by the concerned Bar Council. Gradually the Bar Councils can assist the Bar Associations at the district levels and, in due course of time, have such legal aid services at the taluk level. I cannot find a better way to conclude than to recount what had been said then by me in the "Chairman's Page": "Whatever may be the strategies for attainment of the Constitutional goal of free legal aid, the organised Bar in the country cannot afford to let the initiative slip out of its hand if it is to enjoy the image of a noble profession wedded to the cause of public service".

Besides legal aid there are other general law-related functions that the Bar Councils, and more particularly the BCI, are expected to discharge under the Advocates Act, and these include:

(a) Promotion and support of law reform;
(b) To conduct seminars, organise talks on legal topics by eminent jurists and publish journals and papers of legal interest.

The BCI through its Trust has been publishing a journal, the *Indian Bar Review*, and had also at one time published books on development of law in specific areas, such as constitutional law, taxation, criminal procedure etc. Seminars and conferences are conducted occasionally by the BCI and the other Bar Councils. These activities have remained merely symbolic and cannot be said to have made any significant contribution for either disseminating knowledge in law or promoting law reform.

The Bar Councils have very limited financial resources. The enrollment fee of Rs. 250/- was to be shared by the concerned State Bar Council and the BCI. It was only recently by the amendment introduced in 1993 that the enrollment fee has been raised to Rs. 750/-. The elected representatives of the councils are practitioners of law hailing from different places. For instance the BCI has 16 elected members and two ex-officio members namely, the Attorney General for India and Solicitor General of India. Such being the composition, its members have barely enough time to discharge their functions, such as exercise of disciplinary jurisdictions, inspections of colleges etc. In any event it will be wholly impracticable for the BCI to carry out its general functions such as promoting 'law reform', conduct of seminars and legal publications in the absence of requisite infrastructure. The Council at the national level and State Councils must be provided with sufficient resources to enable them to build research units with competent academics and professionals to assist them in the discharge of their functions. Funding, earmarking the same for such specific purpose is I think an essential requirement, if there is to be any meaningful contribution by the BCI and other councils in these areas.

Having said that, one has to admit that there is considerable apathy and lack of enthusiasm amongst the professional bodies in taking up causes material for administration of justice and maintenance of the rule of law. Even in matters concerning the Bar and the Bench, one does not often find initiatives taken by the councils. I can recall the decision taken by the BCI in the year 1987 to constitute a committee of three retired judges of the Supreme Court to advise the BCI in matters concerning the judiciary and administration of justice. While announcing the said decision, when reference was made to the erosion of the image of the judiciary, the correspondents of the media tried to extract information of specific instances of want of probity among the judges, from me as Chairman of the Council. One senior journalist, noted for his sound reporting, avoided publishing the item altogether, presumably on account of a doubt entertained as to whether such a statement would amount to contempt of court. Sometime thereafter we had seen the concerned Bar Association expressing their strong views with respect to some judges of the Bombay High Court and also the initiation of proceedings for impeachment of a judge of the Supreme Court. There may have been other decisions of the BCI and other councils addressing fundamental issues concerning administration of justice. The fact however remains that the constructive role of the statutory and voluntary professional bodies of the Bar is not generally visible, and hence the need for introspection.

Appendix 5

'Judges and Medals'
V. R. Reddy's article published in The Indian Advocate, The Journal of Bar Association of India, 21: 27–31, 2003.

'THE smile is back', exclaimed the newspapers with a picture of Sunita Rani holding the medals won at the Asian Games, which were restored to her, having been withdrawn earlier for the suspected use of banned drugs. Behind the pleasant smile of Sunita is the deep sense of hurt, and she has reportedly recited a verse: 'In times of trouble no one is around you, but there is everybody to share your happiness'. Sunita's return to glory reminds one of the recent news report of the Supreme Court of India giving a 'clean chit' to three judges of the Karnataka High Court, who are alleged to have been involved in a brawl at a resort near Mysore while in the company of women judicial officers/advocates, after an enquiry by a committee of senior judges. One is tempted to visualize the presentation of 'clean chit' certificates at a public function to the three learned judges, as was done in the case of Sunita Rani, and if ever such a thing could happen, one wonders if any smile could be seen on the faces of the three learned judges.

In the recent months there has been considerable adverse projection of the judges of the higher judiciary. 'They think that they are demigods' is the muted protest often heard from lawyers and litigants who have had a rough deal from a judge. Strangely, when the judges are reported to have displayed their human face with all its frailties, there is much ado in the media and in the corridors of courts. I am referring to the three recent unseemly episodes publicized with gusto, which have caused considerable unease in the minds of those who would like to believe in the purity of justice. The episodes which occupied much space in the media are: the involvement of three judges of the Punjab and Haryana High Court in the 'jobs for sale' scam of the Public Service Commission of Punjab; the Registrar of the Rajasthan High Court propositioning a woman doctor on behalf of a judge of the High Court; and the one involving the judges of the Karnataka High Court.

One common feature noticeable in the three episodes, which, sadly, had gained notoriety owing to the instant hype created by the media and the gossip mills, is the absence of financial impropriety linked directly to the decision making by the judges concerned. It has lately become open talk that corruption has crept into the citadels of justice, and a former Chief Justice of India had to, with anguish, concede that 20% of the judiciary is of doubtful integrity, which seems to be a modest estimate, particularly if one is to go by the reputation enjoyed by the judiciary in general and the lower judiciary in particular. If so, how come there is hardly any instance of such corruption coming to light? The reasons for this are perhaps not far to seek. When there is such monetary consideration passing, it is invariably a clandestine operation shrouded in secrecy. The beneficiary would be the last one to go on record revealing—though it may not be uncommon for the person to brag in private—how smartly he managed or how much it had cost him. The conduits which might include the brethren at the bar would also find it highly damaging to divulge the details, though as a promotional strategy, it may become necessary to drop hints of closeness or capacity to reach out to a judge. In the absence of the promoters of tainted justice revealing the truth, we have only the unsuccessful party crying foul, such complaints being prone to being ignored as the tantrums of a bad loser.

As an eminent judge of the High Court of Australia, Michael Kirby, observed in the days of the British Empire, the spectre of a corrupt judge or magistrate was so horrible that it could largely be dismissed as impossible. This fundamental assumption, regrettably, cannot today be taken for granted, particularly in developing countries, our own being no exception. Finding the existing law inadequate, a special enactment, namely, the Prevention of Corruption Act was brought into force in the year 1947. Despite the clear language including a judge within the expression 'public servant' under the Prevention of Corruption Act, when a former Chief Justice of a High Court, Justice K. Veeraswami, was sought to be prosecuted, profound legal and constitutional issues were raised challenging the same. A Constitution Bench of the Hon'ble Supreme Court by a majority of 4:1 upheld the prosecution by holding that the expression 'public servant' includes every judge, including judges of the High Court and Supreme Court. Such decisions notwithstanding, one does not very often hear any significant number of prosecutions of judges under the said enactment. It is common knowledge that the authorities had to wait for conducting search and seizure in the premises of a judge of the Calcutta High court for violation of FERA till after his retirement. Let alone prosecution in criminal courts, even if one takes into account disciplinary action, the number of judicial officers against whom such action has been initiated cannot by any means arithmetically accord even with the modest figure of 20% of the 'black sheep' referred to by the former Chief Justice of India.

A Conference of Chief Justices adopted a resolution by way of 'Restatement of Values of Judicial Life', listing 16 principles. The problem is not one of any differing views on judicial ethics. It is basically one of enforcement. Different procedures are followed in different jurisdictions. The endeavour in every society, based on the rule of law, is to ensure that the independence of the judiciary is in no manner compromised by any overzealous mechanism for the enforcement of a code of conduct amongst judges. This has led to the judiciary evolving an in-house procedure. One serious shortcoming of any in-house procedure or 'peer group justice' is that its impartiality and efficacy is often doubted. Besides, while an in-house procedure within the judicial family might be effective in dealing with minor violations of the norms, when it comes to serious misconduct such as financial corruption, an in-house procedure may not enjoy adequate credibility.

Initiating a cleansing process is without doubt a must, and it should necessarily start from the top. This process of 'removal' of a judge of a High Court or the Supreme Court under the Constitution, besides being cumbersome and time-consuming, is impracticable, as can be seen from the past experience in the case of Justice V. Ramaswami, a judge of the Supreme Court. A similar procedure for impeachment of federal judges under the American Constitution is also found to be a 'very difficult and protracted process and most infrequent'. The American Congress therefore passed the Judicial Conduct and Disability Act in 1980, conferring powers on judicial councils comprising judges to take such action against a federal judge as is appropriate, short of removal. A statistical survey of the functioning of the judicial councils has led to the comment that 'in practice it is simply another form of ineffective self-discipline by federal judges'.

Though the precise nature and functioning of the in-house mechanism evolved by the judiciary is not known, the recent experience in dealing with the unflattering episodes involving judges of three of the High Courts in the country does not reveal any well-structured in-house procedure. In the case of three judges of the Punjab and Haryana High Court, Chief Justice Saharia had submitted a report as desired by the Chief Justice of India and his colleague judges. News of the impending transfer of one of them to the Guwahati High Court led to strong protest from the members of the bar at Guwahati, refusing to allow their High Court to be made into a 'dumping ground for undesirable judges'. With respect to the judge of the High Court of Rajasthan, Chief Justice G. B. Patnaik, after demitting office, had reportedly said that enquiry into the allegation of sexual harassment of the lady doctor has given rise to the need for investigation into other serious misconduct which is particularly grave.

This takes us to the more disturbing episode relating to the judges of the Karnataka High Court. The popular adage 'all is well that ends well' is wholly inappropriate in this case. What seems to have started with a very short report in one of the local newspapers, of an alleged brawl at a resort near Mysore involving 'legal bigwigs', gradually developed into a shocking story implicating three of the judges of the High Court. The media literally 'went to town' with it, and no one was prepared to take the emphatic refutation by the Commissioner of Police of Mysore seriously. Some dailies and magazines carried not only the story, but also pictures of the three learned judges. The story, with all the embellishments lent to it over a period, brought the judiciary into disrepute. Now comes the announcement that the Supreme Court of India has, on the basis of the report of the committee of the three senior judges that had enquired into the matter, exonerated the three learned judges. Can it ever be the same for the three learned judges who were made to go through such ignominy for weeks and months? Can anything now be effective reparation for the damage caused to the reputation of the judges concerned and the institution itself? All this unpleasantness, [was] to a great extent, on account of the absence of any definite and effective mechanism and the resultant adhocism in dealing with the whole matter. If there were to be an autonomous, organized, constitutional or statutory body, it could have seized the matter on day one, without giving room [for] sensationalization of such a serious matter.

Hitherto the disturbing factor was only the whispering campaign against the deviant conduct of some judges. Now we have seen how judges themselves have become vulnerable to unjustified suspicions. Eminent [figures] of law like Justice Krishna Iyer, Fali Nariman and others [...] The composition of the [judicial] commission is a matter of detail, given the consensus that it ought to be meaningfully plural, with representatives of the judiciary having a greater say. Exercise of contempt of power would prove itself to be counterproductive in the long run, leading to truth itself being inhibited. Besides preventing the erosion of the image and credibility of the judiciary, even to protect the fair name and reputation of its worthy members, such a judicial commission is without doubt the need of the hour.

Appendix 6

'V. R. Reddy's Elevation Welcomed'
Report in the Deccan Chronicle, *4 August 1991, Hyderabad, on V. R. Reddy's appointment as Additional Solicitor General of India.*

THE appointment of Mr V. R. Reddy (Velakacherla Rajagopal Reddy) Advocate-General of Andhra Pradesh, as the First Additional Solicitor-General of India, has been hailed in the legal and judicial circles here.

Fifty-three-year-old Mr V. R. Reddy had his legal education from the University of Madras and the University of London, and was enrolled as advocate in the year 1964. He was appointed Government pleader in the A.P. High Court in 1974, and continued as such till 1978. He was designated Senior Advocate by the High Court in 1989. He practised in the High Court as well as the Supreme Court.

Apart from being the legal adviser to many institutions, Mr V. R. Reddy was elected twice to the Bar Council of India from the State for a total period of 10 years. He was the managing trustee of the Bar Council of India Trust for four years before being elected as its Chairman. He held the position for three years till March 1990.

Mr V. R. Reddy was also the Chairman of the General Council of the "National Law School of India University," Bangalore, a prestigious institution for legal education and presently continues as member of its Executive Council. He also represented the Indian Bar in conferences, including the biennial conference of the International Bar Association in Buenos Aires, Argentina and also led a delegation of the Indian Bar to the People's Republic of China at the invitation of the Chinese Law Society.

With the appointment of Mr V. R. Reddy as the First Additional Solicitor-General of India, the post of Advocate-General of Andhra Pradesh falls vacant. According to legal circles, three prominent advocates are being considered for the post. They are Mr S. Venkat Reddy, Mr S. Ramachandra Rao, who was the Counsel for several Congress (I) leaders in cases filed against the then Chief Minister Mr N. T. Rama Rao, and Mr R. Venugopal Reddy, a leading lawyer and former Advocate-General of A.P.

Appendix 7

'Sydney to Sydney—A Lawyer's Lament'
V. R. Reddy's article sent to the President of the District Court Bar Association, Kadapa, along with his covering letter of 20 February 2008.

V. R. Reddy
Senior Advocate
Former
Addl. Solicitor General of India

D-223, Defence Colony, New Delhi-24
Ph. 24694334. 24652345.
E-mail: vrreddy@vsnl.co
February 20, 2008

Dear Mr President,

At the outset, I wish to thank you and your colleagues for inviting me to the Bicentenary celebration of the District Court of Kadapa. Shri Ch. Siddha Reddy, Senior Member of your Association and my esteemed friend for over four decades had called me to ensure my acceptance and wanted me to send an article for publication in the *Souvenir*, to be brought out on this historic occasion. Knowing that Shri. Siddha Reddy, who is always known for sincerity of purpose in whatever he does, will not easily accept a 'no' from me I meekly submitted to his demand, only to realise later that time at my disposal for preparing an article is too short. I am hence taking the liberty of sending an article which I had prepared immediately after the test match at Sydney. I had sent this to a columnist, who seemed enthusiastic in having it published in a national daily with which he is associated. Since it did not happen at the right time, I am withdrawing it and sending it across to you.

As you may notice, it is not strictly speaking, on a topic in the realm of law, but then, I strongly believe that it is time that the legal fraternity started focusing on issues of vital importance to the civil society such as primary education, sports, health care etc. As lawyers, I believe we can contribute a great deal in promoting such causes, using our exposure to the field of law and life generally. Incidentally, I may mention that it would have given me far greater satisfaction if you had thought of felicitating Ms. Karnam Malleshwari (who I had learnt had spent some years in her younger days in Kadapa District) for bringing some solace to the distressed minds of the people of our country by securing a bronze medal at the Sydney Olympics. The relevance of the topic of the article lies in these thoughts and sentiments. If you are to publish the article in the *Souvenir*, please do publish this letter, which could serve the purpose as a prefatory note, along with it.

Yours sincerely,
[V. R. Reddy]

To,
The President,
District Court Bar Association,
District Court,
Kadapa [AP]

'Sydney to Sydney—A Lawyer's Lament'

THE (saving grace) of the recently concluded test match at the Sydney Cricket ground was the opportunity it afforded at least to two of our accomplished players, Sachin Tendulkar and VVS Lakshman, who put up splendid performances.

While it is so at an individual level, when we think of the country's honour, Sydney is by no means an auspicious venue for India. Going back a few years down the memory lane, we are reminded of the dismal performance at the Sydney Olympics in the year 2000 where the large Indian contingent, mostly of office bearers and officials besides some sportspersons, returned home with one Bronze for the near Billion population that they represented. I distinctly recall the mood of depression and despair on the morning after the meet concluded, and the irresistible urge to do something whatever be one's capability, or to at least express one's concern (if not a solution to the problem). That evening there was this get-together of the Bar Association of India, of which I have the honour of being a Vice President, on the eve of the conference organized to discuss and deliberate upon what as members of the Legal Profession we perceive as a matter of profound importance. There I went up to our esteemed President Shri F. S. Nariman, Senior Advocate and Member, Rajya Sabha, and sought his opinion as to whether we could focus on matters which may not be strictly law related. Fali with his usual warmth and large-hearted generosity said, "Why not?" and then asked me what I had in mind. Buoyed by the response I rushed home to pick up the model advertisement I had prepared, which was to have vertically half a page of one of the dailies with black background and a shining Bronze medal in the middle, followed by the words: 'Bronze for a Billion'. The idea was to shock the conscience of the powers that be and rouse a sense of concern in the public mind. When I carried it back and showed it to Fali, he was quite appreciative of the idea and referred me to the Hon. Secretary. It is a different matter that decisions particularly involving substantial expenditure are not easily forthcoming, and since I could see that effect would not be same if this is not done on the very next day, with the proverbial public memory being short its impact cannot be the same if the publication is delayed, I did not follow it up.

Despite the passage of time, the thought coupled with the urge to act persisted in my mind, and finally I decided that effort should be made to create a forum for persons concerned to meet and try to figure out ways and means to help improve matters. I tried reaching out to some of the sports columnists of national dailies, without much success in enthusing them. Then I took out a full page announcement/advertisement in one of the popular sports weeklies, *Sports Star*, dated November 25, 2000.

By then I had thought of a name for the group, which was to be 'PIPS': "People's Initiative for Promotion of Sports", and had decided to involve some of my young lawyer friends.

The exercise of the group started with the question posed to the concerned to ponder whether sports was too serious a matter to be left to the sports authorities; and the statement of the then Minister for Sports: "*Khel ke saath khilwaad ho raha hai*", and what the *Time* magazine had to say were prominently quoted while seeking views, opinions, suggestions and involvement of sports enthusiasts and concerned citizens by way of an appeal.

It is a different matter that like many well-intended plans and programmes that flounder owing to lack of adequate positive response, 'PIPS' also became a victim of diminishing intent with passage of time. Though lawyer friends, particularly from the younger section of the bar, were ready and willing to assist in promoting the cause, taking into account the practicalities of the situation, the consensus was that as a first step the endeavour should be to identify a person with requisite exposure and background to take over as a full-time executive of the organization. We were conscious of the fact that the proposal entailed substantial funds to be generated for meeting even the bare administrative expenses besides the cost of the other proposed activities. Though we were optimistic about the latter, we failed in securing the services of a competent person to give shape to our ideas, many of which were perhaps nascent, and in launching programmes for achievement of the same.

Now that 2008 Beijing Olympics are round the corner, I am tempted to recall what a noted sports columnist had to say in 2000 referring to the 2004 Olympics: "By the time Olympics 2004 comes ... our officials would be drawing up comparative charts to fool you that India was better prepared than in the past."

Alas, in the run up to the 2008 Olympics even that has not come true since the officials seem far too busy with the Commonwealth Games, presumaby to prove our organizational ability, if not sporting prowess. Just in case they have not noticed the reports it might be useful to quote a report which reads: "The ruling Communist Party envisions the games as a public relations showcase and, leaving no detail unattended, scientists are cross-breeding chrysanthemums to ensure that flowers bloom in August".

But then I suppose we need to remind ourselves of what an analyst had to say in *Time* after the Sydney Olympics, while comparing the medal tally of China with the beautiful Bronze that the First Woman Olympic Medalist, Karnam Malleshwari secured for our country.

"India on the other hand, with its chaotic but pluralistic political system and weak Central Government, has neither the money, the will, nor the competence, to achieve official Sports success." But then the Sensex never soared this high then, nor the GDP. Can we not now look to brighter prospects at Beijing in 2008?

The problem really is not lack of competence. Have the sports authorities tried to activise someone like Laluji, our Dynamic Minister for Railways? After all, speed matters even in athletics. I remember the bygone era when China arrived with a bang in the field of table tennis to outnumber most in the medals tally. I had learnt from some knowledgeable source that one of the measures that may have helped in producing so many champions by popularizing the game was making available a table tennis table in the waiting rooms of railway stations. If it is true, with the kind of time many spend on our railway platforms, you need not be a spoil sport to make them leave the game midway. Wasn't the same thing not said about billiards becoming popular because of the facilities in railway clubs in our country, particularly when Michael Ferreira became the world champion? Aren't these reasons enough to rope in Ministers like Laluji to help in one's endeavour in averting the ignominy that a billion plus population appears doomed to face in many Olympics to follow?

Reverting back to the more recent Sydney episode concerning cricket, which has 'willy nilly' become a religion which most in our country are passionately practicing. While such enthusiastic support to any sporting activity should be welcomed, the downside of it in this case is the manner in which cricket is tending to occupy the whole space, denying many of the other sporting activities room to thrive, making India a one sport nation—'Chak de India' notwithstanding. When we try to believe that we play this game in the true spirit which we imbibed as true legatees, the charge of racial slur against one of our better behaved accomplished cricketers, Harbhajan Singh, came as a rude shock, compounding the hurt of being at the receiving end of inept umpiring. Whatever may be the reservations many of us have against the foray of politicians into the field of sports, one cannot but appreciate the deft and diplomatic handling of the ticklish issue by the President of BCCI, Shri. Sharad Pawar.

In the absence of any authentic information regarding the alleged utterances by Bhajji perceived as constituting racial slur, the whole episode is presently in the realm of speculation. Going by the complaint earlier lodged against one of the spectators for imitating a monkey by gestures, presumably directing the same to Australian all-rounder Andrew Symonds, the offending utterance attributed to Bhajji is also assumed to be monkey related. Normally, one's reaction would be as was expressed by one of the West-Indian cricketers—"What's the big deal? We all had them as our ancestors." If there is something more to it then it will be for consideration whether the player who is alleged to have uttered the offending word had knowledge of the same, since the nature of the charge being something akin to a criminal offence, 'mens rea' or criminal intent is required to be established. For determining the intent, the surrounding circumstances have necessarily to be taken into account. While watching the match one had seen Harbhajan Singh giving expression to his boundless joy when he secured the wicket of Ricky Ponting by repeatedly rolling on the ground. If one of the spectators were to point it out to the child accompanying him saying—"Hey look at the hairy bear rolling there", would it amount to a racial slur? Further, whatever be the sensitivities involved, it is common knowledge that we have in India innumerable temples where people throng to pray to Hanuman, the monkey god. With many such diverse considerations having to be factored in, one should seriously and objectively deliberate before treating what might otherwise be merely a language offensive to another player as one having racial overtones as under Clause 3.3, which is a level 3 offence under the ICC Code of Conduct. In the absence of such racial overtones/slur it will be an offence under Clause 2.8 of level 2, which parenthetically provides that: "It is acknowledged that there will be verbal exchanges between players in the course of play. Rather than seeking to eliminate these exchanges entirely, Umpires will look to lay charges when this falls below the acceptable standard". I have no doubt that with the task of an inquiry having been left to a judge, all relevant aspects will be duly considered* and the required legal assistance from the Board in India to defend its player will not be wanting. A fair and acceptable solution to the avoidable controversy that had arisen in Sydney would go a long way to restore the enthusiasm of sports persons from India for heading to Sydney when it is the chosen venue next.

---

*The expectation has come true and the learned Judge of New Zealand High Court Mr Justice John Hansen has since pronounced his decision.
**The numerous errata in the original, previously published texts included here under Appendices have been corrected, within due constraints and to the extent possible, for publication in this volume.

Appendix 8

'Kadapotsavam'
An invitation to V. R. Reddy from the Kadapotsavam Committee, Cuddapah, to attend the first Kadapotsavam, from 28 January to 1 February 2003.

KADAPOTSAVAM
28-01-2003 to 01-02-2003
INVITATION

To Sri V. R. Reddy, Advocate General of India,
D.No. 223, Defence Colony, New Delhi-24

I would like to inform that the first "KADAPOTSAVAM" is being organized at Cuddapah from 28.01.2003 to 01.02.2003 to highlight the composite culture, heritage and tourism potential of the district.

The history and culture of the Kadapa District is very antiquated and can be dated back to the pre-historic period. The name itself is highly evocative and it brings forth fond memories steeped in history and folklore. The district has played a significant role in every historical event. The contribution of the district to the fields of literature, arts, the freedom movement etc. is invaluable. The pioneers of "Prabhandha Poetry" of the Vijayanagara Period, Allasani Peddana, Ramaraju Bhushanadu etc., the renowned Tallapaka Annamacharya who wrote more than 32 thousand "Keertanas" praising Lord Venkateswara Swamy, the great social reformer Vemana, Sri Veera Brahmendra Swamy who predicted the future and condemned the caste system and superstitious beliefs, Sri Puttaparthi Narayanacharyulu, an eminent poet, and C. P. Brown who dedicated his total life for the development and growth of the Telugu Language as a senior civil servant at Cuddapah during the British period, belonged to Cuddapah District. Further, great visionaries like the B. N. Reddy brothers who helped in the growth of the film industry in South India, and the famous Surabhi artists are also from this district. The history of the freedom movement in Andhra Pradesh is not complete without mentioning the great services rendered by Kadapa Koti Reddy.

Appendix 8

In this regard, the District administration desires to felicitate the great "sons of soil" of Cuddapah who have excelled in different fields. The people of Cuddapah consider it a great privilege to felicitate and honour you for your services rendered in the field of Judicature on 28.01.2003 at 7.00 PM. Your participation in this event will serve as an exemplary example for the people of Cuddapah to strive for excellence and perfection.

[Jayesh Ranjan, I.A.S.]
Collector & Organizing Chairman,
Kadapotsavam Committee, Cuddapah

PLATE 92 VRR and other delegates on a visit to China, with the Vice Minister for Justice, China.

PLATE 93 VRR with Ashok Desai and other Indian delegates at the IBA Conference, Buenos Aires.

PLATE 94 VRR and Anil Divan in Rio de Janeiro in front of the statue of Christ the Redeemer.

PLATE 95 VRR and Anil Divan with Anjali Varma and her husband in Peru.

Plate 96 VRR with former IBA president Kumar Shankar Das, his wife, and the incumbent IBA president.

Plate 97 VRR at IBA's Asian Regional Conference in Delhi.

Plate 98 VRR and Radha at the Law Asia Conference in Manila.

Plate 99 VRR (as Vice President BAI) at the All India Lawyers Convention organised by BAI; on the dais, Fali Nariman (President BAI), Anil Divan and Gaurishanker.

Plate 100 VRR with Lalit Bhasin at the BAI conference on criminal justice.

Plate 101 VRR at dinner hosted by P. S. Narasimha, to felicitate him and his family during their visit to Delhi on the occasion of Deepika receiving the National Sangeet Natak Akademi Award from the President of India; (L to R) Justice Madan Lokur, Umapathi, Dayan Krishan, Nikhil Nayyar, Sunil, VRR, R. S. Suri, Sharma.

Plate 102 P. H. Parekh with VRR.

Plate 103 Parasaran with Deepika, P. S. Narasimha and VRR.

Plate 104 VRR receiving Soli Sorabjee.

Plate 105 VRR and Deepika with Abhishek Singhvi.

Plate 106 VRR with K. K. Venugopal, Attorney General.

Plate 107 VRR with M. L. Verma.

Plate 108 VRR and P. S. Narasimha with Vikas Singh.

Plate 109 VRR with Jaideep Gupta and Justice V. K. Rao.

PLATE 110 (L to R) Pragasam, Venkat Reddy, Nageshwar Reddy, Venkat Ramani, Sanjay Hegde, Krishnan Venugopal.

PLATE 111 VRR and Deepika with Justice L. Narasimha Reddy.

PLATE 112 (Sitting L to R) P. S. Narasimha, Pragasam, Radha, VRR and Deepika; (standing L to R) Siddharth, Vijayabhaskar, Venkat Reddy, Nageshwar Reddy, Shyam, Choudhury, Abhilasha and Kannan.

PLATE 113 At conference commemorating 60 years of BAI on 3 December 2019, VRR with Parasaran, BAI President Lalit Bhasin; seen Krishnayan Sen.

Plate 114 VRR with Vikramjit Banerjee, Justice Ravindra Bhat, Prof. Upendra Baxi, Priya Hingaroni.

Plate 115 VRR receiving the plaque of honour and distinction from Justices Indira Banerjee and Ravindra Bhat; seen Ashok Desai, Prashant and Lalit Bhasin.

PLATE 116 The plaque being presented to VRR.